Keyboard Shortcuts

File Shortcuts

New	⌘-N
Open	⌘-O
Close	⌘-W
Save	⌘-S
Document Setup	⌘-Shift-D
Print	⌘-P
Quit	⌘-Q
General Preferences	⌘-K

Object Editing Shortcuts

Undo	⌘-Z
Redo	⌘-Shift-Z
Cut	⌘-X
Copy	⌘-C
Paste	⌘-V
Select All	⌘-A
Select None	⌘-Shift-A
Paste In Front	⌘-F
Paste In Back	⌘-B
Repeat Transform	⌘-D
Move	⌘-Shift-M
Bring to Front	⌘-=
Send to Back	⌘-hyphen
Group	⌘-G
Ungroup	⌘-U
Lock	⌘-1
Unlock All	⌘-2
Attributes	⌘-Control-A
Join	⌘-J
Average	⌘-L
Make Guides	⌘-5
Release Guides	⌘-6
Lock/Unlock Guides	⌘-7
Make Compound Paths	⌘-8
Release Compound Paths	⌘-9

For every kind of computer user, there is a SYBEX book.

All computer users learn in their own way. Some need straightforward and methodical explanations. Others are just too busy for this approach. But no matter what camp you fall into, SYBEX has a book that can help you get the most out of your computer and computer software while learning at your own pace.

Beginners generally want to start at the beginning. The **ABC's** series, with its step-by-step lessons in plain language, helps you build basic skills quickly. For a more personal approach, there's the **Murphy's Laws** and **Guided Tour** series. Or you might try our **Quick & Easy** series, the friendly, full-color guide, with **Quick & Easy References**, the companion pocket references to the **Quick & Easy** series. If you learn best by doing rather than reading, find out about the **Hands-On Live!** series, our new interactive multimedia training software. For hardware novices, there's the **Your First** series.

The **Mastering and Understanding** series will tell you everything you need to know about a subject. They're perfect for intermediate and advanced computer users, yet they don't make the mistake of leaving beginners behind. Add one of our **Instant References** and you'll have more than enough help when you have a question about your computer software. You may even want to check into our **Secrets & Solutions** series.

SYBEX even offers special titles on subjects that don't neatly fit a category—like our **Pushbutton Guides**, our books about the Internet, our books about the latest computer games, and a wide range of books for Macintosh computers and software.

SYBEX books are written by authors who are expert in their subjects. In fact, many make their living as professionals, consultants or teachers in the field of computer software. And their manuscripts are thoroughly reviewed by our technical and editorial staff for accuracy and ease-of-use.

So when you want answers about computers or any popular software package, just help yourself to SYBEX.

For a complete catalog of our publications, please write:

SYBEX Inc.
2021 Challenger Drive
Alameda, CA 94501
Tel: (510) 523-8233/(800) 227-2346 Telex: 336311
Fax: (510) 523-2373

SYBEX is committed to using natural resources wisely to preserve and improve our environment. As a leader in the computer book publishing industry, we are aware that over 40% of America's solid waste is paper. This is why we have been printing the text of books like this one on recycled paper since 1982.

This year our use of recycled paper will result in the saving of more than 15,300 trees. We will lower air pollution effluents by 54,000 pounds, save 6,300,000 gallons of water, and reduce landfill by 2,700 cubic yards.

In choosing a SYBEX book you are not only making a choice for the best in skills and information, you are also choosing to enhance the quality of life for all of us.

TALK TO SYBEX ONLINE.

ADOBE

ILLUSTRATOR™ 5.5

FOR THE MAC®

Designer's Guide

Cynthia S. Williams

SYBEX®

San Francisco ■ Paris ■ Düsseldorf ■ Soest

DEVELOPMENTAL EDITOR: *Steve Lipson*
EDITOR: *James A. Compton*
TECHNICAL EDITOR: *Chris Boccucci*
BOOK DESIGNER: *Helen Bruno*
SCREEN GRAPHICS: *Aldo Bermudez*
DESKTOP PUBLISHER: *Ann Dunn*
PRODUCTION ASSISTANT: *Renée Avalos*
INDEXER: *Nancy Guenther*
COVER DESIGNER: *Joanna Kim Gladden*
COVER ILLUSTRATOR: *Hank Osuna*
Screen reproductions produced with Collage Plus
Collage Plus is a trademark of Inner Media Inc.

Library of Congress Card Number: 94-68476
ISBN: 0-7821-1304-4

Manufactured in the United States of America
10 9 8 7 6 5 4 3 2 1

For Eric

Acknowledgments ▰ ▰ ▰ ▰

would like to thank those at SYBEX, Inc. who have worked hard to make this book a reality: Steve Lipson, Jim Compton, Kris Vanberg-Wolff, Ann Dunn, Renee Avalos.

Special thanks to Chad Kubo for his extraordinary color illustrations.

Thanks also to Adobe Systems Inc., not only for providing me with information and assistance, but also for creating such a great application in the first place.

A big Thank You goes to those around me who gave of their time and patience when I needed it most, especially Lisa Parkinson.

And last, but far from least, eternal thanks to Eric Webb for love, support, and everything else.

CONTENTS

AT A GLANCE

Introduction   xxi

1	Welcome to Adobe Illustrator	1
2	Getting to Know Adobe Illustrator 5.5	13
3	Illustrator Basics	29
4	Object Editing and Transformation	71
5	Getting the Most Out of Illustrator	99
6	Working with Type in Illustrator	117
7	Using Colors, Patterns, and Trapping	155
8	Special Effects	179
9	Plug-In Filters	203
10	Creating Graphs	245
11	Adobe Acrobat, Adobe Separator, and Adobe Type Manager	267
12	Special Projects	277
APPENDIX	Adobe Illustrator Menu and Keyboard Shortcuts	301

Index   333

Table of Contents

Introduction   xxi

1 WELCOME TO ADOBE ILLUSTRATOR   1

What is Adobe Illustrator?   2
  Where Did Adobe Illustrator 5.5 Come From?   3
  New Features in Illustrator 5.5   3
Who Can Use Adobe Illustrator?   5
What Will I Need to Use Illustrator 5.5?   5
  Hardware Requirements   6
  Software Requirements   8
Compatibility   9
  Troubleshooting Your Compatibility Problems   9
  Backward, Forward, and Cross Compatibility   10
Summary   11

2 GETTING TO KNOW ADOBE ILLUSTRATOR 5.5   13

Making Friends with Adobe Illustrator   14
Starting Adobe Illustrator   15
Touring the Desktop Interface   16
  The Drawing Surface (Artboard)   16
  Dialog Boxes and Palettes   18
  Keyboard Shortcuts   19
  The Menu Bar and Menus   19
  The Toolbox and Tools   20
Setting Preferences: Personalizing the Program   25
  Tool Behavior Preferences   26
  Keyboard Increments   27
  Edit Behavior   28
  Other Preference Controls   28
Summary   28

3   ILLUSTRATOR BASICS   **29**

Viewing Modes in Illustrator   30
Drawing with Tools   31
  Drawing Lines   31
  Drawing Basic Shapes   39
  Designing as You Learn: The Flower Drawing   42
Manipulating Objects   46
  Moving Objects   47
  Duplicating Objects   48
  Grouping Objects   49
  Designing as You Learn: The Five-Ring Logo   51
Adding Type to a Document   53
  Entering Type into a Document   54
  Selecting Type   55
  Editing Type   56
  Designing as You Learn: The Sale Ad   56
Styling Text and Objects   58
  Painting: Filling Objects with Color   58
  Stroking: Adding Lines and Frames   61
  Changing the Style of Type   62
  Designing as You Learn: The Food Label   65
Summary   70

4   OBJECT EDITING AND TRANSFORMATION   **71**

Understanding Points and Paths   72
  Path Types and How They Work   73
  Types of Points and How They Work   74
  Adding Points to a Path   77
  Curving Those Straight Lines: Converting Anchor Points 78
  Deleting Anchor Points   80
  Designing as you Learn: The Half-Circle   81
  Moving the Line Segments of a Path   82
Transforming Objects—A Closer Look   83
  Rotating Objects with the Rotate Tool   84
  Scaling Objects with the Scale Tool   86
  Designing as you Learn: Rotating and Scaling an Object Group 89

Mirror, Mirror: Using the Reflect Tool   91
Using the Shear Tool   93
Designing as You Learn: Reflecting and Shearing   95
Summary   97

5   GETTING THE MOST OUT OF ILLUSTRATOR   99

Using Templates in Adobe Illustrator   100
Creating Templates   101
Tracing the Template   102
Using the Auto-Trace Tool   102
Setting Tracing Preferences   103
Styling a Traced Template   104
Creating Guides   104
Ruler Guides   105
Importing Artwork into Illustrator   105
Styling Imported Images   107
Saving the Imported Image with the File   107
Exporting Your Illustrator Files   108
Saving Images as EPS Files   108
Saving Images as PICT Files   109
Working with Layers in Adobe Illustrator   109
Creating Layers   110
Hiding and Locking Layers   110
Positioning and Page Options   111
Tiling a Page   111
Positioning with the Page Tool   114
Document Information at a Glance   114
Summary   116

6   WORKING WITH TYPE IN ILLUSTRATOR   117

Getting Type into Your Design   118
Inserting Type into a Document   118
Importing Text   122
Linking Text Blocks   124
Setting Up Rows and Columns   125
Creating Text Wraps around Graphics   127

Designing as You Learn: Wrapping Columns around a Graphic   130
Word Processing Features in Illustrator   133
   Using the Spelling Checker   133
   Auto Hyphenation   135
   Smart Punctuation   137
   Changing the Case of Letters   139
   Designing as You Learn: Using the Word Processing Features   140
Styling Text in Adobe Illustrator 5.5   140
   The Wonderful World of Fonts   141
   Searching and Replacing Fonts in a Document   143
   Sizing Type: Changing the Point Size   145
   Leading Lines of Type   146
   Adjusting the Kerning and Tracking   147
   Specifying Word and Letter Spacing   149
   Changing the Baseline Shift   151
   Horizontally Scaling Type   151
   Changing the Alignment of Type   152
   Setting Indentation   152
   Setting Tabs in Text   152
Summary   154

7   USING COLORS, PATTERNS, AND TRAPPING   155

Working with Colors   156
Using the Paint Style Palette   157
   Using the Paint Swatches   158
   Using the Color Selector and Slider Tint Bars   159
   Dashed Lines, Caps, and Joins   161
Custom Colors   163
   Creating a Custom Color   164
   Deleting Custom Colors   165
   Using Colors from Color Matching Systems   165
   Converting Colors to Process   167
Using Gradient Fills   168
   Creating a Gradient   168
   Duplicating an Existing Gradient   170
   Deleting a Gradient   171

Creating a Gradient with Three or More Colors   171
Positioning a Gradient within an Object   171
Printing and Exporting Gradients   171
Creating Fill Patterns   172
Using the Preset Patterns   172
Creating Your Own Patterns   173
Modifying an Existing Pattern   173
Deleting a Pattern from the List   174
Trapping   174
Creating a Trap   175
Trapping Text   176
Summary   177

8   SPECIAL EFFECTS   179

Dividing Paths—Creating That Woven Look   180
Drawing in Three Dimensions   183
Creating a Three-Dimensional Box   183
Creating a Three-Dimensional Cylinder   185
Creating Spheres   187
Keeping in Perspective   188
Special Effects with Type   190
Creating Type Outlines   190
Masking—Creating "Windows" Out of Type   191
Creating Drop Shadows   192
Embossed or Chiseled Type   193
Creating Metallic Type   194
Adding Other Elements to Type   196
Moving Beyond Color
with the Blend Tool   197
Simulating Motion with the Blend Tool   199
Morphing with the Blend Tool   200
Summary   201

9   PLUG-IN FILTERS   **203**

Colors   204
  Adjust Colors   204
  Blend Front to Back   205
  Blend Horizontally   206
  Blend Vertically   207
  Custom to Process   208
  Desaturate   209
  Desaturate More   209
  Invert Colors   209
  Saturate   209
  Saturate More   210
Create   210
  Fill & Stroke for Mask   210
  Mosaic   210
  Polygon   212
  Spiral   213
  Star   213
  Trim Marks   214
Distort   215
  Free Distort   215
  Roughen   216
  Scribble   217
  Tweak   218
  Twirl   218
Objects   219
  Add Anchor Points   219
  Align Objects   220
  Distribute Horizontally   221
  Distribute Vertically   221
  Move Each   221
  Offset Path   221
  Outline Path   222
  Rotate Each   223
  Scale Each   223

Other   224
    Document Info   224
    Overprint Black   226
    Make Riders   227
    Delete Riders   228
Pathfinder   229
    Unite   229
    Intersect   229
    Exclude   230
    Minus Front   231
    Minus Back   231
    Divide   231
    Outline   232
    Trim   233
    Merge   233
    Crop   234
    Hard   235
    Soft   235
    Trap   236
    Options   237
Select   237
    Same Fill Color   238
    Same Paint Style   238
    Same Stroke Color   238
    Same Stroke Weight   238
    Select Inverse   238
    Select Masks   239
    Select Stray Points   239
Stylize   239
    Add Arrowheads   240
    Bloat   240
    Calligraphy   241
    Drop Shadow   242
    Punk   242

Round Corners 243
Text 243
Summary 243

10 CREATING GRAPHS 245

Using the Graph Style Dialog Box 246
Graph Type 247
Selecting the Axis 248
Graph Options 249
Other Graph Style Preferences 252
Drawing a Graph 252
Manually Drawing a Graph Outline 253
Drawing a Graph Outline
with Predetermined Dimensions 253
Entering Graph Data 254
Manually Entering Information 255
Importing Data into the Worksheet 256
Pasting Data into the Worksheet 257
Editing Graph Data 257
Manipulating Graph Data Elements 258
Transposing Data in Rows and Columns 258
Transposing the Axes in a Scatter Graph 258
Customizing the Cells 259
Customizing Graphs 259
Selecting and Changing Elements 259
Using and Creating Specialized Graph Designs 261
Summary 266

**11 ADOBE ACROBAT, ADOBE SEPARATOR,
AND ADOBE TYPE MANAGER 267**

Adobe Type Manager 268
The ATM Control Panel 268
Increasing the Font Cache 269
Line Spacing and Character Shapes 269

Adobe Acrobat   270
  Saving a File as PDF   270
  Opening a PDF File in Illustrator   270
Adobe Separator   271
  Opening a File in Adobe Separator   271
  Setting the Specifications   272
  Adding Printer Marks   274
  Making Separations   274
  Saving the Separations   275
  Printing the Separations   275
Summary   276

12 SPECIAL PROJECTS   **277**

Designing a Business Card   278
  Drawing the Card Outline   279
  Adding the Rules   280
  Adding the Business Name and Address   280
  Adding the Employee Name   281
Creating a Poster Advertisement   282
  Setting Up the Design   282
  Drawing the Orange   284
  Creating the Ducks   285
  Creating the Background   287
  Adding the Type   288
  Adding the Finishing Touches   290
Creating a Magazine Layout   290
  Setting Up the Spread   291
  Adding Text Blocks to the Spread   294
  Creating the Text Wrap   295
  Adding the Headline, Deck, and Byline   296
  Adding the Flying Bees   298
  Adding the Pop Cap   299
Summary   300

**APPENDIX ADOBE ILLUSTRATOR MENUS AND
          KEYBOARD SHORTCUTS**   **301**

The Illustrator Menus   302
   The File Menu   302
   The Edit Menu   304
   The Arrange Menu   306
   The View Menu   307
   The Object Menu   310
   The Font Menu   315
   The Type Menu   316
   The Filter Menu   321
   The Window Menu   326
Keyboard Shortcuts   329
   File Shortcuts   329
   Object Editing Shortcuts   329
   Viewing Shortcuts   330
   Type Editing Shortcuts   331
Palette/Dialog Box Shortcuts   332

Index   333

Whether you're a designer looking for a new medium or a computer user interested in design, this book will help you get more out of one of the most powerful designing applications available for the Macintosh, Adobe Illustrator 5.5.

Since its conception, Illustrator has grown from an already excellent designing program into a multifaceted designing, painting, and layout program. Each new version has brought with it a wealth of new features, making it the foremost Macintosh designing application available on the market today.

Who Is This Book For?

Appropriate for both beginners and more experienced users alike, this book is filled with detailed instructions to guide you through Illustrator's many complex functions. As an added bonus, numerous "hands-on" examples have been included, allowing you to work through concepts as you learn them. By doing this, even novice users will find themselves creating sophisticated, professional designs almost immediately.

new Throughout this book, the many new features included in Illustrator version 5.5 are highlighted by a special icon, like the one at left. If you're familiar with past versions of Illustrator, be on the lookout for this icon to learn about new and updated features of the application.

Not much time is spent introducing you to basic Macintosh features. I've assumed that you already know how to use a Macintosh, and that you're here to learn about Illustrator, not the machine. Still, wherever I've deemed it appropriate, I have included a few tidbits about the Mac interface, just for the beginners.

Hardware Requirements

Chapter 1 describes in detail the hardware and software you need in order to use Adobe Illustrator 5.5 efficiently. The most important requirement is that you have a Macintosh with at least 8 MB of RAM. The program can run on only 4 MB, but you'll find that it runs better and faster if you have at least 8 MB on your machine.

Another requirement for using Illustrator efficiently is a color monitor. While you *can* view Illustrator on a gray-scale monitor, doing so defeats the purpose of having a program with such powerful color capabilities.

How This Book Is Arranged

This book is arranged so that even novices can easily find information, learning the program as they progress chapter by chapter through the book. If you already have some experience with Illustrator, you may wish to skim over some parts, pausing whenever you see the NEW symbol to update yourself on new additions to the program.

Throughout each chapter, you will find several exercises that give you hands-on experience by taking you step-by-step through the information just presented. In addition, the final chapter of the book contains three complete projects that you can work on at your leisure. It is important, especially if you have had limited Macintosh experience, to spend time working through these exercises and projects. Not only will it make you more familiar with the material, but you'll also learn some tricks along the way that you can use in your own projects in the future.

Get Started

Turn the page now and begin your quest for designing excellence. Adobe Illustrator will provide you with the medium for your creativity; all you need is your imagination…

Welcome to Adobe Illustrator

Welcome to one of the most popular and sophisticated drawing programs available today, Adobe Illustrator 5.5. Whether you're a designer with little computer experience or a computer enthusiast who wants to learn more about design, both this book and Illustrator have been designed to help you quickly become proficient in computer design skills.

What is Adobe Illustrator?

Adobe Illustrator is a comprehensive design program containing tools much like those on an artist's work table: a pen, a brush, scissors, a drawing surface, rulers, and so forth. The computerized versions of these tools found in Illustrator work the same way as their traditional counterparts—and then some.

For instance, a traditional pen can be used to draw lines and shapes. The Adobe Illustrator pen tool can be adjusted to draw curves that either tightly or loosely follow the guide of the cursor as you draw. The curve can be manipulated once it is drawn to further adjust its shape and curvature. It can then be styled, to change its width and color, again and again until you find the combination you like best. If you want to start over, the original drawing (or any small part of it) can be deleted and redrawn in a flash.

Illustrator's tools aren't limited to drawing curves, though. There are tools that let you draw lines, rectangles, squares, ovals, circles, stars, spirals and more. Still other tools can apply text in a variety of ways to any part of your design. All of these elements can be combined, layered, and manipulated to achieve your own unique look.

Both text and graphics can be painted in a limitless array of color combinations, including blends and specialized patterns. This is only the beginning of what you can do with Illustrator 5.5—a wealth of other special effects are possible.

In addition, designs and artwork produced in Adobe Illustrator can be output directly into color separations, high-resolution film that is ready for use in any publication. This takes several intermediary steps out of the production process and guarantees that the design you originally create is the one that gets published.

In short, the tools in Adobe Illustrator 5.5 are an "advanced form of life" compared to their manual predecessors. They take the labor out of drawing, painting, and designing and make these tasks what they should be—a work of art.

Where Did Adobe Illustrator 5.5 Come From?

Adobe Illustrator 5.5 is the culmination of years of research and development by Adobe Systems, Inc. to produce a comprehensive design package that is useful and accessible to designers, not programmers. As the program evolved, working artists and designers took part in its development, giving valuable suggestions that the technical wizards then implemented in the program. The result is an amazing designing program that is easier and more intuitive for an artist to use, regardless of his or her technical background.

New Features in Illustrator 5.5

 Those of you with previous Illustrator experience will be happy to note that version 5.5 contains lots of exciting new features. Most of these enhancements are so advanced and slick they make older versions of Illustrator seem absolutely prehistoric. Throughout this book, look for the **NEW!** icon shown at left to alert you to additions or changes in version 5.5.

To whet your appetite, here is a brief review of some of the more outstanding additions to the program. I think you'll agree just on the basis of these features alone that Adobe Illustrator 5.5 was well worth the wait.

Improved Text Handling

If Adobe keeps improving the text-handling features of Illustrator as they have for version 5.5, they'll be competing with page layout applications very soon. That's pretty good for a designing program that is already leading the pack in its own field. If you've been clamoring for an all-inclusive design package that can whip text into shape as well as give you powerful design tools, then check out what version 5.5 can offer you.

First, it is now possible to set tabs in Illustrator (we should be setting off fireworks for this addition alone). The Tab Ruler palette works like those included in other word processing and page layout programs, allowing you to set left, right, centered, and decimal tabs for a block of text.

Other text-handling additions to version 5.5 include:

- the **Check Spelling** filter, which includes a user-customizable dictionary,
- the **Smart Punctuation** filter, which searches for keyboard text symbols (em dashes, quotation marks, and so forth) and replaces them with true "typesetter's" punctuation,
- the **Change Case** filter, which changes text to all uppercase, lowercase, or mixed case letters,
- the **Find Font** filter, which lets you search for and replace the fonts used in the current document, and
- the **Rows & Columns** filter, which lets you create rows and columns of text, as well as adjust the height, width, and gutter spacing between columns.

More Plug-in Filters

One of the most remarkable enhancements of Illustrator 5.0 over earlier versions was the addition of more than forty plug-in filters. First introduced by Adobe in their Photoshop package, filters can create unique objects and special effects by automating several steps that were previously tedious but necessary manual manipulations. Adobe has added a few more of these filters to version 5.5, as well as cleaned up versions of some of the filters that were included (but not documented) in version 5.0.

The most notable addition to the filter collection in Illustrator 5.5 is the Trap filter. This filter helps you control the amount of trapping, or overlap, between two adjacent colors in a design. If you are printing your designs on a high-speed press, the small addition of trapping between the colors keeps the images looking clean despite any misregistration. The Trap filter lets you adjust the amount and type of trapping that is applied directly in Adobe Illustrator to the colors in your design.

This is only a sampling of the many features included in Adobe Illustrator 5.5. All of them are discussed in detail in appropriate sections later in this book, but I'm sure you'll agree that Illustrator just keeps getting better with each new version.

Who Can Use Adobe Illustrator?

Everyone! Illustrator is well suited for anyone interested in design and illustration. Beginners can learn the program as they go, improving their skills with practice. Advanced users can design complex drawings effortlessly, increasing their productivity while saving valuable time and money.

Illustrator is used every day by people in varied occupations: publishing, marketing, advertising, public relations, and design, to name a few. If you need a way to create professional designs suitable for publication or display, then Adobe Illustrator is the program for you.

Regardless of your skill level, Illustrator 5.5 is sure to greatly enhance the ease with which you create your designs, as well as your creativity itself.

What Will I Need to Use Illustrator 5.5?

There are a few hardware and software requirements for running Adobe Illustrator 5.5 efficiently on your machine. The following sections list both the recommended requirements and some added extras that you may find useful.

Hardware Requirements

Adobe Illustrator needs in excess of 4 MB of RAM (random access memory) that can be dedicated solely to running the program. But let's get real—the System software is going to hog a lot of memory, and as soon as you start working on a large and complicated design in Illustrator, you're going to start moving pretty slow if you don't have a little more muscle on your Mac. If you like to keep a wealth of fonts at your fingertips (as I do), you'll find that all those fonts demand more than their fair share of memory, too.

I recommend starting with 8 MB of RAM. If you plan on spending a lot of time in Illustrator every day (or in two or more programs at once), then you may want to consider more—a lot more. The more RAM you have, the faster your machine will work when drawing, editing, and printing complex files. Yes, 8 MB will run the program, but you should see how it rips with 12 MB, 16 MB, or more. As a friend of mine once said, "You can never have too much RAM…"

Getting Colorized: Monitors

Unless you *really* enjoy working in gray-scale, a large color monitor is a sensible addition to your system. Adobe Illustrator is such a color-intensive workhorse that it would be a shame to condemn it to the monotony of a gray-scale monitor. Similarly, once you've used a 21″ monitor, it's hard to go back to anything smaller. The luxury of being able to see (and even work on) your entire design at once—legibly—has no comparison. The price of larger color monitors has dropped enough in the past few years that you should be able to find a reasonable deal that fits within your budget. But shop around—monitors vary widely in quality as well as price.

Video Cards

If you want or need the most accurate color representation on your screen, a 24-bit video card is another option worth investigating. Using a 24-bit number to specify the color of each pixel on the screen means that your machine can display more than 16 million color gradations, giving you a more accurate representation of the finished product. Without 24-bit color, your machine will be limited to rendering 256 or 16K colors at once (standard issue for Macs), and the colors you see on your screen are almost guaranteed to be different from their printed counterparts.

Depending on your line of work, the type of designs you create in Illustrator, and of course, your budget, a 24-bit video card may or may not be a viable alternative for you.

Printing and Printers

For proofing purposes, you will need a Macintosh-compatible PostScript printer of some sort. There are several types on the market today: gray-scale laser, color laser, and thermal wax, to name a few. Do some investigative work before you buy—again, the prices continue to drop for color printers and you may find a good deal or an alternative you haven't considered.

Above all, it is important that the printer be compatible with PostScript, since Adobe Illustrator files are saved in Encapsulated PostScript (EPS) format. Without a PostScript printer, your illustrations will print bit-mapped and distorted—if they print at all.

If you cannot afford to purchase a PostScript printer for your own use, find a local service bureau that is capable of printing your Illustrator files for you. This can become quite expensive; in the long run it is more economical to have your own printer for proofing purposes if nothing else.

Other Peripherals to Consider

It goes without saying that you will need a keyboard and a mouse. Some designers prefer to use a trackball instead of a mouse. Others prefer to use a pressure-sensitive digital drawing tablet and stylus for some operations, which can be easier to use if you're used to drawing with a pen. Regardless of the peripheral tools you choose, Adobe Illustrator 5.5 is compatible with any of them. Choose and use whatever you are most comfortable with, and whatever best fits your needs for the type of designing you do.

Software Requirements

In order to do anything on your Macintosh, you must have Macintosh System software resident on your machine. While Adobe Illustrator 5.5 can run on Apple System software version 6.0.7, System 7 is definitely preferable. If you are still using System 6, upgrade. *Now.*

Adobe Type Manager (ATM)

Adobe Illustrator 5.5 comes with Adobe Type Manager (ATM). This is a useful font utility that can generate a sharp image of any size Type 1 font on your computer screen as well as on any printer that supports QuickDraw. When using ATM, you only need to install the outline fonts and at least one bit-mapped version of each font you wish to use. ATM will then generate the font in the appropriate sizes.

ATM is automatically installed when you install Adobe Illustrator 5.5.

Fonts, Fonts, and More Fonts

As a working designer, you'll need access to many fonts on your machine at once. Not only does it keep your designs from all looking the same, it makes it easy to try different looks just by changing the font.

Illustrator 5.5 comes with 40 Type 1 Adobe fonts that are installed automatically on your system along with the application. This is a welcome bonus to the program. For those of you who want even more creative access in your type design, there are literally thousands of fonts available on the market from Adobe as well as other type foundries. While some of these fonts can be quite expensive, there are cheaper alternatives available. Most software stores sell font packages—several fonts bundled together for one low price.

If you expect to send your Illustrator files to be printed at a service bureau or printing press, or to anyone else who will need to print your file, it is best to stick with Type 1 fonts; they are the industry standard.

Compatibility

Adobe Illustrator 5.5 files are saved in Encapsulated PostScript (EPS) format. PostScript is a page-description programming language that is device-independent. (In other words, any output device that "understands" PostScript can successfully print an EPS file.) Essentially, an EPS file is a "script," containing instructions, in the PostScript language, that describe the image in terms of mathematical formulas. As a result, EPS files usually output sharper and more consistently than bit-map files, making EPS the format of choice for higher-grade output systems.

Because they use the EPS format, Illustrator 5.5 files are compatible with many other software programs. Files created in Illustrator can be imported into programs such as Adobe Photoshop and Aldus Freehand for additional work. They also work beautifully as art files imported directly into page layout programs such as QuarkXPress and PageMaker.

In addition, EPS files from other sources can be imported and placed as objects within an Illustrator file. Illustrator 5.5 also has a new option that allows you to import and convert certain PICT images into EPS files. We'll discuss this at greater length in Chapter 5.

Troubleshooting Your Compatibility Problems

You may have trouble importing extremely large and complex Illustrator files into some page layout programs. Large files often take much longer to redraw and print when they are imported into another program. Some problems can be overcome by increasing the amount of RAM in your machine or the amount of memory allotted to the layout program itself. You may alleviate some printing problems by printing the file to a more sophisticated output device.

If you encounter more problems such as these, consult the user's guide for the page layout program in question, or call their technical support line.

INSIDE INFO

> **Before you call anyone's technical support line for solutions to import problems, try shutting down any other applications you may have running. This may give your machine the boost it needs to import a larger file. In addition, if you have printing problems, uncheck all of the Printer Effects in the Page Setup dialog box before printing.**

Backward, Forward, and Cross Compatibility

Forward compatibility usually isn't a problem between versions of any software program on a Macintosh. Files you create in Adobe Illustrator 5.5 will be compatible with any future version of Illustrator. For example, a file created in Illustrator 3.0 can be opened seamlessly in Illustrator 5.5, and saved as either an Illustrator 3.0 or 5.5 file.

Going Back in Time

Unlike most software packages, Adobe Illustrator also provides for backward compatibility. A file created in Illustrator 5.5 can be saved in any other version of Illustrator, all the way back to Illustrator 1.1. However (and this is a big however), while the file itself can be saved in a previous version, not all of the Illustrator 5.5 embellishments will travel with it.

For instance, certain color blends created in 5.5 will not hold when the file is opened in an older version of Illustrator. The technology that makes it possible for you to create such a blend in 5.5 simply doesn't exist in the older versions of the program. When you save a file in which this problem could occur, a warning message will appear on your screen.

WATCH OUT!

> **In some cases, Illustrator 5.5 files may need to be saved as Illustrator 3.0 files to be compatible with other programs. For instance, QuarkXPress 3.2 can't process some of the new gradient color blends in Illustrator 5.5, and Adobe Premier 3.0 cannot read Illustrator 5.5 files at all. In both cases, saving the file in question as an Illustrator 3.0 file gets around this bug. You may experience similar incompatibilities with other applications; if you do, saving the file in the Illustrator 3.0 format may be a solution.**

Bridging the Cross Compatibility Gap

Illustrator files can be saved for use on non-Macintosh systems as well. Illustrator 5.5 allows you to save an EPS file that will be IBM PC-compatible. You can then import the file easily into a page layout program on a DOS system.

You can also save files for use in Illustrator 4, which is the Windows version of Adobe Illustrator. This makes it easy to edit the file once it is on a different system.

With the addition of Adobe Acrobat to Illustrator 5.5, files can also be saved in Portable Document Format (PDF). This format is convenient because PDF files can be viewed on other machines where Illustrator 5.5 is not installed.

Summary

Adobe Illustrator is a comprehensive drawing program containing sophisticated tools for creating intricate designs with graphics, text, color, and special effects. The addition of several new features to version 5.5 has made Illustrator more powerful and yet more accessible than ever before. Whether you're a professional artist or a novice designer, you will find Illustrator 5.5 a valuable and exciting artistic outlet for your creativity.

Getting to Know
Adobe Illustrator 5.5

T W O

Now that the introductions are over, it's time to get to know Adobe Illustrator 5.5 a little better. This chapter surveys the basic tools and elements that make up the Adobe Illustrator application. You don't need to memorize all the information in this chapter before continuing on. As you use the application, you'll gradually become familiar with how it works. You'll also get a more concrete sense of what the Illustrator terminology introduced in the following pages actually means—how those terms relate what you do with the program.

new
Experienced Illustrator 5.0 users won't need to do more than glance at this chapter. Although you'll find that some of the features of Adobe Illustrator have been rearranged for version 5.5, most of the information in this chapter is provided for the benefit of first-time users. Look for a NEW symbol like the one in the margin for quick reference to exclusive changes or additions to version 5.5.

Making Friends with Adobe Illustrator

If you have used any Macintosh application before, you probably feel somewhat at home already with Adobe Illustrator. But for novices to the program, the thought of tackling such a complex and sophisticated set of tools may be a bit overwhelming. Don't worry—you're not alone!

The easiest way to learn *any* program on the Macintosh is to sit down and play with the application. Don't work, don't memorize commands and functions—just play. Become familiar with the way things work, try each of the tools out, and experiment with the palettes a little. This makes learning much less stressful and yes, even fun. As you learn the lingo and how everything works, you'll feel at home in no time at all.

AUTHOR'S NOTE

Later chapters present exercises—complete design projects—
you can work through to develop your Illustrator skills. In this
chapter, however, you should simply try out each tool that
interests you, playing with it as much as you want before moving
on to the next one.

Starting Adobe Illustrator

When you installed Illustrator on your hard drive, a new folder titled Adobe Illustrator 5.5 was created. This folder contains everything you need to run Illustrator. Open the folder and locate the application icon. Double-click on this icon to start the program.

When you open the application for the first time, the program will prompt you to personalize your copy of Illustrator. A dialog box will ask for your name, organization (optional), and the serial number of your copy of the application. You will not be able to use the program unless you enter your name and serial number. Your serial number can be found in four places among the Adobe Illustrator program materials:

- on the back of Disk 1 (the installation disk)
- on the first page of the application's User Guide
- on the *Read This First* registration card
- on the bottom of the application's box

Once you have entered the appropriate information, click on the OK button to start Adobe Illustrator 5.5. In the future, you will only need to double-click on the Adobe Illustrator 5.5 icon to start the application.

INSIDE INFO

If you have previously created and saved an Illustrator 5.5 file, you can open both Illustrator and the file at the same time by double-clicking on the file's icon in a Macintosh directory.

Touring the Desktop Interface

The Adobe Illustrator interface is designed much like an artist's traditional workspace. With a drawing surface, numerous tools in a handy tool box, and a palette of colors to paint with, Illustrator provides a familiar working atmosphere for artists through the medium of the computer. Although it may seem strange at first to draw with a mouse while looking at a screen, as you become more familiar with the Illustrator interface this method will soon feel quite natural.

The Illustrator interface is organized into several key components:

- A drawing surface
- Dialog boxes and palettes
- A menu bar and menus
- Keyboard shortcuts
- A toolbox and tools

Let's take a closer look at each of these elements.

The Drawing Surface (Artboard)

When you open the Adobe Illustrator application, a blank page will appear in a document window labeled *Untitled art 1*. This is the drawing surface, or *artboard*, and it's the digital equivalent of a blank piece of paper (see Figure 2.1).

You can draw directly on this surface, or modify it to your own liking by using the Document Setup command under the File menu (see Figure 2.2). This dialog box lets you change the size and orientation of the page, and you can set your preference for ruler units and other items. We'll use the Document Setup dialog box in various contexts throughout the book.

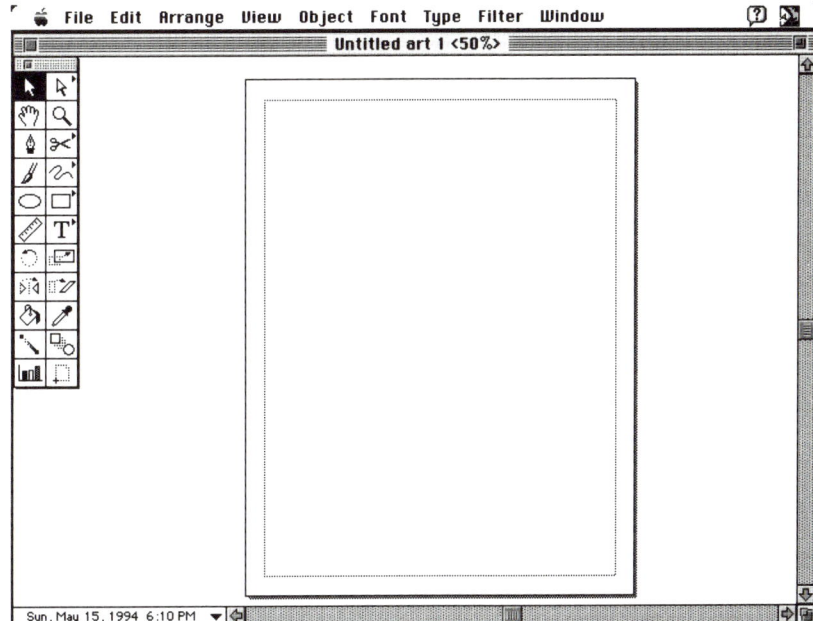

To the right and bottom of the document window are slider bars and arrows, which allow you to move the view of your page around as needed. If you have selected Rulers under the View menu, rulers will appear across the right and bottom sides of the window next to the slider bars.

In the bottom-left corner of the window is the status bar, which can be set to display four different types of information as shown in Figure 2.3. Click and hold on the small black triangle in the bar to reveal a sub-menu containing the four display options.

2.3

The user-definable status bar with four options.

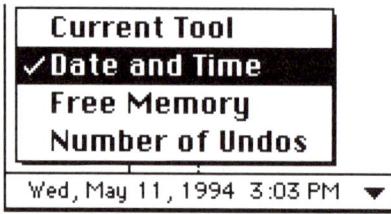

- **Current Tool**—displays the name of the tool currently selected.
- **Date and Time**—displays the current date and time as set in your machine.
- **Free memory**—displays the amount of memory currently free in your system as both a percentage and a numerical figure in megabytes (MB).
- **Number of Undos**—displays the number of undos (steps of your work that you can "undo") currently available, as well as the number of redos (undos that you can reinstate) available. The number for both undos and redos is limited by the level selected in the General Preferences dialog box (discussed later in this chapter).

Dialog Boxes and Palettes

Many of the features of Adobe Illustrator are accessed through dialog boxes and palettes. In a *dialog box* you tell the program what to do by selecting options from lists or typing values into text boxes (as illustrated in Figure 2.2). Once you have entered the information, you must exit the dialog box (usually by clicking OK) in order for the changes to take place.

A *palette* is a dialog box that floats freely on your screen. It does not need to be closed in order for its commands to take effect in your document. You can reposition a palette on your screen as you wish and use it simply by clicking on one of its fields and typing in information. When you hit the Return key, the changes will take effect in your document.

Keyboard Shortcuts

Both dialog boxes and palettes can be accessed through the menus arranged in the menu bar. Many of them can also be called by invoking keyboard shortcut commands, a handy feature found in all Macintosh applications. Using a shortcut command is the fastest way to do *anything* in Illustrator. By pressing a simple combination of keys (for example, the ⌘ Command key plus a letter key), you can perform most routine operations quickly without fussing with the menus.

If you start using the shortcuts now, in no time at all they'll become second nature. Another good reason to use the shortcuts is that many of them are universal across programs—for instance, ⌘-S always means Save. For a complete listing of keyboard shortcuts, see the Appendix at the end of this book.

The Menu Bar and Menus

Across the top of your screen you will see the Adobe Illustrator menu bar, with nine menu options (in addition to the standard Apple menu). Each of these menus contains commands that operate different aspects of the Illustrator program. If you click on any of the menu headings and hold down your mouse key, you will see a listing of the commands in that menu.

When you see a command listed in gray instead of black, it means that the command is not available for use, based on the objects you have currently selected on your desktop. For example, if you have only one object selected on a page, it would not make sense to use the Join command, so it is "grayed out." If a small black triangular arrow appears to the right of a command, it means that the command leads to a "submenu" of further choices. Move your cursor over the command, and the submenu will appear.

A command followed by an ellipsis (…) calls a dialog box to the screen. Many dialog boxes contain several related commands in one convenient location. As you become more familiar with the menu commands, you will be able to accomplish more in less time by taking advantage of the collections of commands found in dialog boxes.

If a keyboard shortcut is available for a command, it also appears in the menu listing. The following abbreviations apply to the keyboard shortcuts:

⌘ = Command key

↑ = Shift key

option = Option key

control = Control key

You'll learn the most important menu commands over the next few chapters. For a complete reference to all the menus and keyboard shortcuts in Illustrator, see the Appendix.

The Toolbox and Tools

The Toolbox palette contains numerous tools that are used to design and style elements in an Adobe Illustrator drawing (Figure 2.4). Like other palettes, the Toolbox freely floats on the desktop and is usually kept in the upper-left corner of your screen.

The tools in the Toolbox each perform differently. Some of them are drawing tools, which can be used to draw directly on your desktop. Others are application tools, which are used to apply options to existing objects. Still other tools perform other various operations when used.

2.4

The Toolbox pal-
ette contains a
wide variety of
tools for designing
and styling ele-
ments of a drawing.

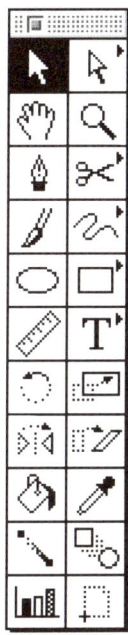

Some of the tools are not displayed directly in the toolbox. Five of the displayed tools in the Toolbox have small black triangles in their upper-right corners. If you click on one of these triangles and hold it, other available tools will appear in a submenu to the side of the palette.

Selection Tools

There are three selection tools: Selection, Direct Selection, and Group Selection.

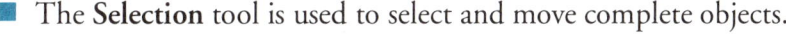
- The **Selection** tool is used to select and move complete objects.

- The **Direct Selection** tool is used to select points and path segments in objects.

- The **Group Selection** tool lets you select groups of objects by clicking on just one of the objects in the group.

Viewing Tools

There are three viewing tools: Hand, Zoom In, and Zoom Out.

- The **Hand** tool lets you grab and move your page as needed to better view your document. Double-clicking on the Hand tool changes your document view to Fit to Window.

- The **Zoom In** tool lets you zoom in for a closer look at your design. It has a plus sign in the middle of the magnifying glass icon.

- The **Zoom Out** tool lets you reduce the view of your document. When you hold down the Option key, the Zoom-In tool becomes the Zoom-Out tool, and the plus sign changes to a minus sign.

Point and Path Editing Tools

There are four tools that edit points and paths: Scissors, Add Anchor Point, Delete Anchor Point, and Convert Direction Point.

- The **Scissors** tool inserts end points into the middle of a path, splitting the path into two different objects or converting a closed path into an open path.

- The **Add Anchor Point** tool adds an anchor point when clicked on a segment of a path.

- The **Delete Anchor Point** tool deletes an existing anchor point.

- The **Convert Direction Point** tool changes an existing anchor point into a direction point.

The Drawing Tools

There are seven tools for drawing: Pen, Brush, Oval, Rectangle, Rounded-Rectangle, Freehand, and Auto Trace. These tools allow you to draw lines and shapes of any dimension, as well as automatically trace imported templates.

- The **Pen** tool draws straight lines and curves.

- The **Brush** tool simulates a brush stroke, and will create a closed path object instead of an opened path line. Double-clicking on this tool brings up a dialog box in which you can modify its effect.

■ The **Oval** tool draws ovals. By holding down the Shift key while you draw, you will constrain the oval to a perfect circle. Double-clicking on this tool changes its effect to center-draw.

■ The **Rectangle** tool draws rectangles. By holding down the Shift key while you draw, you will constrain the rectangle to a perfect square. Double-clicking on this tool changes its effect to center-draw.

■ The **Rounded-Rectangle** tool draws rectangles with rounded corners.

■ The **Freehand** tool is a sketching tool, and reacts more like a pencil would when used to make rough sketches of a design.

■ The **Auto Trace** tool is used in conjunction with an opened template. When selected and clicked on the edge of an image in a template, it will trace around the perimeter of that image.

The Measure Tool

The **Measure** tool measures the distance between any two selected points in your document (Figure 2.48). When used, it automatically opens the Info palette to display the distance measured by the tool.

The Type Tools

There are three tools for working with type in Adobe Illustrator: Type, Area Type, and Path Type.

■ The **Type** tool lets you enter type at the insertion point (the point where you click on your document).

■ The **Area Type** tool turns any object into a graphic area into which you can add type.

■ The **Path Type** tool can insert type along any path.

The Transformation Tools

There are four transformation tools in Adobe Illustrator: Rotate, Reflect, Scale, and Shear. Each one transforms objects or text in a different manner. Double-clicking on any of these tools brings up a dialog box where you can modify its effect.

- The **Rotate** tool rotates objects either clockwise or counter-clockwise.

- The **Reflect** tool reflects an object across either the vertical or horizontal axis, deleting the original. It can also leave the original in place and reflect a copy of the original instead.

- The **Scale** tool changes the horizontal and vertical scale of objects in either even or uneven proportions. It can also leave the original at 100 percent and create a scaled copy.

- The **Shear** tool skews an object at an angle along either the horizontal or vertical axis. It can also leave the original in place and shear a copy of the original.

The Color Tools

There are four tools in Adobe Illustrator that apply, manipulate, and sample color: Paint, Eyedropper, Gradient Fill and Blend. Chapter 7 is a complete guide to working with color in Illustrator.

- The **Paint** (Paint Bucket) tool paints a selected object with the attributes currently set in the Paint Style palette. Double-clicking on this tool brings up a dialog box where you can modify its settings.

- The **Eyedropper** tool samples (copies) the color of a painted object on your screen and paints other selected objects the same color. Double-clicking on this tool brings up a dialog box where you can modify its settings.

- The **Gradient Fill** tool repositions a gradient fill inside an object.

- The **Blend** tool creates a series of stepped shapes and/or colors between two selected objects.

The Graph Tool

The **Graph** tool is used to create the dimensions for a graph. Once you have drawn the dimensions with the Graph tool, the Graph Data dialog box automatically appears, ready to accept data. Then, once you have entered the data, the graph will appear on your screen. The graph can be styled further using the Graph submenu controls in the Object menu; double-clicking on the Graph tool brings up this dialog box.

Chapter 10 offers a detailed look at graphing in Illustrator.

The Page Tool

The **Page** tool repositions the artboard page around your design. This is a handy way to center a complex design on a page without disturbing the design itself.

Setting Preferences: Personalizing the Program

Illustrator offers several preference settings that you can adjust to suit your own needs and tastes. Some of these, such as the ruler units, are settings you will probably change infrequently. Others, such as the cursor key increments, you may change several times during the course of one project. As you progress through the examples in this book, you will become more familiar with these preferences and how they can benefit your working environment.

The File menu contains the Preferences submenu, with four preference options: General, Color Matching, Hyphenation Options, and Plug-ins. The three latter options are specific to certain functions, and will be discussed in depth with their respective topics later in this book. However, since the General Preferences dialog box contains settings for modifying the behavior of the tools and controls we have just discussed, let's take a look at that dialog box now.

The General Preferences dialog box (Figure 2.5) has three main sections and a few added extras. In the upper-left corner are the Tool Behavior controls, in the upper-right corner are the Keyboard Increment controls, and below them on the right is the Edit Behavior control box. Also in this dialog box are preferences for measurement units and type greeking. Each of these areas controls a different preference aspect, so let's look at them individually.

2.5

The General Preferences dialog box sets user-preferred measurements for a variety of areas within the Adobe Illustrator application.

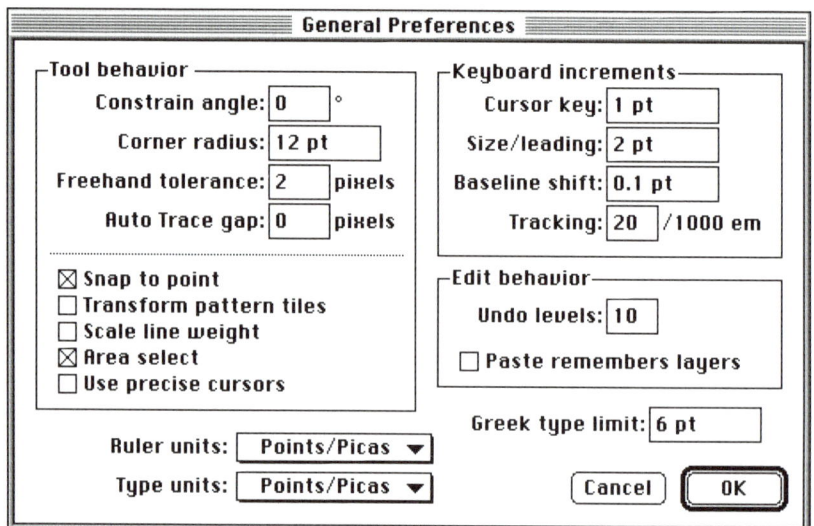

> **General Preferences**
>
> ┌─Tool behavior ──────────────────
> Constrain angle: `0` °
> Corner radius: `12 pt`
> Freehand tolerance: `2` pixels
> Auto Trace gap: `0` pixels
>
> ☒ Snap to point
> ☐ Transform pattern tiles
> ☐ Scale line weight
> ☒ Area select
> ☐ Use precise cursors
>
> ┌─Keyboard increments─────
> Cursor key: `1 pt`
> Size/leading: `2 pt`
> Baseline shift: `0.1 pt`
> Tracking: `20` /1000 em
>
> ┌─Edit behavior─────
> Undo levels: `10`
> ☐ Paste remembers layers
>
> Greek type limit: `6 pt`
>
> Ruler units: Points/Picas ▼
> Type units: Points/Picas ▼
>
> [Cancel]   (OK)

Tool Behavior Preferences

■ **Constrain Angle** resets the *X* and *Y* axes to the angle you prefer. The default setting (0°) sets the *X* axis parallel to the sides of the document window and the *Y* axis parallel to the bottom. Changing this setting will affect the axis on which new objects are drawn.

■ **Corner Radius** sets the curve radius for rounded rectangle corners.

■ **Freehand Tolerance** sets how closely the program will follow the dotted line created by the Freehand tool when it is used to draw a line. A higher setting will cause the program to generate fewer points along the path, resulting in a smoother line. A low setting will cause the program to follow your cursor more closely, resulting in a more jagged look.

■ **Auto Trace Gap** sets how closely the program will trace around a template when the Auto Trace tool is used. Setting a lower number tells the program to follow the template more closely, while a larger number gives it more flexibility to ignore small bumps and gaps it encounters while tracing.

■ **Snap to Point** causes objects and lines to snap to the closest anchor point, guide or intersection when drawing.

■ **Transform Pattern Tiles** tells the program to transform the fill pattern within an object when the object itself is modified using one of the transformation tools. When this option is left unchecked, the fill pattern will remain positioned and scaled the same, despite the transformation of the object.

■ **Scale Line Weight** sets the default for how line weights will be scaled when an object is transformed.

■ **Area Select** will allow you to click anywhere inside a filled object to select it when in Preview mode.

■ **Use Precise Cursors** changes the cursor icons for the Pen, Brush, Freehand, Paint and Eyedropper tools into cross hair cursors. This makes it easier to draw and apply color to smaller objects than with the pictorial icons normally displayed as cursors for these tools.

Keyboard Increments

■ **Cursor Key** sets the increments by which the cursor will move when you press the up, down, left and right arrow keys on your keyboard.

■ **Size/Leading** determines the default keyboard increment values for size and leading of type.

■ **Baseline Shift** sets the increments in which type will be shifted above and below the baseline.

■ **Tracking** sets the default value for tracking and kerning of type.

Edit Behavior

- **Undo Levels** sets the number of operation that you can "undo" as you work.
- **Paste Remembers Layers**, when checked, pastes a cut object back onto the same layer from which it was cut, regardless of where it is moved.

Other Preference Controls

- **Ruler Units** gives you a choice of points/picas, inches, or millimeters that can be used as the measurement units on the horizontal and vertical rulers.
- **Type Units** sets the increments in which type units are measured.
- **Greek Type Limit** sets the point size at which Illustrator will begin to greek smaller text on your screen. When type is greeked, it appears as a gray bar on screen. This speeds up the redraw process for your machine. The type itself is not affected, just the way it is viewed.

Summary

Adobe Illustrator 5.5 is a well-organized drawing program that is designed to be easy for anyone to use, whether you're a novice or seasoned professional. This chapter reviewed the dialog boxes, tools and preferences that are important for you to become familiar with as you learn the program. As you use the program, most of these elements will become second nature and you'll soon find yourself flipping to the correct tool or palette automatically as you work.

With all of these thoughts in mind, let's proceed to the next chapter and start using Adobe Illustrator. Chapter 3 is a detailed presentation of the beginning tools and commands, designed to get you on your feet and running with Illustrator by the end of the chapter. Also included are four exercises that will give you hands-on experience with the material as you go. Are you ready to become an Illustrator power user? Just turn the page.

Illustrator Basics

Although it's a feature-rich program that allows you to do complex things, Adobe Illustrator consists of some very basic tools and operations. Once you get a feel for how these work, the rest of the program will be icing on the cake. As a designer, you already have an instinctual grasp of how traditional design tools work, and the tools in Illustrator behave very similarly. Learning to use them will come naturally to you. This is an added bonus, since you will be able to jump right in and express your ideas in Illustrator all the faster.

This chapter takes a look at some of the more basic tools in Illustrator and how they work. You will learn how to use the line- and shape-drawing tools and how to fill (paint) the objects you create with color. In addition, you will also begin learning about manipulating objects and adding type to your designs.

To reinforce what you learn, get some hands-on experience by completing the four exercises offered in this chapter. As you work each one, you will be using the skills and concepts you've just learned. By the end of this chapter you should feel comfortable enough to begin using Illustrator on your own.

We'll begin by trying out Illustrator's drawing tools. Before you start drawing, however, it's useful to know about Illustrator's three viewing modes.

Viewing Modes in Illustrator

Illustrator offers three ways of looking at your document on the screen:

The **Artwork** (⌘-E) mode shows only the outlines of objects as they are drawn and styled. This is the fastest mode to work in, especially with a complex design. It's the mode you'll use in this chapter and throughout the book, except where instructed to switch to another mode.

Preview (⌘-Y) shows your design on screen the way it will actually look when printed, with all styles and color in place. Unlike earlier versions of Illustrator, version 5.5 lets you edit a file directly in Preview mode. However, depending on the complexity of your file and the amount of RAM in your Mac, the program is almost sure to run slower in Preview mode. Also note that in this mode you can't see anything you have not given a color and line weight.

Preview Selection (⌘-Option-Y) is essentially a blend of the first two viewing modes. In Preview Selection mode, all objects are shown in Artwork mode except for the currently selected object or objects, which will appear in Preview mode.

Drawing with Tools

As you would pick up a pencil and begin to draw on a piece of the drawing tools in Adobe Illustrator allow you to work in the manner on your screen. It may take some time before you feel able drawing with the mouse in your hand, but keep trying. on find that the tools are much more forgiving than a regular eraser, and even fun to use.

There are several drawing tools available in Adobe Illustrator. Each tool creates a line or shape in a different way, and some of the tools even have multiple functions. We'll start by learning to draw lines.

Drawing Lines

In Adobe Illustrator, a line consists of a *line segment* or *path*, the straight portion of a line, and two *anchor points*, the points on each end of a line that show the beginning and ending areas of a path. In addition, a curved line also contains *direction points*, moveable arms that extend from an anchor point that you can adjust to change the shape of a curve (Figure 3.1). Selected anchor points are solid, while unselected points remain hollow.

3.1

3.1

Lines and curves in Adobe Illustrator consist of line segments, anchor points, and direction points.

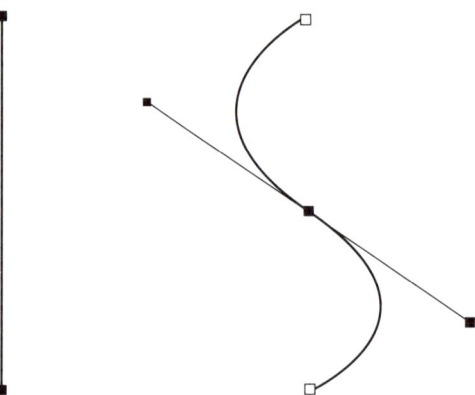

Unlike rectangles and other shapes, lines are considered open paths; that is, they have both a beginning and an ending anchor point. However, lines can be joined together to create closed-path shapes such as polygons.

Creating Straight Lines with the Pen Tool

The Pen tool can create both straight lines and curves, depending on how it is used. To draw a straight line with the Pen tool:

1. Click on the Pen tool once to select it.

2. In the drawing area, click once and release the mouse button to create the first anchor point.

3. Move the mouse in any direction and click the button once again. A second anchor point will appear with a line segment stretched between them (Figure 3.2).

3.2

A straight line drawn with the Pen tool.

Since a polygon consists of a series of straight lines, it is an easy shape to create using the Pen tool:

1. With the Pen tool selected, click and move your mouse to create each side and point of the polygon.

2. When you are ready to close the path, move your cursor back over the original anchor point. A small circle will appear to the right of your pen cursor on the screen (Figure 3.3). This indicates that two points will be joined if you click on that spot.

3. Click over the first anchor point to join the paths and finish the polygon.

3 . 3

The Pen tool can be used to create straight-sided shapes. To join the two ends, place your cursor over the original anchor point and click.

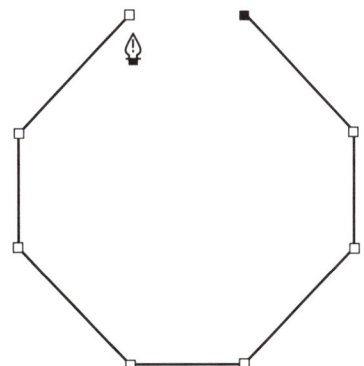

INSIDE INFO

The Undo command can be a real lifesaver when you accidentally take a wrong turn in the middle of a design. Use the keyboard shortcut ⌘-Z to undo the last step or sequence of steps performed; then pick up from there and keep drawing.

To adjust the size of any straight line, click on the Direct Selection tool and then click on an anchor point and drag it. The point you select will become solid, while the rest of the points in the line will remain hollow.

To constrain a line so that it can only be drawn at 45-degree angles, hold down the Shift key while drawing. This is an easy way to draw a perfectly straight line, especially over long distances.

Creating Curves with the Pen Tool

Curved lines are similar to straight lines in composition, but with a difference—curves have *direction points*. Direction points extend from the anchor points in a curve on *direction lines*, so that you can easily adjust the curvature in a line (Figure 3.4). They are only visible when you select an anchor point containing direction points, and disappear when you select another point or object.

3.4

A curved line consists of direction points, which extend away from anchor points on direction lines.

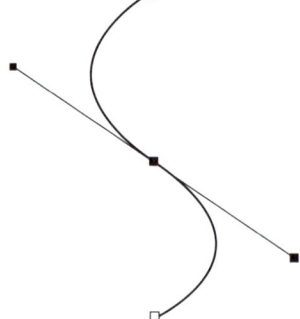

There are a few rules to remember when creating curves. First, a curve will be smoother if its anchor points are located on the sides of the curve, rather than on the top or bottom "bump." Second, the fewer anchor points in a path, the smoother the curve will be. When using the Pen tool, you have tight control over the placement of anchor points since you are placing each one by hand.

To create a curve using the Pen tool:

1. Click once and move your mouse to the right.
2. Now click again and hold the mouse button down, moving the mouse downward. A line will appear between the two points and begin to curve.

3. You will see direction points and lines appear at the tip of your cursor as you pull away from the last anchor point. Depending on how much you pull down and away from the anchor point, the height and angle of the curve will change.

4. Release the mouse button when the curve is complete.

How a line curves depends on the position of the direction lines and points. The angle of each direction line sets the angle for the curve. How long you extend the direction point away from its anchor point sets the curve's height or depth (Figure 3.5). Learning how to adjust the direction points correctly to manipulate curves takes a little practice. As you work with Illustrator, however, it will become second nature.

3.5

To change the
shape of a curve,
adjust the angle of
the direction point,
and the length of
the direction line.

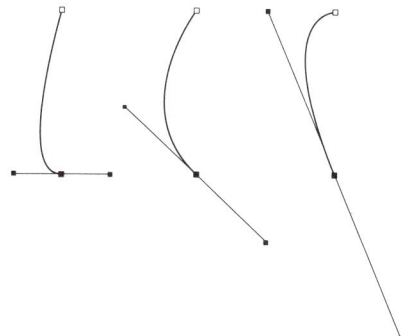

To create a continuous wavy line, you only need to adjust the direction points of every other anchor point you create:

1. Click once to place the first anchor point and move your cursor to the right.

2. Now click and pull to place another point and adjust the curve's direction points.

3. Move your cursor to the right and click again—another curve will appear on its own.

4. Again, move your cursor to the right, click, and then drag on the point to adjust the curve.

5. Move once more to the right and click to place the next curve.

Continue this pattern to create a wavy line of any length (Figure 3.6).

3.6

A wavy line is created using a series of curves.

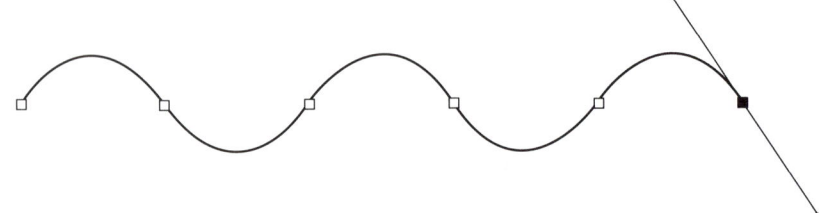

Creating a Curve with the Freehand Tool

The Freehand tool (not to be confused with Aldus Freehand, a competing drawing program) also creates curves, but with less precision than the Pen tool. As the name implies, it reproduces your mouse movements, irregularities and all. Unlike the Pen tool, the Freehand tool gives you little control over where and how the anchor points are placed while you are drawing. Everywhere the line you sketch curves, this tool adds another anchor point. However, you do have complete control over editing the points in a Freehand curve once it has been drawn.

You can set how closely the Freehand tool will trace the movements of your mouse in the General Preferences dialog box (⌘-K). The Freehand Tolerance setting determines whether Illustrator will follow the line you draw closely (within one or two pixels), or more loosely (within ten pixels). The more closely the program follows what you draw, the more points will be added to the shape. This will result in curves that look more angular than smooth (Figure 3.7).

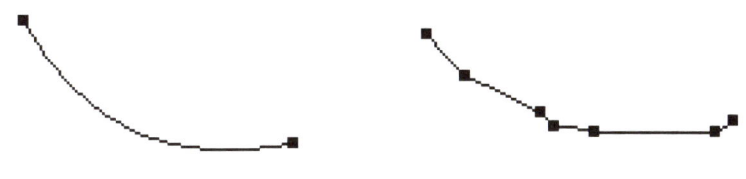

3.7

When the Free-hand Tolerance is set at ten pixels, the shape appears smoother.

INSIDE INFO

I find it easiest to keep the freehand tolerance set to 10 pixels when drawing with a mouse. I've found that even at 10 pixels, a curved line of any length is still rendered with a few too many points. Unfortunately, the mouse cannot move as gracefully as a pen.

To use the Freehand tool:

1. Click on the tool.
2. Click and drag on your page to draw.

Like the Pen tool, the Freehand tool can also create open or closed paths. When you're drawing with the Freehand tool, a small circle will appear to the right of the cursor when you place it back over the beginning anchor point (Figure 3.8). Clicking on this point will join the two open ends, closing the path.

3.8

Two anchor points will be joined if you click when a small circle appears next to your cursor.

If you want to erase part of your Freehand tool creation as you draw, simply hold down on the Command (⌘) key and your cursor will turn into an eraser. Move the eraser back over the line to delete a portion of it; then release the Command key to start drawing again.

Creating a Curve with the Brush Tool

 The Brush tool creates broad stroked lines, much as a real brush would. Unlike the Pen and Freehand tools, the Brush tool does not create a single open path when you draw a line. Instead, it creates a closed-path object that follows the movement of your mouse (Figure 3.9). To use the Brush tool, select it and then click and drag to draw a line.

3.9

The Brush tool creates a stroked line (left) by rendering a closed-path object (right).

You can modify the Brush tool to some extent by using the Brush dialog box (Figure 3.10), which you'll find by double-clicking on the Brush tool in the Tool palette. Here you can select a brush width in points, as well as whether you want angled or smooth corner joins and line ends. The dialog box also offers a calligraphic mode, which when selected will give a ribbon-like effect to lines drawn with the Brush tool (Figure 3.11).

AUTHOR'S NOTE

If you are using an electronic drawing tablet and pen, you can also use the Brush dialog box to select a variable line width. This will give you the feel of a real brush, since the line width will vary depending on the pressure you use with the pen on the drawing tablet.

3.10

In the Brush dialog box, you can adjust the width of a Brush stroke and turn the calligraphic mode on or off.

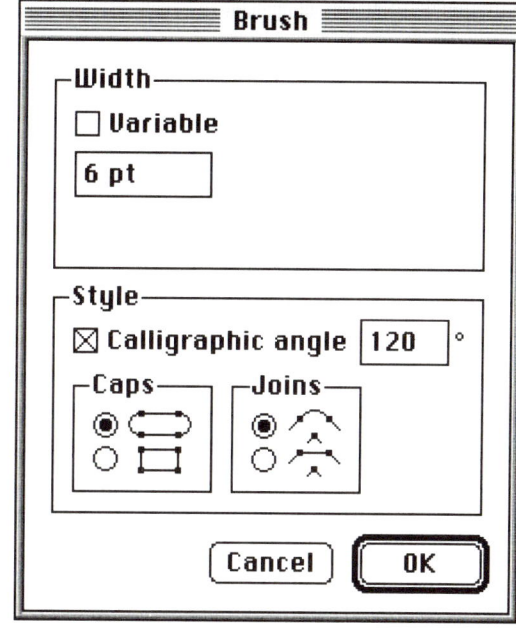

3.11

When the calligraphic mode is turned on, a line drawn with the Brush tool will take on a ribbon-like effect.

Drawing Basic Shapes

There are tools for creating shapes in Adobe Illustrator: the Oval, the Rectangle, and the Rounded Rectangle, illustrated at left. In addition, each can be constrained to create a circle, square, or a rounded square, respectively. Since the three tools all work in the same way, let's use the Rectangle tool as an example.

1. Select the Rectangle tool from the Toolbox.

2. Click on your page where you want the upper-left corner of the rectangle to be positioned.

3. With the mouse button still depressed, drag down and to the right. The outline of a rectangle will form on your screen as you drag the mouse.

4. Release the mouse button when the rectangle is the size you prefer (Figure 3.12).

3.12

The Rectangle tool creates a rectangular shape when dragged down and to the right.

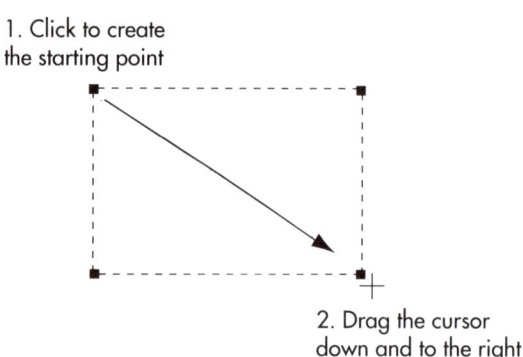

1. Click to create the starting point

2. Drag the cursor down and to the right

Drawing Shapes from the Center Out

If you prefer to draw shapes around a center point instead of from the upper-left corner, you can modify any of the tools to work in this mode simply by double-clicking on the tool in the Toolbox. A small plus sign will appear in the middle of the tool, indicating that its shape will be drawn from the center out (Figure 3.13).

Using a Dialog Box to Create Precisely Sized Shapes

There is a third method of creating shapes, which works best if you already know the precise size that a shape needs to be.

1. Click on your preferred shape tool.

2. Click on your page and release the mouse button.

3. A dialog box will appear, where you can enter the height and width of your shape (Figure 3.14).

3 . I 3

Shapes can also be drawn from the middle out when you modify one of the shape tools.

1. Click to create the starting center point

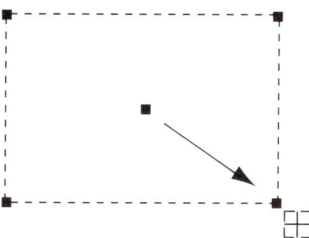

2. Drag from the center down and to the right

3 . I 4

If you know the dimensions of an object ahead of time, you can use the Rectangle dialog box to enter the precise dimensions.

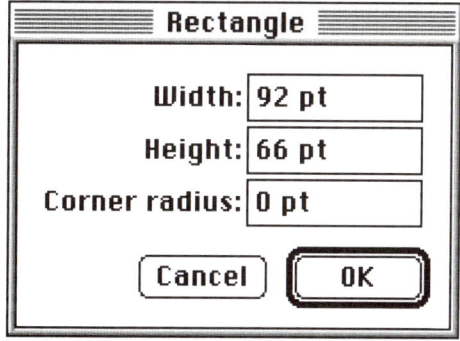

4. Click OK. The shape will appear on your page.

Creating "Constrained" Shapes—Circles and Squares

As mentioned before, you can constrain any of the main shape tools to create a circle, square, or rounded square object, simply by holding down the Shift key. This time, let's use the Oval tool to create a circle in our example:

1. Select the Oval tool from the Toolbox.

2. Click on your page and begin to drag. An oval shape will appear.

3. Push and hold the Shift key as you drag with the mouse. The oval will snap to a circular shape.

4. With the Shift key *and* the mouse button still depressed, adjust the size of the circle with the mouse.

5. When the circle is the proper size, release the mouse button and *then* the Shift key. If you release the Shift key first, the object will snap back to an oval shape.

Designing as You Learn: The Flower Drawing

To reinforce what you have just learned, you can use your new skills in the following exercise. The easiest way to learn something is by doing it yourself, so throughout this book you'll find exercises such as this one following each new section. This will give you the chance to practice and visually understand what is going on before diving into more advanced material.

Our first exercise uses a combination of lines, curves, and objects to create a flower. This is not a complex design—in fact, it is rather rudimentary. But it does combine the proper elements in a simple design that should be familiar to everyone.

Setting Up

First, you will need a new document window. If you have just started Adobe Illustrator 5.5, a new document window will automatically open when the application is started. If there isn't a new document window open on your screen, open one now by choosing New under the File menu (⌘-N).

Make sure you are working in Artwork mode (⌘-E). This will give you a better view of what you are working on during this lesson.

You will need to have the Info palette on your screen during this exercise. It will list measurements that will be helpful in keeping your drawing proportional. You can open the Info palette by selecting Show Info in the Window menu (⌘-Control-I).

Last, but not least, make sure your document window is set to 100 percent. Look at the top of your document window in the title bar—this is where the percentage of your current view is listed. To change the view to 100 percent, double-click on the Zoom tool in the Toolbox or press ⌘-H.

Drawing the Center of the Flower

1. Click on the Oval tool.

2. With the Shift key depressed to constrain the shape, click and drag on your page to create a circle that is approximately 35 points high and wide (check the Info palette for the measurements).

3. Release the mouse button. You should see a circle that closely resembles Figure 3.15.

3.15

Check the Info palette as you draw to adjust your dimensions.

X: 220 pt	W: 35.355 pt	
Y: 174 pt	H: 35.355 pt	

Drawing the Petals

We want the petals to have a slightly asymmetrical look, so we'll use the Freehand tool to draw them:

1. Go into the General Preferences dialog box (⌘-K) and set the Freehand Tolerance to 10 pixels. Click on the OK button to exit.

2. Select the Freehand tool from the Toolbox.

3. You will be drawing the petals of the flower now. Click your cursor on the top edge of the circle you just drew and begin to draw large loops around the perimeter of the circle.

4. When you have drawn petals around the entire perimeter, move your mouse over the beginning anchor point and release the mouse button.

5. Your flower should now resemble the one in Figure 3.16.

3.16

Using the Free-
hand tool, add
petals to the flower.

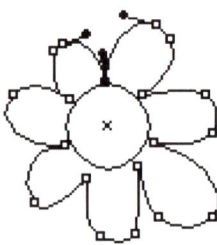

Drawing the Stem

For the stem we'll draw a simple vertical line:

1. Select the Pen tool from the Toolbox.

2. Click at the base of the flower's center circle and release the mouse button.

3. Move your cursor down approximately 100 points below the first place you clicked. The upper-right corner of the Info palette will give you a depth reading, using the first point as reference.

4. Hold down the Shift key and click again. A vertical line will appear between the two anchor points. Holding down the Shift key constrained the line to the nearest 45-degree angle, which in this case was straight up and down.

5. With the line still selected, move it behind the rest of the flower by selecting Send to Back in the Arrange menu (⌘-hyphen). Since you are working in Artwork mode your screen view will not change, so don't be alarmed.

Adding Leaves to the Flower

We'll again use the Freehand tool to draw the leaves:

1. Select the Freehand tool from the Toolbox.

2. Click on a point midway down the stem and draw a leaf shape by curving out to a point, clicking, and moving back to click again on the original point to close the path.

3. On the opposite side of the stem, draw another leaf by repeating the last step (Figure 3.17).

3.17

The leaves are created using the Freehand tool.

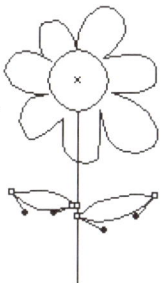

Drawing the Planter Box

The planter box is a simple rectangle:

1. Select the Rectangle tool from the Toolbox.

2. Click on your page below and slightly to the left of the flower stem, and drag a rectangle down and to the right, until it is approximately 100 points wide by 50 points high (check the Info palette to adjust your dimensions as you draw).

3. Release the mouse key. Your drawing should resemble Figure 3.18.

3.18

The completed flower drawing.

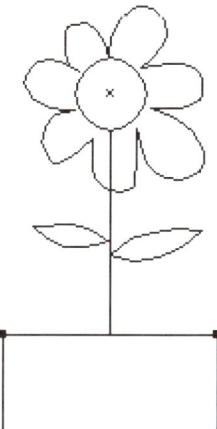

4. Print your drawing now to see the finished results on paper.

Saving Your Drawing

You can save this exercise now by selecting Save in the File menu (⌘-S). The Save As dialog box will appear (Figure 3.19). Name the file Flower and save it as an Illustrator 5 document. To keep things organized, create a new folder on your hard drive to store this and future exercises as you complete them.

3.19

Saving a new document gives you easy access to the drawing in the future.

Manipulating Objects

One of the nicest things about using a computer drawing package is that designs aren't set in stone after they're drawn. You still have the freedom to move objects around until you are completely satisfied with the way your design looks.

In this section you will begin to learn about manipulating objects you've drawn. Since this is a broad subject in Adobe Illustrator, we'll focus on moving, duplicating, and grouping objects for now. In later chapters you will learn more advanced object manipulation techniques.

Moving Objects

Moving any object—whether line, curve, or shape—in Adobe Illustrator is easily accomplished using the Selection tool. This tool selects the entire path and all points so that they can be moved as one object. Make sure you are using the Selection tool (the solid black arrow at left). The Direct Selection tool (the white arrow) will not initially select an entire object at once.

To move any line, curve, or shape in Adobe Illustrator:

1. Click on the Selection tool (the solid black arrow) in the Toolbox.

2. Click and hold on any side or point of the object you wish to move. The object will become selected, showing solid anchor points.

3. With the mouse button still depressed, begin to drag the object in any direction (Figure 3.20).

3.20

To move an object, just click and drag using the Selection tool.

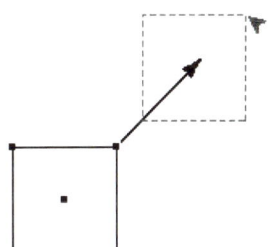

4. Release the mouse button when you have placed the object in its new location.

INSIDE INFO

Regardless of the tool you have selected, you can temporarily change it into the Selection tool simply by holding down the Command key. The tool will switch and behave as the Selection tool so that you can select or move an object before continuing on with your drawing. To return to your original tool, release the Command key.

If you know the precise amount that an object needs to be moved, you can use the Move dialog box (⌘-Shift-M) to enter the horizontal and/or vertical movement amounts (Figure 3.21). When you click the OK button, the object will move to the new location you specified. The Move dialog box can also copy the selected object and place the copy in a new location, leaving the original untouched.

3.21

The Move dialog box lets you move objects, as well as create and offset a copy of the original.

```
╔══════════════ Move ══════════════╗
║                                   ║
║    Horizontal: │ 0 pt          │  ║
║      Vertical: │ 12 pt         │  ║
║   ─────────────────────────────   ║
║      Distance: │ 12 pt         │  ║
║         Angle: │ 90          │ °   ║
║                                   ║
║      ⊠ Objects  □ Pattern tiles   ║
║   ( Copy )  ( Cancel )  (( OK ))  ║
╚═══════════════════════════════════╝
```

Duplicating Objects

Objects in Adobe Illustrator can be duplicated in numerous ways. Many of the advanced transformation tools you'll explore in Chapter 4 let you create a copy of an object as it is transformed. The Move dialog box, as mentioned above, can also create and place a duplicate copy of the selected object in a new location.

By far the easiest and most direct way to duplicate an object, though, is to use the traditional Copy and Paste commands. These commands are fairly standard throughout most applications and are applicable to both graphics and text.

When you invoke the Copy command on a selected object, that object is copied to the Clipboard, a temporary "holding cell" of sorts. When you give the Paste command, the object is copied from the Clipboard and pasted into the document in a new location. As long as you don't Copy or Cut anything else to the Clipboard first, you can Paste an object from the Clipboard as many times as it is needed.

To duplicate an object using the Copy and Paste commands:

1. Click on the Selection tool in the Toolbox.

2. Click on the object you wish to duplicate so that it is selected.

3. Invoke the Copy command by selecting Copy from the Edit menu or by using the keyboard shortcut, ⌘-C.

4. If you need to move to a new area of your design in order to place the copy, do so now.

5. Select Paste from the Edit menu (⌘-V) to paste a copy of the object back into the document.

6. If necessary, click on the copy and drag it to a new location.

Grouping Objects

There will be times when you'll find it convenient to manipulate several objects at once. In order to do this efficiently, Adobe Illustrator allows you to group an unlimited number of objects together. Once you've created a group, it becomes, in effect, a single "object" that you can transform in numerous ways: moving, rotating, deleting, duplicating, and painting, just to name a few.

To group two or more objects, first you must select them. This can be done in three ways:

- Hold down the Shift key and click on each object with the Selection tool, or

■ Use the Selection tool to draw a marquee (also called "marching ants") around the objects to be grouped (Figure 3.22), or

■ If there are no other objects in the document, use the Select All command in the Edit menu (⌘-A) to select all the objects in your document.

3.22

To select items for a group, you can draw a marquee around the items. The marquee only needs to touch an object to select it; it does not need to enclose the object completely.

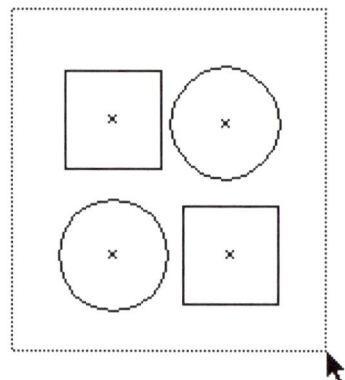

INSIDE INFO

If you have accidentally selected the wrong object, hold down the Shift key and click on the object again to deselect it.

Once you've chosen the proper items, select Group from the Arrange menu (⌘-G) to create a group. From now on when you click on any of the grouped items with the Selection tool, all of the items in the group will be selected and travel as a group. You can still edit individual items within a group, however, by using the Direct Selection tool.

To release the grouping feature, simply select the group and in the Arrange menu choose Ungroup (⌘-U). You will need to click on a neutral area on the page to deselect the items before the Ungroup command will take effect.

Designing as You Learn: The Five-Ring Logo

Take some time out now to practice what you just learned in the previous section. In this exercise you'll create a familiar design—a variation on the Olympic logo, a pattern consisting of five rings. This is an easy design to create, and perfect for practicing moving, duplicating, and grouping skills.

Open and Save a New Document

1. Select New from the File menu (⌘-N). A new document window with an empty page will appear.

2. Use the keyboard shortcut ⌘-S to open the Save dialog box.

3. Enter a new name, Ring Logo, for this document and click on the Save button.

4. Make sure your document is set to Artwork mode (⌘-E).

Duplicating Circles

Now we're ready to begin drawing. We'll create a circle and make four copies of it.

1. With the Oval tool selected, hold down the Shift key and draw a circle on your page. Make it about the size of a quarter.

2. With the circle still selected, use the Copy command (⌘-C) to copy the circle to the Clipboard.

3. Invoke the Paste command (⌘-V) four times. You will only see one new circle appear on your screen, but it is really four copies of the circle stacked on top of each other.

Moving the Circles into Position

1. With the Selection tool, click and drag on the stack of duplicated circles. One of the circles will follow your cursor as you drag.

2. Position the circle to the right of the original circle.

3. Continue to click and drag on the stack of duplicated circles, putting the second circle to the right of the third, and placing the fourth and fifth circles next to each other below the first row, overlapping the top row. Figure 3.24 shows this stage in progress.

3.23

Duplicating the Circle.

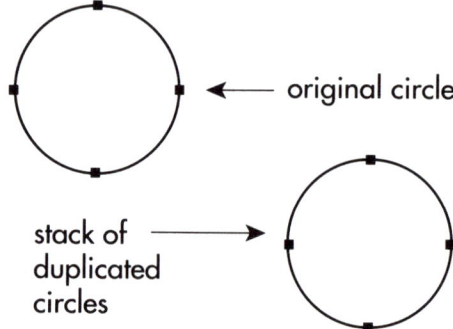

stack of duplicated circles

original circle

3.24

Dragging the circles into position.

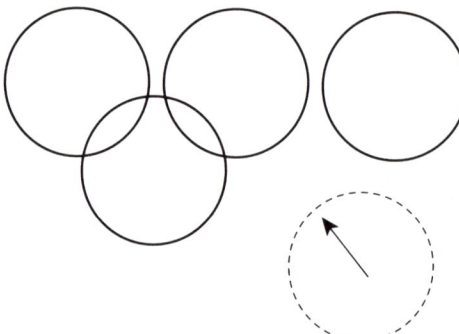

Grouping the Circles

It's a good idea to group the items of a design together before closing the file, in case you accidentally click on one and move it out of place.

1. Hold down the Shift key now, and with the Selection tool click on each circle to select them all. You can also use the Selection tool to simply draw a marquee around all the objects to select them.

2. Group them together by using the keyboard shortcut for the Group command, ⌘-G.

3.25

The finished Olym-
pic logo.

3.25

The finished Olym-
pic logo.

INSIDE INFO

When using the marquee method to select a group of objects, you do not need to draw the marquee completely around the objects. As long as the marquee touches any part of the object, it will become selected.

Saving Your Document

It is always a good idea to save your files every few minutes while you work on them. Not only does it ensure that your hard work becomes a permanent fixture on your computer, it also safeguards against unforeseen catastrophes (power failures being a popular one).

Save your document by selecting the Save command under the File menu (⌘ S).

Adding Type to a Document

Type is often an integral part of a design. Whether you're designing an advertisement, a technical drawing, or a book cover, the type you choose and how you display it will be an important factor to consider.

In this section, we'll discuss the basics of placing and editing type in a document. Chapter 6 will get more in depth about Adobe Illustrator's amazing new type handling features, but first we need to cover the principles that will make all that designing excitement possible.

AUTHOR'S NOTE

The words type and text are used interchangeably in this section and, for these purposes, have the same meaning.

Entering Type into a Document

Type is entered into a document using any of three type tools located in the Toolbox palette. In this section we will only be using the main Type tool.

1. Click on the Type tool in the Toolbox palette. Your on-screen cursor will become an I-beam cursor.

2. Click the cursor on your document window in the area where you want the type to be placed. This will create an anchor point for the type, and a blinking insertion point cursor will appear.

3. Begin to type the words you want to place in your document.

4. When you are finished typing, move your cursor back to the Toolbox and click on the Selection tool (Figure 3.26).

3.26

Type is entered into a document at an insertion anchor point.

.Come one, Come all
to the Big Sale!
Shop 'til you drop!

With the Clipboard, you also have the option of copying and pasting type into your document from another Illustrator file, or from any Mac application. You can do this either by copying and placing the entire text block as you would an object, or by copying a section of type and inserting it into an existing text block.

Selecting Type

In order to edit and style type, you need to be able to select it. There are two ways to select type: by text block or with the I-beam insertion cursor.

Selecting Type by Text Block

1. Click on the Selection tool in the Toolbox.
2. Click on the small × in front of the first word in a text block, or anywhere along the baseline of type on any line of a text block.
3. The small × at the start of the text block will become a solid anchor point, and each line of text will become underlined, as you saw in Figure 3.26.

This block of text can now be moved, copied, deleted, or styled as a block. It cannot, however, be edited. For that purpose you need to select the text with the insertion cursor.

Selecting Type with the Insertion Cursor

1. Click on the Type tool in the Toolbox palette.
2. Click the I-beam cursor in front of the area of text you wish to select.
3. With the mouse button still depressed, drag the cursor across the words to be selected. To indicate that the words have been selected, you'll see reversed type against a dark bar (Figure 3.27).

3.27

Text that has been selected with the Type tool's insertion cursor becomes reversed out of a dark bar.

Come one, Come all to the Big Sale! Shop 'til you drop!

4. This selected section can now be edited for content, as well as styled, deleted, and copied for insertion in another text block. It cannot, however, be moved as an object.

Editing Type

Type can be edited by using the Type tool's I-beam cursor to highlight, insert, or replace text.

1. Click on the Type tool in the Toolbox.
2. Click at the point where you wish to insert type, or click and drag over an area of existing type that you wish to replace.
3. Begin typing. The new text will be entered at the insertion point, or will replace the text that was highlighted for removal.
4. To move to a new section of text to edit, move your mouse to position the I-beam cursor, and repeat the above steps.

Designing as You Learn: The Sale Ad

This is a short exercise that will give you a little experience in entering and editing type in a document. If you don't already have a document open, open a new one now by using the keyboard shortcut ⌘-N.

Adding Type to a Document

1. Click on the Type tool in the Toolbox.
2. Click your cursor anywhere on the blank page. As illustrated in Figure 3.28, it will change to a flashing insertion point. Type the words **Announcing the Year-End Clearance Sale!**
3. With the Zoom tool selected, click on your page to enlarge the view until you can comfortably read the type you have entered.

3.28

When you click the I-beam cursor on your page, it becomes a flashing cursor. This means it is ready to enter text.

I-beam cursor ⟶

insertion point ⟶

INSIDE INFO

To return to 100 percent of your screen size at any time, simply double-click on the Zoom tool in the Toolbox.

Selecting and Editing the Type

1. With the Type tool selected, click and drag your I-beam cursor over the words **Year-End** to highlight them.

2. Type in the word **Spring** to replace the highlighted words (Figure 3.29). You do not need to delete the words first before you begin typing—Illustrator will do that work for you.

3.29

Type is easy to edit in Adobe Illustrator.

Announcing the ▮Year-End▮ Clearance Sale!

Announcing the Spring Clearance Sale!

Moving a Block of Type

1. Switch now to the Selection tool. You'll notice that your selected type will become underlined, with an anchor point at the beginning of the line.

2. Click with the Selection tool on the anchor point (or anywhere on the underline) and drag to reposition the line of type.

Save Your Drawing

Get in the habit of saving your drawings often. Use the keyboard short-cut ⌘-S, and name this drawing Text Test. Click on the Save button to exit the dialog box.

Styling Text and Objects

What is style? In desktop publishing, this catch-all term refers to various aspects of an object's (or a text block's) appearance. Much more than editing for size, shape, or content, changes in style can directly affect the emotional impact that your design conveys. Changing the style of an item includes changing its color, texture, and outline or border. With type, it also includes changing the font, point size, and scale, among other elements.

While other chapters will cover each of these subjects in greater depth, this section is a styling sneak preview to get you rolling. In this section you will learn to fill and stroke objects with color, as well as learn how to change some basic text styling elements.

Painting: Filling Objects with Color

Adding color to a design is like turning on a light in a darkened room. Color adds detail, depth, and interest to a design, visually stimulating the viewer. It is amazing what even the smallest addition of color can do to bring an image to life.

The Paint Style palette in Adobe Illustrator offers an unlimited choice of colors that you can use to colorize any object or piece of type in a design. You can create your own color combinations, or choose from one of the many preset colors offered in the palette.

To fill any object with color:

1. Open the Paint Style palette (shown in Figure 3.30) by selecting Paint Style from the Object menu (⌘-I), or by choosing Show Paint Style from the Window menu..

2. Using the Selection tool, click on an object in your design to select it.

3. In the upper-left corner of the Paint Style palette there is a box labeled Fill. Click on this box to indicate that you want to change the fill color of the selected object.

4. The right side of the palette shows a series of boxes across the top. For the purposes of this lesson, we'll just use the first four of these boxes, as shown in Figure 3.31. In order from left to right, these boxes represent No Color, White, Black, and Process Color Fills. Click on the Process Color box.

5. Slider bars for each of the four process colors (Cyan, Yellow, Magenta, and Black) will appear below the color boxes, as shown in Figure 3.32. Adjust the levels of each slider bar to achieve the mixed color you prefer.

3.30

The Paint Style dialog box.

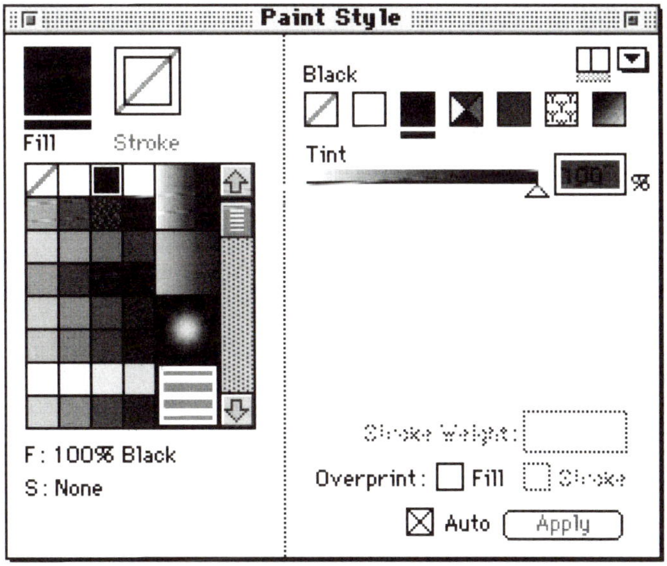

6. As you adjust the color levels, the fill box in the upper-left corner of the palette will show the current color combination. If you are working in Preview mode, the selected object on your page will also change each time you adjust a slider bar.

7. When you are finished selecting a color, just click on your page to return to your document. You can either leave the Paint Style palette open or close it to free up room on your screen.

3.31

Four of the color option boxes in the Paint Style dialog box, and what each represents.

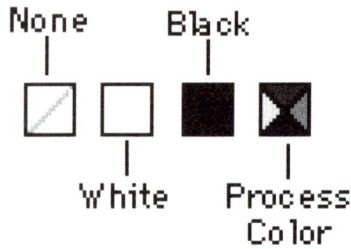

3.32

The slider bars in the Paint Style dialog box let you change the percentages of each color to obtain a custom color combination.

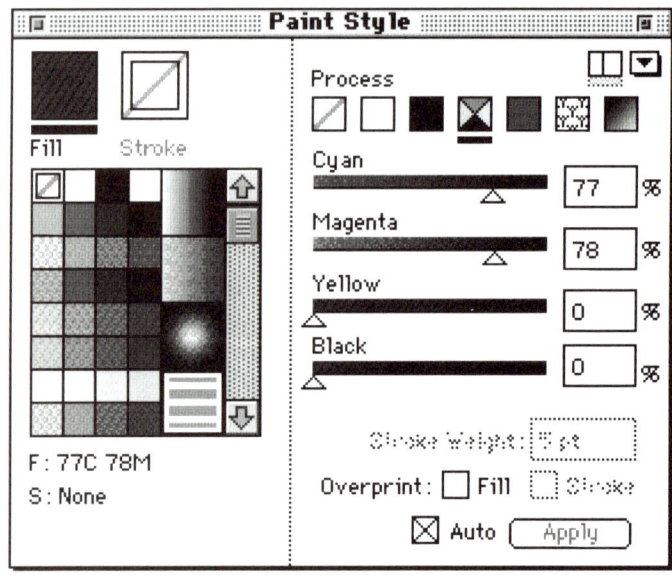

You can use this method of painting to fill any object or type in your document with color. In Chapter 7, you will learn more about color, including advanced color options and how to create customized patterns that can be used to fill objects.

Stroking: Adding Lines and Frames

The Paint Style palette is also used to create stroked lines. *Stroking* means to add a certain color at a certain width to color a line or curve, or to create a frame around a box.

It is important to remember that stroking always refers to lines of some sort. You *fill* an object with color, but you *stroke* a line or the border around an object. Often users will forget to stroke a line, leaving it "filled" with color instead. This produces an inconsistent, wimpy line that often disappears when printed. For consistent solid lines, always use the stroke feature.

To create a stroked line or border:

1. Open the Paint Style palette by selecting Paint Style from the Object menu (⌘-I), or by choosing Show Paint Style from the Window menu.

2. With the Selection tool, click on the object you wish to stroke.

3. In the upper-left corner of the Paint Style palette, next to the Fill box, there is a box labeled Stroke. Click on this box (Figure 3.33).

4. Once again, click on one of the smaller color boxes to the right to pick the type of color you want.

5. Adjust the slider bars until the color that borders the Stroke box is correct for your needs. Most often, you will probably just want to use black, but color is an option for stroked lines as well as filled objects.

6. To select the weight of the stroked line, enter a width (in points) in the Stroke Weight field. Then hit Return to make the width setting take effect in your drawing. Figure 3.34 shows several different line widths.

3.33

When you click on the Stroke box, you can adjust the color levels for the stroke of a line or border around an object.

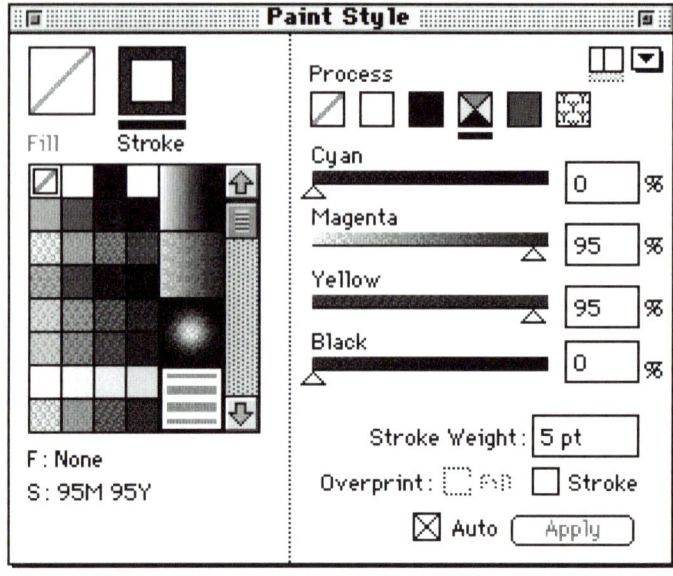

3.34

Adobe Illustrator measures line widths in points. Here are some examples from a half-point line to a 10-pt line.

Changing the Style of Type

In styling type you work with some elements that don't come into play when styling objects—font, point size, and scale. Type can also be filled with color and stroked to give it a solid outline, using the same techniques as with objects. This gives you a lot of freedom in designing with type and, in fact, your creativity may be limited only by the number of fonts you have loaded in your system.

Chapter 6 is a complete guide to working with type in Illustrator. For now, let's take a quick look at how you can style type using the Character palette.

Using the Character Palette

The Character palette (⌘-T) is a conglomeration of several handy type commands, all grouped in one convenient box (Figure 3.35). Instead of running back and forth to the menus to make changes, you can keep the Character palette on your desktop as you work with your text.

3.35

The Character palette combines several type style commands in one place.

To use the palette, just highlight a section of text and enter new commands in the palette for that section. If you use the pop-up menus next to the font, point size, and leading fields, you can scroll directly to a new selection and see the changes take effect immediately on your screen. If you type in new commands in the palette, you must hit the Return key to see the changes take place in your document.

Styling Text with Fonts

Selecting the appropriate font is one of the most basic decisions a designer can make about a piece of text. Each font has a personality all its own. Since the type of font you use can change the whole feel of a design, you should take into account the mood you want to create when choosing a font. For example, despite the fact that each line in Figure 3.36 says the same thing, each takes on a different personality from its chosen font.

3.36

These five lines of type say the same thing literally, but convey five different moods because of the fonts chosen.

You are cordially invited to the party.

You are cordially invited to the party.

You are cordially invited to the party.

You are cordially invited to the party.

You are cordially invited to the party.

Sizing and Shaping Type

Size is another important factor to consider. Headline type should be considerably bigger than the text of the story placed underneath. Likewise, the labels on a technical drawing should not be so large that they detract from the design, yet they shouldn't be so small that they are unreadable.

You may enlarge or reduce the point size of type depending on the font you choose. As you can see in Figure 3.36, not all fonts take up the same amount of room on a page, even at the same size. If you are using two or more fonts in a design, but want them to look symmetrical, you will probably need to set them to different sizes.

Another way to change the visual size of type is to change the horizontal scale of the letters. While a scaled version of type will remain the same height as normal, the horizontal width of each letter is either enlarged or reduced. This can create some unique effects, although it should be done in moderation (Figure 3.37).

3.37

This type is scaled at 100 percent (top), 120 percent (middle), and 75 percent (bottom).

You are cordially invited to the party.

You are cordially invited to the party.

You are cordially invited to the party.

WATCH OUT!

Type that is scaled down lower than 75 percent of normal begins to lose its readability—this can be disastrous in large blocks of small text. For the most part, save the horizontal scaling effects for larger display type.

Designing as You Learn: The Food Label

In this exercise, you'll add color to objects, stroke various lines, and style some type. Excited? You should be. You're getting into the fun part of learning the program now. Feel free to unleash your creativity as you do this exercise. If you prefer different colors or styles than the ones I suggest, by all means go for it.

In this exercise, you'll be designing a simple label for a food product. To better see what you are doing, you'll be toggling between Artwork (⌘-E) and Preview (⌘-Y) modes.

Setting Up the Exercise

1. Open a new document (⌘-N) and save it (⌘-S). Name it Food Label.
2. Open the Info palette (⌘-Control-I).
3. Make sure you are in Artwork mode (⌘-E).
4. Open the rulers in your document (⌘-R).

Getting Started

1. With the Rectangle tool, draw a rectangle that is 300 points wide by 200 points high. Check your dimensions in the Info palette as you draw.
2. Enlarge your view of the rectangle with the Zoom tool so that it fills the screen view.

3. To move the ruler zero point to the top-left corner of your rectangle, click in the lower-right corner of your document window where the two rulers meet and drag that point up to the upper-left corner of the rectangle (Figure 3.38).

3.38

Reset the ruler so that it coincides with the upper-left corner of your rectangle.

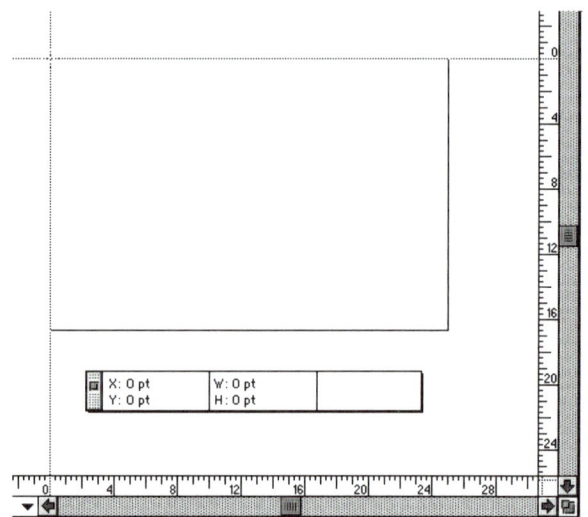

Adding to the Rectangle

1. With the Rectangle cursor still selected, move the cursor to the coordinate *X:0 pt, Y: −46 pt* (check the Info palette for this information).

2. Click on this point and drag to create another rectangle that is the same width as the first, and 14 points high.

3. With the Selection tool, click on this rectangle and copy it (⌘-C). Paste the copy back into your document (⌘-V), and use the Selection tool to position it at *X:0 pt, Y: −160 pt*.

4. Click on the Oval tool in the Toolbox. Move the cursor to the coordinate *X:146 pt, Y: −32 pt*. Click and drag to create an oval that is approximately 100 points wide by 20 points high.

5. With the Oval tool still selected, move your cursor to the coordinate *X:144 pt, Y: −80 pt.* While holding down both the Shift and Option keys, click and drag out a circle that is approximately 30 points in diameter.

6. While this circle is still selected, Copy (⌘-C) and Paste (⌘-V) two duplicates of the circle back on your page.

7. Use the Selection tool to move the circles into a triangular formation under the first, as shown in Figure 3.39.

3.39

The label design with the objects in place.

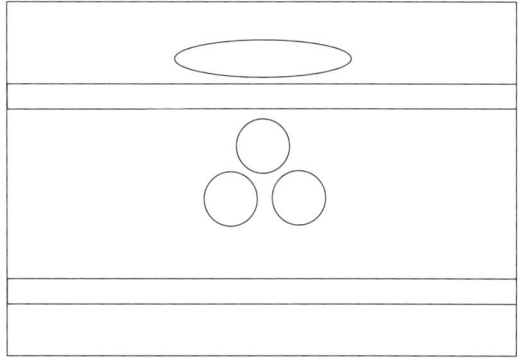

Adding Type to the Design

1. Click on the Type tool in the Toolbox.

2. Click your cursor in the middle of the top oval and type the words **Circus Brand.**

3. Center the words using the keyboard shortcut ⌘-Shift-C.

4. Use the Type tool to highlight the words. Open the Character palette (⌘-T) and change the font to Garamond Bold. If you don't have Garamond, choose any serif font that you like.

5. Use the Selection tool to adjust the centering of the words in the oval.

6. Click on the Type tool again and center your cursor vertically and horizontally in the space under the three circles.

7. Type in the word **PEANUTS** in all caps. Use the Selection tool to reposition it, if necessary, so that it is centered.

8. In the Character palette, change the font to Garamond Bold (or your preferred font), and the size of the type to 24 pt. Your drawing should now resemble Figure 3.40.

3.40

**The label design
with type added.**

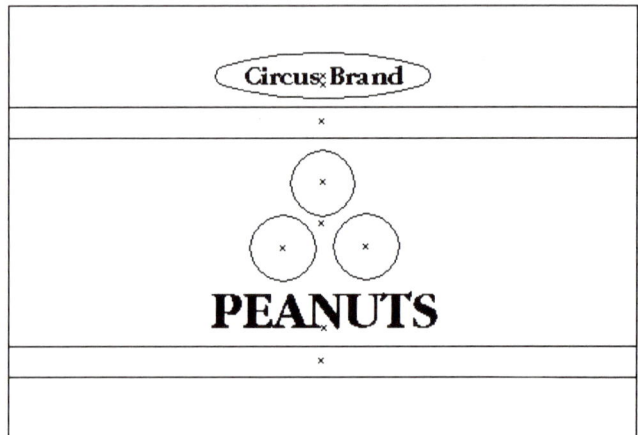

Coloring the Label

Now comes the fun part, where you see your design in living color (or a close facsimile). Since Illustrator's default for color is to fill everything with black (very unhelpful), let's change that first.

Use the Selection tool to draw a marquee around the design and then open the Paint palette (⌘-I). Click on the Fill button in the upper-left corner and then click on the "no color" button in the list to the right (it has a gray slash through it). Change to Preview mode (⌘-Y). Don't be alarmed—if you did this procedure correctly, you should see absolutely nothing. Why? Because you've yet to add any color to the objects you have created. Although the design is there in Artwork mode, the image will not show in Preview mode until after you have painted and stroked the design with color. Change back to Artwork mode now, and let's get started coloring.

1. Using the Selection tool, click on the large rectangle. In the Paint palette, fill the rectangle with 75% yellow and 20% magenta.

2. Holding down the Shift key, click on each of the smaller rectangles with the Selection tool to select them. Fill them with 100% yellow and 100% magenta.

3. Holding down the Shift key, click on each of the three circles to select them. Fill them all with 100% yellow and 100% magenta. Now give them a stroke of 1 point in black.

4. Click on the larger oval at the top of the drawing. Fill it with 100% yellow and 100% cyan. Give it a stroke of 0.5 point in black.

5. Click on the type within the oval with the Selection tool. Fill it with white.

6. Click on the PEANUTS type below. Fill it with 100% black, and give it a white stroke of 0.5 point.

7. Go to Preview mode (⌘-Y) now to check the results (Figure 3.41).

3.41

The completed label. Your screen version will look slightly more colorful than this.

Summary

We've reviewed the basic procedures for creating drawings in Adobe Illustrator 5.5. You should feel comfortable and confident enough now to sit down with Illustrator and create a simple drawing on your own. Although future chapters will go more in depth on much of the material presented in this chapter, you now hold the fundamental keys to designing with Illustrator in your hands.

In the next chapter, you will learn more about editing points and paths, as well as further object manipulation techniques. This will give you greater freedom in editing and transforming objects as you design.

Object Editing
and Transformation

Let's face it—no one is perfect, but as designers, most of us *are* perfectionists. We spend valuable time trying to get a design to look "just right" by editing and adjusting its elements over and over again. And, unfortunately, no two people have the same idea of what looks "just right," so if a design has to be approved by anyone else, it most likely will come back for more editing. No matter how you look at it, editing is a necessary and important step in the designing process.

Editing a design in Adobe Illustrator is a little like thinking aloud on your screen. As you move and resize the points and line segments of an object, often you'll be inspired to veer away from your original idea and try something different. Illustrator gives you this flexibility—you can always undo small changes or go back to the original design, should your burst of inspiration suddenly go sour.

This chapter expands on the basic object editing features of Adobe Illustrator that were described in Chapter 3. We'll discuss the different kinds of points an Illustrator object contains: what they are, how to manipulate and edit them, and even how to add them to and delete them from existing paths. Along with this, we'll talk about editing paths and how to perform object transformations, such as scaling, rotating, reflecting, and shearing.

Understanding Points and Paths

All objects in Adobe Illustrator contain *points* and *line segments*. In an angular object such as a square, each corner of the shape contains a single point. These points are joined together by line segments, which create the sides of the square (see Figure 4.1). This combination of points and line segments is called a *path*.

4.1

All objects are
made up of paths,
which in turn con-
tain points and line
segments.

points   line segments

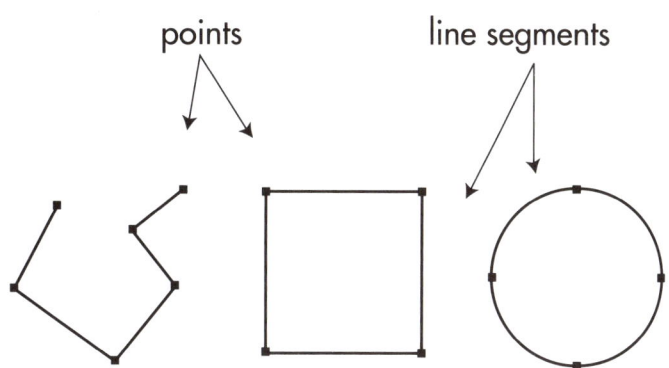

Path Types and How They Work

Since all objects are really paths, paths themselves come in several varieties. A *closed path*, such as a circle, is an unbroken circuit with numerous directional anchor points but no endpoints (see Figure 4.2). When a closed path is filled with color, all areas inside the path are colored.

An *open path*, such as a line, has a definite beginning and ending point. When an open path is filled with color, Adobe Illustrator will draw an imaginary line between the endpoints and fill the contained area with color.

WATCH OUT!

If you try to fill an open path consisting of a single straight line, it won't work. A single line has only two endpoints, and Illustrator (bound by the rules of geometry) needs three points on slightly different planes to define an area it can fill. A filled straight line may look all right on screen, but usually will print out looking wimpy (if it prints at all). For this reason, straight lines should be always be stroked instead of filled and assigned a definite line width to maintain their integrity.

4.2

A closed path (left) has no endpoints, while an open path (right) has a definite beginning and ending.

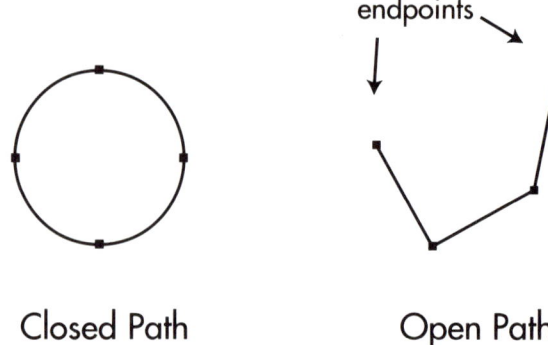

endpoints

Closed Path   Open Path

You can manipulate paths in numerous ways to adjust the shape of an object. Most often, these manipulations will involve adjusting the various points along a path. Since Adobe Illustrator uses several types of points to create shapes, let's examine each of them separately.

Types of Points and How They Work

While any independent line or the outline of any object can be considered a path, the elements that really define a path are its points. Illustrator uses several varieties of points that function in different ways to create specific shapes.

Anchor Points

Anchor points (Figure 4.3) are the most fundamental type. They define where one line segment ends and the next begins in a path. To move any anchor point, use the Direct Selection tool to click and drag the point to a new location.

When you've selected an anchor point with the Direct Selection tool, you can also move it by using the directional arrow keys on your keyboard. These arrows move the point up, down, right, or left, according to the Cursor Key increments set in the General Preferences dialog box (⌘-K).

4.3

Anchor points separate the line segments in a path.

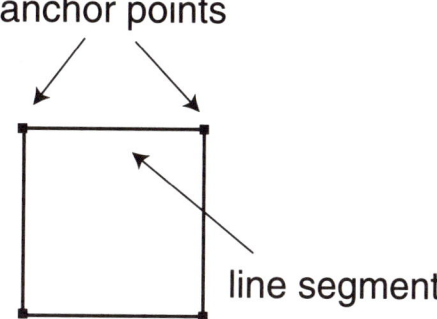

Endpoints

Endpoints (Figure 4.4) are the beginning and ending anchor points of an open path. When both are selected and the Join command is given (⌘-J), the two endpoints can be joined to create a closed path.

4.4

Endpoints are the beginning and ending anchor points of an open path.

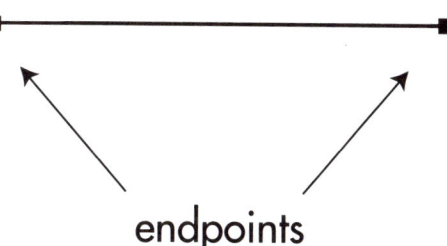

Direction Points

When an anchor point falls on a curved line segment, it will have one or two *direction points* associated with it. These are used to control the slope and depth of the curve. Direction points extend from their anchor points on *direction lines*, and appear when you click on any anchor point that falls on a curved line segment (Figure 4.5).

Once you have clicked on the appropriate anchor point, simply click and drag on a visible direction point to manipulate its curve. The angle of the direction line determines the slope of the curve, while the length of the direction line decides the height or depth of the curve.

4.5

Direction points extend on direction lines from anchor points that fall on curved line segments.

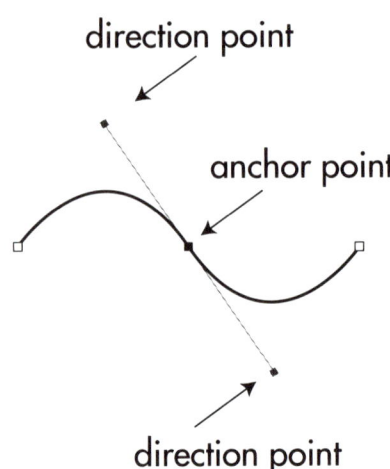

Smooth Points

Smooth points are anchor points that connect curved paths containing no angles (continuous curved line segments). A smooth point has two direction points that move symmetrically whenever either one is adjusted to keep the curve smooth and in alignment (Figure 4.6).

To adjust a smooth point, click on the point with the Direct Selection tool and then click and drag on either of its direction points. The angle of both direction points will move as you adjust the one—however, you can change the height or depth of the twin direction points separately by increasing or reducing the length of each direction line.

4.6

Smooth points have associated direction points that move synchronously whenever one is adjusted.

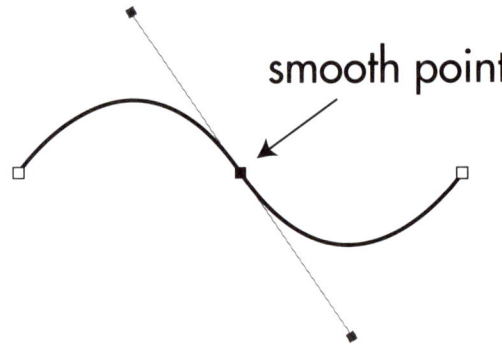

Corner Points

Corner points connect curved line segments that are separated by an angle, as in Figure 4.7. When you adjust one of the direction points associated with a corner point, it moves independently of its companion direction point, and adjusts the curve only on its side of the line segment.

4.7

Corner points con-
nect curves at an
angle.

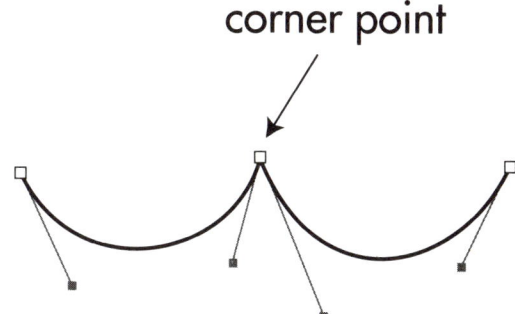

corner point

To adjust a corner point, click on the point with the Direct Selection tool and then click and drag on the direction point that falls on the side of the curve you wish to manipulate. As you move one direction point, you will notice that its companion direction point and line remain stable.

Center Points

Although they cannot be edited, all closed-path objects drawn with either the oval or rectangle tools will also contain a center point. The center point makes it easy to align text over an object such as a box, or to align the objects themselves. It also gives you a handy central point for rotating objects.

Adding Points to a Path

Since things rarely come out perfect the first time, Adobe Illustrator has made it possible to add anchor points to any path. This gives you the flexibility of changing the shape of any path without having to redraw it—just add an extra anchor point or two, manipulate them a little and you're set.

You add points to a path using the Add Anchor Point tool (at left). This tool may not be readily displayed in the Toolbox, since it shares its slot with three other tools. Click and hold on the Scissors tool (the default for that slot in the Toolbox), and you will see the other available tools pop up. The Add Anchor Point tool looks like the Pen tool with a small plus sign to the right.

With this tool selected, click on the path where you wish to insert an anchor point, as in Figure 4.8. An anchor point appropriate to the path will be inserted where you clicked. This means a directional anchor point will be inserted on a curve, while a regular anchor point will be inserted on a straight line segment.

4.8

The Add Anchor Point tool lets you add anchor points to any path.

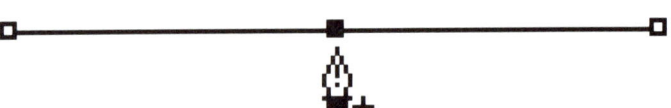

INSIDE INFO

 **You do not need to select a path before inserting a point on that path. Just click the Add Anchor Point tool on the edge of the path where you need another anchor point. However, if there are two or more paths intersecting at that position, you will need to select and bring the chosen path to the front before inserting a point. Otherwise, the point may be added to the wrong path.**

Curving Those Straight Lines: Converting Anchor Points

Straight lines are all very good and fine, but what happens if you suddenly need to turn a straight line into a curve? Rather than force you to redraw, Illustrator lets you convert regular anchor points into directional anchor points easily and painlessly. (To achieve the look you really want, you may also need to add another point or two to the path.)

 To begin the conversion process, you must first select the path using the Direct Selection tool. Next, select the Convert Direction Point tool from the Toolbox (it looks like a directional anchor point). Like the Add Anchor Point tool, it may not be readily visible in the Toolbox at first glance, but it is in the same slot as the Scissors and Add Anchor Point tools.

With the Convert Direction Point tool selected, move the triangular cursor over a point on the selected path, click, and hold down the mouse button. Now drag your mouse to the right and up a little. You will see the selected anchor point turn into a directional anchor point, and the straight line segment will have become a curve (Figure 4.9). Release the mouse button when you have adjusted the direction points of the anchor point appropriately.

4.9

The Convert Direction Point tool lets you change a regular anchor point into a directional anchor point.

WATCH OUT!

 **When adjusting direction points, be careful of the direction in which you move them. You can easily cross them in the wrong direction and end up with a loop instead of a smooth curve. Take the time to practice manipulating direction points correctly before you get in the middle of a project and get frustrated. They're not difficult to learn to work with—just different.**

Deleting Anchor Points

There are many reasons why you might need to delete anchor points from a drawing. For example, the Freehand tool often generates too many points along a path, leaving the line a little too angular. Or, when combining paths by joining points, you may end up with several unnecessary points left over that encumber further manipulation. Regardless of the reason, Illustrator has provided an "aim and shoot" Delete Anchor Point tool that cleans up point problems beautifully.

 To delete an anchor point from a path, you must first select the path with the Direct Selection tool. Next, locate the Delete Anchor Point tool (in the pop-up menu with the Add Anchor Point and Scissors tools) in the Toolbox.

Click on the offending anchor point with the Delete Anchor Point tool (Figure 4.10) and it will be deleted from the path. This will not break the path—the path itself will continue on to the next anchor point. However, deleting points may cause the shape of your object to change drastically. Use the Direct Selection and Convert Anchor Point tools, if necessary, to readjust the shape of your object.

4.10

The Delete Anchor Point tool removes unwanted anchor points from a path.

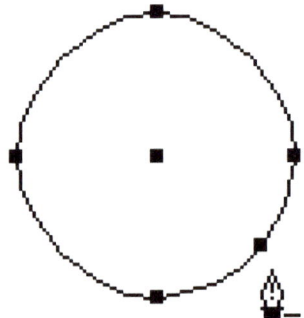

WATCH OUT!

> You can only delete anchor points with the Delete Anchor Point tool. It cannot be used to delete direction points or line segments. Should you click the tool on anything "illegal," Illustrator will give you the warning message Can't delete the anchor-point. Please use the delete anchor-point tool on the anchor point of a path.

Designing as you Learn: The Half-Circle

Although there are many ways of creating a half-circle in Adobe Illustrator, let's take a moment to learn how it can be done using the Delete Anchor Point tool. This brief exercise gives you some experience with the Delete Anchor Point tool as well as with direction points.

1. Make sure you are working in Artwork mode (⌘-E).

2. Using the Oval tool, hold down the Shift key and draw a circle on your page (Figure 4.11a). Make the circle fairly large so that it will be easy to work with—you can use the whole width of the page if you want.

3. Click on the Delete Anchor Point tool in the Toolbox.

4. Look at your circle. Notice that Illustrator has generated four anchor points in the path: one at the top, one at the bottom, and one on each side of the circle. Click the Delete Anchor Point tool on the bottom anchor point to delete it from the path. Your circle will now resemble Figure 4.11b.

5. Click on the Direct Selection tool. You'll notice that each of the side anchor points in the path now is extending a direction point downward towards the missing anchor point. Click on a direction point and pull it back up so that it is positioned over its own anchor point (Figure 4.11c). This operation requires care—you don't want to upset the position of the other direction point extending from that anchor point. Repeat the procedure for the other side anchor point.

6. If you need to adjust the remaining direction points to keep the curve of the half-circle in alignment, do so now. You will probably only need to move the direction line back to its vertical position.

7. Your finished half-circle should resemble the example shown in Figure 4.11d.

4.11

A perfect half-circle is created by using the Delete Anchor Point tool and adjusting direction points.

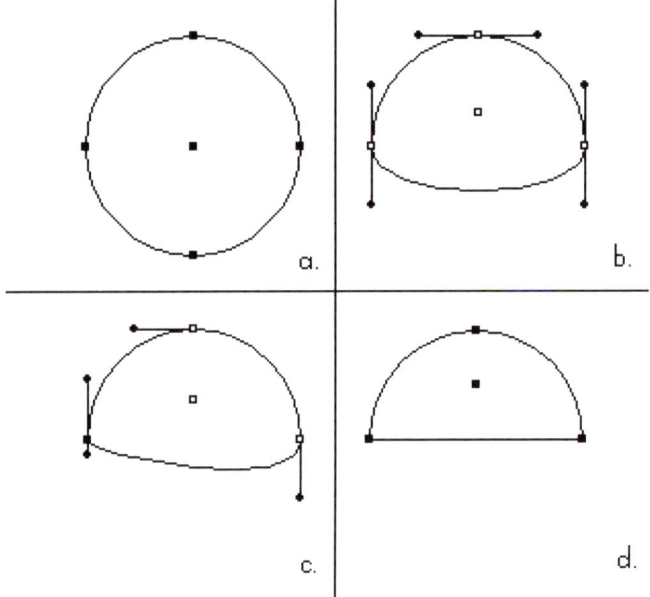

a.

b.

c.

d.

Moving the Line Segments of a Path

Now that we've discussed the ins and outs of working with points, let's enlarge our view of editing to include entire line segments. It is often easier to move several points along a path all at once. For instance, say you have a design that contains a rectangle. As you are drawing, you realize that the rectangle needs to be slightly wider to match the rest of your design. Instead of redrawing the rectangle, it makes more sense simply to grab the end of the rectangle and stretch it into position.

Adobe Illustrator lets you do precisely that. The Direct Selection tool (introduced in Chapter 3) allows you to select *anything* and move it: a single line segment, a group of points, several objects, or only selected portions of an object. To solve the problem above, you can use the Direct Selection tool to click on and drag the end of the rectangle until it reaches the correct width (Figure 4.12). Alternately, you can use the Direct Selection tool to click on the line segment and then use the arrow keys on your keyboard to move the segment in exact increments.

4.12

Use the Direct Selection tool to move a portion of an object.

To move only part of an object containing several points and line segments, use the Direct Selection tool to draw a marquee around the points and line segments to be moved. Once you've highlighted the area (the points will appear solid in contrast to the unselected parts of the object), you can use the arrow keys on your keyboard to move the selected portion into a new position.

By moving points and line segments, adding and deleting points, and converting points, you'll begin to see the many ways you can easily edit and transform objects in Adobe Illustrator. However, this is only the beginning. Illustrator also contains several transformation tools that automate some of the work and speed up the designing process.

Transforming Objects—A Closer Look

The Rotate, Scale, Reflect, and Shear tools in the Toolbox allow you to quickly transform whole objects or groups of objects in a design. Each tool can be used in two different ways, depending on the kind of results you want. The first method involves clicking directly on an anchor point in the object with any of the tools and then clicking and dragging to transform the object. This is a more visual, although inexact, way to use the tool.

For a more precise transformation, hold down the Option key while clicking with the selected tool on an anchor point in the object. This will bring up a transformation dialog box, specialized for each tool, that will let you enter the appropriate angles, dimensions, and other pertinent information to complete the transformation. Using the dialog box method also gives you the option of creating a transformed replica of the original, leaving the original intact.

INSIDE INFO

When using any of the transformation tools, remember that the transformation will take place using the selected anchor point as a central point of focus. For example, when using the Rotate tool, your object will be rotated around the anchor point you select. (You can actually select any point as the focus; however, it's generally easier to make transformations from an anchor point.)

As mentioned above, the transformation tools work not only on single objects, but on groups of objects as well. Use the Selection tool to select each object to be transformed—you don't need to use the Group command, just make sure that each object is *completely* selected. (Using the Direct Selection tool won't work unless you can draw a marquee completely around all portions of the objects at once.) Once the group is selected, you can switch to your preferred transformation tool to complete the action.

Rotating Objects with the Rotate Tool

The Rotate tool will rotate objects up to 360 degrees in either direction around a selected anchor point. When you hold down the Option key while selecting this tool, a dialog box lets you rotate either the original object or a copy of it by a specified angle.

To use the Rotate tool directly on an object (Figure 4.13):

1. Using the Selection tool, select the object(s) to be rotated.

2. Click on the Rotate tool in the Toolbox.

3. Click on the anchor point that will be used as the pivot point for the rotation.

4. Click and drag on any other anchor point in the object to rotate the object either clockwise or counterclockwise around the pivot point.

5. Release the mouse button when the transformation is complete.

4.13

Use the Rotation tool to rotate objects around a selected anchor point.

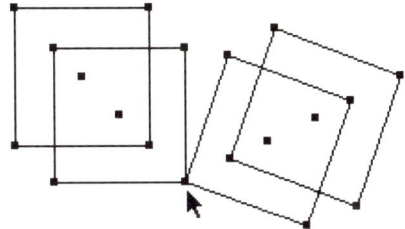

When you need to rotate an object (or its duplicate) by a precise number of degrees, use the Option key to display the Rotate dialog box (Figure 4.14):

1. Select the object(s) to be rotated using the Selection tool.

2. Click on the Rotate tool in the Toolbox.

3. Hold down the Option key and then click on the anchor point to be used as the pivot point for the rotation.

4. The Rotate dialog box will appear. Enter the rotation angle in degrees.

5. To rotate a duplicate of the object, click on the Copy button. To rotate the object itself, click on the OK button.

4.14

Measurements entered in the Rotate dialog box are used to specify a precise rotation angle for an object.

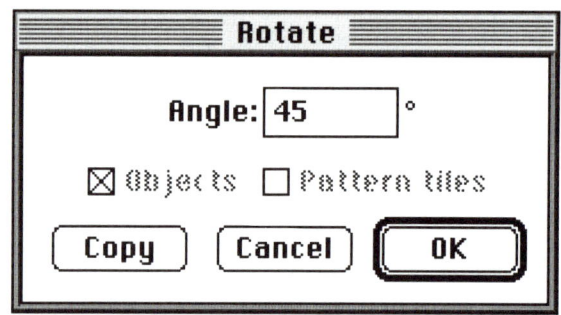

INSIDE INFO

When specifying the angle for a rotation, a positive value indicates a counterclockwise rotation, while a negative value indicates a clockwise rotation.

Scaling Objects with the Scale Tool

The Scale tool make it easy to enlarge or reduce the size of any object or group of objects in your design. When you combine this tool with the Option key, you also have the choice of scaling the horizontal and vertical size of an object to different percentages in the Scale dialog box. When you scale an object uniformly (that is, to the same horizontal and vertical percentages), this dialog box also lets you scale the line weight of objects, making the scaling operation a smooth transformation from one size to another.

To use the Scale tool directly on an object (Figure 4.15):

1. Using the Selection tool, select the object(s) to be scaled.

2. Click on the Scale tool in the Toolbox.

3. Click on a central anchor point in the object. The object will be scaled from this point.

4. Click on any other anchor point in the object and drag to begin the transformation.

5. To scale the object uniformly, hold down the Shift key as you drag.

6. Release the mouse button when you have finished scaling the object.

4.15

The Scale tool en-
larges and reduces
the size of objects.

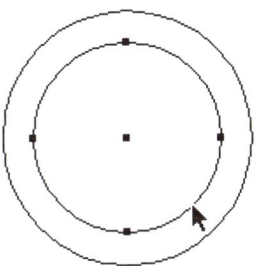

To scale an object uniformly using the Scale tool and dialog box (Figure 4.16):

1. Select the object(s) to be scaled using the Selection tool.

2. Click on the Scale tool in the Toolbox.

3. Hold down the Option key and click on a central anchor point in the object. The object will be scaled from this point.

4. The Scale dialog box will appear. Click on the Uniform button in the top of the box.

5. Enter the percentage for the enlargement or reduction of the object (the object is currently at 100 percent).

6. If you would like the line weight of your object to be scaled accordingly, make sure the Scale Line Weight box is checked.

7. To scale a duplicate of the object, click on the Copy button. If you want to scale the object itself, click on the OK button.

4.16

The Scale dialog box lets you create uniform and non-uniform scaled objects.

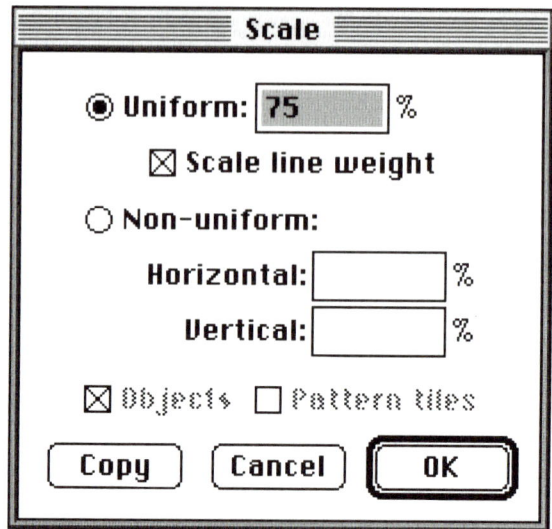

To scale an object to different horizontal and vertical percentages using the Scale tool and dialog box:

1. Select the object(s) to be scaled using the Selection tool.

2. Click on the Scale tool in the Toolbox.

3. Hold down the Option key and click on a central anchor point in the object. The object will be scaled from this point.

4. The Scale dialog box will appear. Click on the Non-Uniform button in the top of the box.

5. Enter separate horizontal and vertical scaling percentages for the object.

6. To scale a duplicate of the object, click on the Copy button. If you want to scale the object itself, click on the OK button.

WATCH OUT!

> When you are using the Scale dialog box and you don't like the results of your first try, always use the Undo command (⌘-Z) to return your object to its original size before scaling the object again. The Scale dialog box does not remember what 100 percent of your object was--to Illustrator, an object's current size will be considered 100 percent for the next transformation. For instance, if you were to reduce a box to 80 percent of its original size, and then decide you really want it to be 50 percent, the Scale dialog box will further reduce the box to 50 percent of the 80 percent size, not 50 percent of the original size. Using the Undo command between transformations saves you the hassle of wondering why your objects are suddenly so small (or large).

Designing as you Learn:
Rotating and Scaling an Object Group

In this exercise, you'll practice using the Rotate and Scale tools on a group of objects.

Rotating the Rectangles

1. Make sure you are working in Artwork mode (⌘-F).

2. With the Rectangle tool selected, draw a rectangle on your page. Draw another rectangle approximately the same size next to the first one. You can overlap the two rectangles if you wish.

3. Click on the Selection tool, and while holding down the Shift key, click on each of the rectangles to select them. You do not need to use the Group command unless you want to—merely selecting the objects at the same time will make them ready for a transformation.

4. With the Rotate tool selected, click on any anchor point in either of the selected paths.

5. You'll notice that your cursor changes from a crosshair to a solid black arrow at this point. Click the black arrow cursor on a *different* anchor point and drag to rotate the selected objects (Figure 4.17). Release the mouse button to end the transformation.

4.17

Click and drag with the Rotate tool to change the rotation of objects.

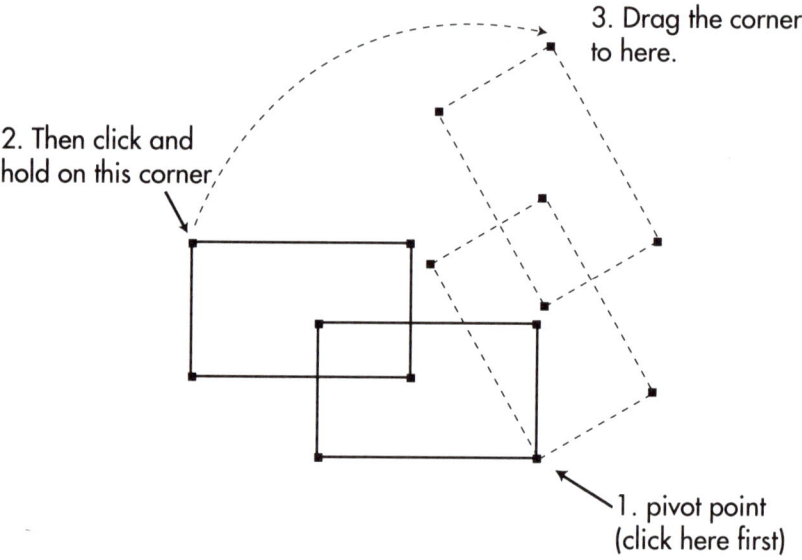

2. Then click and hold on this corner

3. Drag the corner to here.

1. pivot point (click here first)

Scaling the Rectangles

1. Use the Undo command (⌘-Z) to return the rectangles from the above transformation to their original state, or just draw two more rectangles on your page.

2. Click on the Selection tool, and while holding down the Shift key, click on each of the rectangles to select them.

3. With the Scale tool selected, click on any anchor point in either of the selected paths.

4. Your cursor again changes from a crosshair to a solid black arrow at this point. Click the black arrow cursor on a *different* anchor point and drag to scale the selected objects (Figure 4.18). Release the mouse button to end the transformation.

4.18

Click and drag on the rectangle to resize it with the Scale tool.

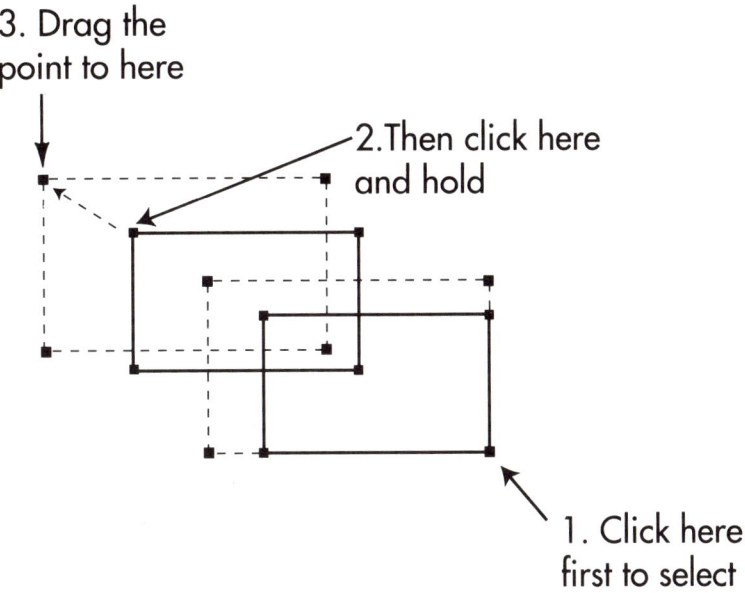

3. Drag the point to here

2. Then click here and hold

1. Click here first to select

Practice each of the above transformations again, only this time hold down the Shift key as you click the selected transformation tool on the object. By entering new measurements in the dialog box when prompted, you can transform an object to a precise size or angle.

Mirror, Mirror: Using the Reflect Tool

The Reflect tool can create a mirror image of an object by reflecting it across either the horizontal axis, the vertical axis, or at an angle. You can use the tool directly on objects or, with the help of the Option key, you can use it through the Reflect dialog box.

To use the Reflect tool directly on a object (Figure 4.19):

1. Select the object(s) to be reflected, using the Selection tool.

2. Click on the Reflect tool in the Toolbox.

3. Click on the anchor point that will be used as the pivot point for the transformation.

4.19

The Reflect tool creates a mirror image of a selected object.

reflecting across
the vertical axis

4. Click on any other anchor point in the object and drag to reflect the object. When used in this manner, the Reflect tool will create a mirror image of the object and let you rotate it into alignment.

5. Release the mouse button when the transformation is complete.

To reflect an object using the Reflect dialog box (Figure 4.20):

1. Select the object(s) to be reflected, using the Selection tool.

2. Click on the Reflect tool in the Toolbox.

3. Hold down the Option key and click on the anchor point that will be used as the center point for the transformation.

4.20

The Reflect dialog box provides a way to create a mirror image of an object across either axis or at an angle.

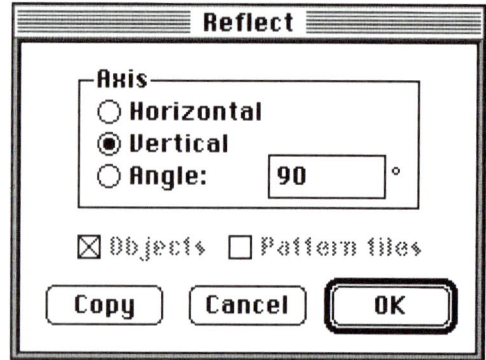

4. The Reflect dialog box will appear. Select Horizontal or Vertical to reflect the object directly across an axis, or select Angle and enter a rotational position in degrees where the program can reflect the object.

5. To reflect a duplicate of the object, click on the Copy button. If you want to reflect the object itself, click on the OK button.

INSIDE INFO

Reflecting an object across the horizontal axis will cause it to flip upward. Reflecting an object across the vertical axis will cause it to flip to the side.

Using the Shear Tool

 The Shear tool skews objects to an angle. Sheared images work well when placed behind unsheared objects, creating a drop shadow effect. When you select the tool while pressing the Option key, the Shear tool dialog box lets you enter both an angle and the axis on which to shear an object.

The Shear tool is probably the hardest transformation tool to control manually, but with practice you can really create some interesting effects with shearing. The tool is easiest to work with when moved at 45-degree angles from the horizontal and vertical axes, but you don't need to stay in this range.

To use the Shear tool manually on an object:

1. Select the object by clicking on it using the Selection tool.

2. Click on the Shear tool in the Toolbox.

3. Click on an anchor point in the object. This will be the pivot point from which the object is sheared.

4. Click on an anchor point opposite from the pivot point and drag at an angle away from the pivot point, as in Figure 4.21. You may need to try dragging the object in several directions before you find the shear angle that looks best.

4.21

The Shear tool skews objects at an angle.

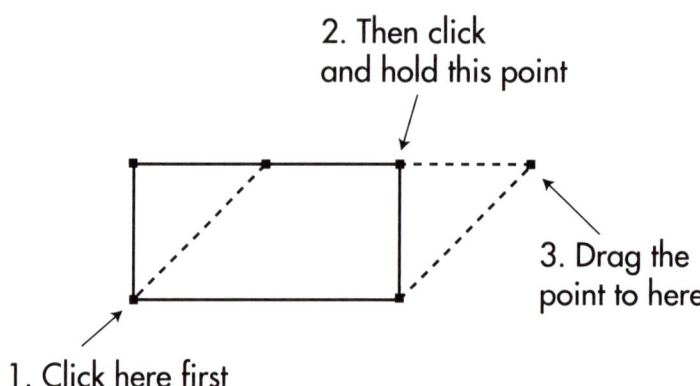

2. Then click and hold this point

3. Drag the point to here

1. Click here first

5. Release the mouse button when the transformation is complete.

To create a sheared object set at precise angles using the Shear dialog box (Figure 4.22):

1. Select the object by clicking on it using the Selection tool.

2. Click on the Shear tool in the Toolbox.

3. Hold down the Option key and click on an anchor point in the object. This will be the pivot point from which the object is sheared.

4. The Shear dialog box will appear. Enter the angle at which the object should be sheared, and select the axis across which the shearing will take place.

5. If you want to shear a duplicate of the original object, click on the Copy button. If you want to shear the object itself, click on the OK button.

4.22

Measurements entered in the Shear dialog box will skew an object to a precise angle across the chosen axis.

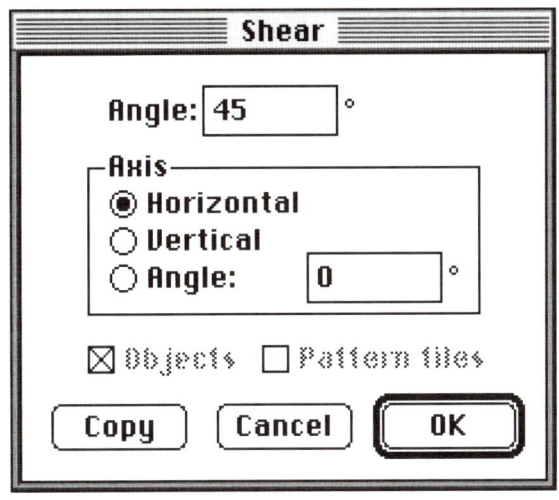

Designing as You Learn: Reflecting and Shearing

The Reflect and Shear tools are a little more difficult to use than the first two transformation tools discussed in this chapter. Those of you who are good with spatial concepts may think this is a piece of cake, but others may still be trying to sort out what the horizontal and vertical axes are. The following exercise uses both tools and will give you a chance to practice reflecting and shearing an object, as well as get you used to the way each tool reacts.

Reflecting the Rectangles

1. As usual, make sure you are working in Artwork mode (⌘-E).

2. Use the Rectangle tool to draw two rectangles on your page. Make one of the rectangles vertical, and the other rectangle horizontal.

3. Use the Selection tool to select both rectangles.

4. Click on the Reflect tool, and while holding down the Option key, click on any anchor point in either of the selected objects.

5. The Reflect dialog box will appear. Select the axis to reflect your objects across—remember, reflecting the objects across the horizontal axis will cause them to flip upwards, while reflecting across the vertical axis will flip them to the side. For this exercise, click on the Vertical button.

6. Click on the Copy button now, and watch copies of your objects reflect across the vertical axis (Figure 4.23).

4.23

The selected objects reflected across the vertical axis.

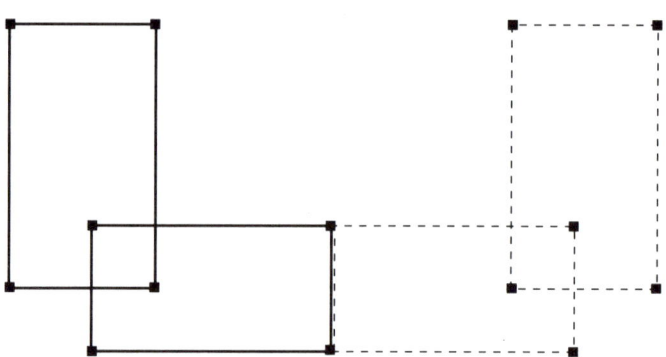

Shearing the Rectangle

1. Use the Undo command (⌘-Z) to remove the rectangles from the previous exercise from your page.

2. Use the Rectangle tool to draw one new rectangle on your page.

3. Click on the Shear tool and then click on the upper-right anchor point in the rectangle.

4. Now click and drag on the lower-left anchor point in the rectangle. The rectangle will begin to slant as it is sheared (Figure 4.24). For this exercise, just move your mouse in a circular pattern as you drag to get a better idea of how the Shear tool works. You can shear an object vertically or horizontally using the tool, or even a combination of both if you move down and out at a 45-degree angle.

5. Release the mouse button to end the transformation.

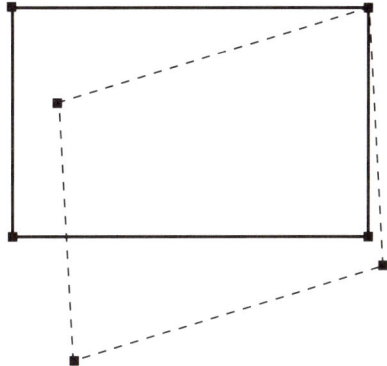

4.24

The rectangle becomes skewed as you drag an anchor point with the Shear tool.

Draw a new rectangle and try shearing it again, this time using the Shift key as you click on the rectangle the first time with the Shear tool. This will bring up the Shear dialog box, where you can enter a precise angle to shear the object (horizontally or vertically). In addition, the box also has an Angle field that will reposition the object on the axis as it is sheared.

Summary

Editing and object transformation are important skills to hone while using Adobe Illustrator. The tools and controls in the program provide tight control over the look of your design, and learning to use them correctly gives you the freedom to create the look you really want. Although some things, such as working with points or using the Shear tool, may be difficult to get the hang of, persistence and continued use will improve your skills dramatically. The more familiar you are with the program, the easier it will be to use. As in the old joke about getting to Carnegie Hall, the best advice I can give is practice, practice, practice.

Getting the Most
Out of Illustrator

Most of us work under deadlines. Projects not only need to be perfect, they need to be on time. To get the most out of Illustrator, you should learn to use the tools it provides for enhancing your productivity. For example, when you're creating a new project, the inspiration for your design may come from several places. You may base your current design on elements from another design, or on a photo, illustration, or any other visual inspiration you might find. Being able to use these other elements as templates for your own design is a clever and creative way to get a project rolling *fast*.

Adobe Illustrator provides several productivity tools. In this chapter, we'll discuss how to use templates, guides, and imported art files as part of the designing process. Along with importing, Illustrator has several exporting options that we'll cover.

We'll also look at how layering and positioning can be employed in your designs to help you work more efficiently. Finally, we'll examine Illustrator's Document Info option, which gives you access to a wealth of information about the current document in a single window.

Using Templates in Adobe Illustrator

The word *template* has many definitions. In Adobe Illustrator, a template is a black-and-white bitmapped image file that you can open and use as a pattern to create a new design.

Think back to when you were a small child learning to write. Remember those letters made up of dotted lines that your teacher had you trace over and over? A template in Illustrator has the same purpose—a bitmapped image file is opened and shown on your screen as a dotted outline. You then use any of Illustrator's drawing tools, including the auto-trace feature, to trace over the dotted template and create a workable design (Figure 5.1).

5 . 1

By tracing over the imported template (left), you can quickly render a design in Illustrator (right).

As you can probably imagine, using templates can greatly increase your productivity, allowing you to spend your time finessing the design instead of drawing it point by point.

Creating Templates

As mentioned above, a template consists of a black-and-white bitmapped image. These images can come from two sources:

- a MacPaint or PICT image file that was created in another program, or
- a scanned image that was saved in the PICT file format.

If you have an image you wish to use as a template, but it is not in one of these formats, check the application it was created in to see if you can save the image as a PICT file.

INSIDE INFO

Sometimes you'll need to use an "intermediary" application to open and save files in the format you want. For instance, since Adobe Photoshop has the ability to open and save files in several different formats, I often use it to convert the image files I receive from clients into a compatible format that I can use. Likewise, a translation software utility such as MacLink (DataViz, Inc., retail $130) can also translate several PC formats into PICT.

To use the PICT file as a template, use either the New command (⌘-Option-N) or the Open command (⌘-O), both of which are located in the File menu. In the dialog box that appears, choose the name of the PICT file to open as a template. (If you choose None in the New dialog box, Illustrator will simply open an empty new document for your use.)

Tracing the Template

Once you've opened a template, you will see the dotted outline of your PICT image (Figure 5.2). You cannot alter the way the image is displayed at this point, nor will this image print as it now exists. You can remove the template from your view (or bring it back) by using the Hide/Show Template command (⌘-Shift-W).

The template is now ready to use as a tracing guide. You can use any of the drawing tools to trace the outline of the image manually, or you can use the Auto-Trace tool to automatically outline the image and areas within the image.

Using the Auto-Trace Tool

 The Auto-Trace tool, located in the Toolbox in a pop-up menu next to the Freehand tool, works just by clicking it on the edge of the template. The point where you click must be within six pixels of the edge, or it will not trace. The tool will automatically trace the perimeter of the shaded area nearest to where you click, creating a closed path (Figure 5.3).

5.2

An opened template is shown as a gray dotted outline.

5.3

The Auto-Trace tool traces the perimeter of the template. Continue to click on different areas of the template in order to trace all parts.

You may need to use the Auto-Trace tool several times to completely trace the entire template image. To trace only part of the image, click on one spot and drag the cursor directly to the spot where you want to finish. Moving clockwise, the Auto-Trace tool will trace the area between those two points instead of the entire perimeter.

Setting Tracing Preferences

Two preference settings affect the way the Auto-Trace tool works. In the General Preferences dialog box (⌘-K), the Freehand Tolerance sets how closely the Auto-Trace tool will follow the template while tracing (Figure 5.4). You can enter a value in this field between zero and 10 pixels, zero being the closest setting. When this field is set to 10, the Auto-Trace tool will create a very loose, curved rendition of the template it is tracing.

5.4

The General Preferences dialog box contain the Freehand Tolerance and Auto Trace Gap settings.

```
┌─Tool behavior ──────────────────
│       Constrain angle: [0      ] °
│        Corner radius: [0 pt        ]
│     Freehand tolerance: [2     ] pixels
│        Auto Trace gap: [0     ] pixels
│ ⋯⋯⋯⋯⋯⋯⋯⋯⋯⋯⋯⋯⋯⋯⋯⋯
```

The Auto Trace Gap setting, in the same dialog box, determines how much the tool will smooth out the sometimes rough edges and bumps that are inherent in bitmapped images. The lowest setting, 0, means that the tool will trace every gap and bump in the image. The highest setting, 2, means the tool will ignore gaps of two pixels or less.

Styling a Traced Template

Once you are done tracing the template, you can style the design as you would any other drawing. To remove the template from your view (leaving the drawing), use the Hide Template command (⌘-Shift-W). In Figure 5.5, I've added a color fill to the drawing and stroked the outline in different shades.

5.5

A tracing from a template can be styled like any other combination of objects on your screen.

Creating Guides

You aren't limited to creating templates from bitmap files. You can use anything you draw in Illustrator as a template by turning it into a *guide*. The Make Guides command (⌘-5) turns any selected path into a guide, a dotted line that, like a template, will not print. However, unlike a template, a guide can be released (⌘-6) and returned to its original form at any time. Even while it is being used as a guide, the element will retain all its styling information for future use. Figure 5.6 shows a guide used as a baseline for aligning text and an object.

5.6

Guides help align
text and objects in
a design.

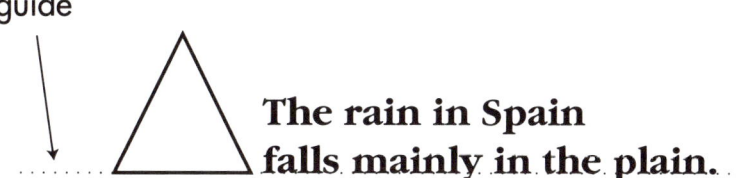

Guides are also very helpful when you need to constrain a design within a certain size. When I'm drawing an illustration for a publication and I know I'm restricted to a certain size, I'll use the Rectangle tool to make a rectangle of that size. By turning the rectangle into a guide (⌘-5), I can see precisely how much room I have and draw to size.

Once you have converted a path to a guide, it is still movable. To avoid moving guides inadvertently, you can lock them down with the Guides Lock command (⌘-7). This command is a toggle; choosing it a second time releases the Guides Lock.

Ruler Guides

Adobe Illustrator also provides *ruler guides*, nonprinting straight guidelines that you can place as needed on your page. To use a ruler guide, you must first open the rulers in your document using the Show Rulers command (⌘-R).

To create a vertical guideline, click on the ruler to the right of your document window and drag. A dotted linc will follow your cursor as you drag (Figure 5.7). Position the line as needed and release the mouse button. For a horizontal guideline, drag from the ruler across the bottom of your document window.

Importing Artwork into Illustrator

Not only does Illustrator let you create unique works of art all on your own, it also lets you import certain image files for placement in an Illustrator document. This thoughtful feature adds to your creativity by allowing you to incorporate photos or outside illustrations into your own design.

Ruler guides can be dragged out of either the horizontal or the vertical ruler to help align objects and text on your page.

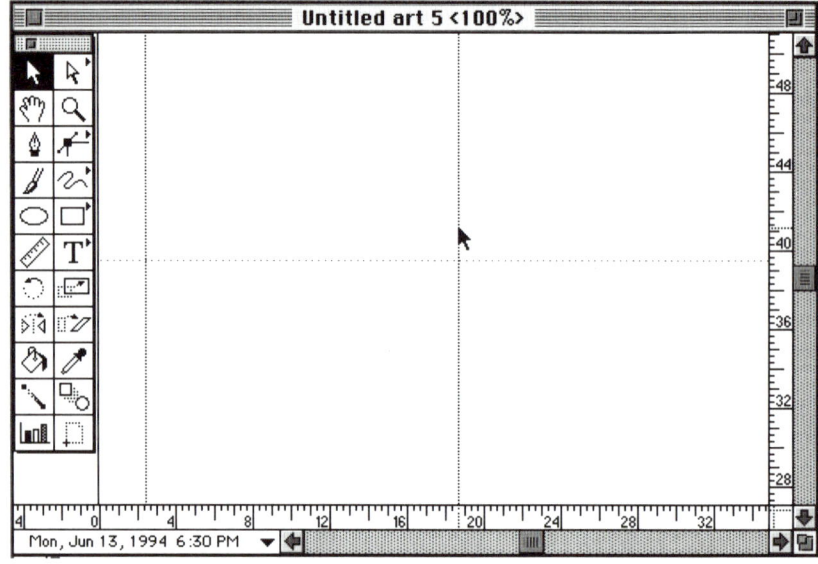

You can import one Adobe illustrator file into another, or you can incorporate EPS files from a scanner or another application. The Place Art command in the File menu lets you select an EPS file for placement. When selected, the image will appear on your screen in a non-printing bounding box (Figure 5.8).

As of version 5.5, you can also import selected PICT images into Illustrator. MacDraw and Canvas images can be imported and converted directly into objects, which can be edited freely. Pixel-based PICT

5.8

An imported image in Illustrator is surrounded by a bounding box.

files, as from MacPaint or Photoshop, can be imported and converted into EPS images for placement (but not for editing) within Illustrator.

Inserted EPS files always appear when you view your file in Preview mode (⌘-Y). However, if you haven't selected Show Placed Images in the Document Setup dialog box, only the bounding box will appear when you view the image in Artwork mode (⌘-E).

Styling Imported Images

Once you've imported a file, you can use any of the transformation tools (discussed in Chapter 4) to scale, rotate, reflect, or shear the image. You can also click on the bounding box and drag it about the screen to position the image. The only thing you *can't* do to style an imported image is change its color.

INSIDE INFO

To automatically exchange the placed image with another, while keeping the same transformations, click on the old image and then select Change Placed Art from the File menu. The new image you select to place will be imported with the same transformations as the old one.

Saving the Imported Image with the File

Before you can print the new file or give it to another user, you need to make sure a copy of the original art file that you imported is available. You must also save the new file in a way that keeps the two files associated.

To connect the two files, select Save As from the File menu. Save the file as an EPS file and click on the Save button. In the second dialog box that appears (Figure 5.9), click on Include Placed Images and once again click on the Save button. Illustrator will then automatically search for the original art file when it is needed in the future for printing.

5.9

It is important to click on Include Placed Images when saving a file that contains an imported image.

```
┌──────────────────── EPS Format ────────────────────┐
│  ┌─ Preview ──────┐   ┌─ Compatibility ─┐  ┌──────┐ │
│  │  ○ None         │   │  ○ Illustrator 1.1 │  │  OK  │ │
│  │  ○ 1-bit IBM PC │   │  ○ Illustrator 88  │  └──────┘ │
│  │  ○ 1-bit Macintosh │ │  ○ Illustrator 3   │  ┌────────┐ │
│  │  ● 8-bit Macintosh │ │  ● Illustrator 5   │  │ Cancel │ │
│  └─────────────────┘   └──────────────────┘  └────────┘ │
│  ☒ Include Placed Images                               │
└──────────────────────────────────────────────────────┘
```

Exporting Your Illustrator Files

Adobe Illustrator files can be exported to other applications in two different ways. If you save your artwork as an EPS file, it will be compatible with other applications that can import images in the EPS format. Illustrator also provides a way for saving files as PICT images on the Clipboard, if necessary for the application you are using.

This flexibility is great for artists who create designs for publications, such as magazines, books, or marketing brochures. You can create an illustration, save it as EPS, and send it on to your client with the confidence that it will be compatible with their layout or presentation application. Once imported, the EPS image will also easily print as part of the new application.

Saving Images as EPS Files

To save an image as an EPS file, select Save As from the File menu. In the dialog box, select EPS from the pop-up Format menu. Click on the Save button. In the EPS Format dialog box, choose the appropriate settings for the type of EPS image you want. The Compatibility box lets you select the version of Illustrator you prefer to save your file in. The Preview box lets you select the quality of the image that will be viewed when it is imported into another application. Click on the OK button when you are finished. The EPS file is now ready to be exported to another application.

Saving Images as PICT Files

If you need to export your Illustrator file to an application that accepts only PICT files, you aren't out of luck. By holding down the Option key while choosing the Copy command (⌘-Option-C), you'll send a PICT version of your image to the Clipboard. The PICT image can be imported from the Clipboard as soon as you open your other application.

WATCH OUT!

Remember, things only stay in the Clipboard until you Copy or Cut another element from your document. If you have created a PICT file for use in another application, go directly to that application to import the image as soon as you've created it.

Working with Layers in Adobe Illustrator

 The Layers feature presents a unique way of organizing and working with the different elements of your design. By grouping objects onto different layers, you can display or hide and lock or unlock each layer at different stages. This can help you avoid time-consuming errors. It prevents you from accidentally moving or editing something you shouldn't, by locking down certain objects while you work on others in the vicinity.

AUTHOR'S NOTE

Don't confuse the Layers feature with the stacking order, the front-to-back apparent layering of objects that Illustrator does automatically (and that you can override with the Bring to Front and Send to Back commands). If you draw two overlapping objects, the second object drawn will appear to be in front of the first, but they will both be on the same layer.

Creating Layers

The Layers palette, shown in Figure 5.10, is found in the Window menu (⌘-Control-L) and controls the creation and status of each layer. A new Adobe Illustrator document starts off with Layer 1 already created. Each object you draw is made a part of that layer.

To start a new layer, simply go to the Layers palette and select New Layer from the pop-up menu. Layer 2 will become activated, and the objects you now draw will become part of that layer. To switch between layers, simply click on the Layer number in the Layers palette, or click on any object in that layer.

You can easily tell the objects in different layers apart, because as you create each new layer, you assign it a color. When an object is selected while in Preview mode, it will be highlighted in the color assigned to its layer.

5.10

The Layers palette organizes the objects on your screen into layers.

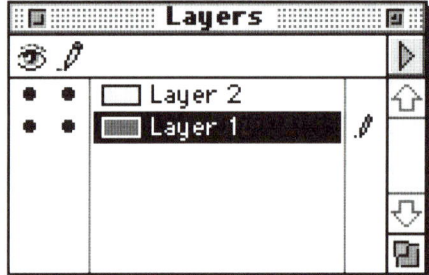

Hiding and Locking Layers

In the Layers palette, two icons and the dots beneath them show the status of each layer. The eye icon represents whether the layer is hidden (no dot) or showing (dot). The pencil icon lets you know whether a layer is locked (no dot) or available for editing (dot).

When a layer is hidden, it will disappear from your page view completely until you turn off the Hide command in the Layer palette. Likewise, when a layer is locked, you will not be able to select any of the elements in that layer.

The Layers palette also gives you the option of putting the elements of all other layers into Artwork mode, leaving only the selected layer in Preview mode. This makes it easy to concentrate on smaller sections of your design at a time.

Positioning and Page Options

When you open an Illustrator document, a single 8.5″ × 11″ page will appear in your document window. However, this standard page may not always fit your needs. What do you do if you need more than one page in the same document, or your image is larger than the default page?

The size and orientation of the page are determined by the dimensions entered in the Document Setup dialog box (⌘-Shift-D). Illustrator pages can be specified for any size, up to 120″ × 120″. However, when selecting a size you will most likely be restricted by the output device where you'll print the design. This is where tiling comes into play.

Tiling a Page

Tiling is the division of a single page into printable sections. There are three tiling options you can choose from in the Document Setup dialog box: Single Full Page, Tile Full Pages, and Tile Imageable Areas. Depending on the combination of these options with the page dimensions, you can most likely achieve the results you'll need when printing. Let's look at each of these tiling options a little closer.

Single Full Page

The Single Full Page option displays the imageable area of a single page on the artboard (Figure 5.11), according to the dimensions entered in the Document Setup dialog box (⌘-Shift-D). The imageable area (shown by a dotted perimeter) will be slightly less than the size of a full page, because Illustrator uses half-inch margins. The Single Full Page option will work for cases when you can constrain your design to the dimensions imposed by the page border.

5.11

The Single Full Page tiling option places one image-able area with margins onto your artboard.

Tile Full Pages

The Tile Full Pages option places as many full-size imageable areas (approximately 8″ × 10″) as possible on the size of artboard you have selected (Figure 5.12). For instance, if you selected a page dimension of 11″ × 17″, Illustrator will place two separate imageable areas on the artboard, each of which will print as a separate page. This option is ideal to use when creating two-page spreads, as for a magazine.

5.12

The Tile Full Pages option will place as many imageable areas (8″ × 10″) on the artboard as space will allow.

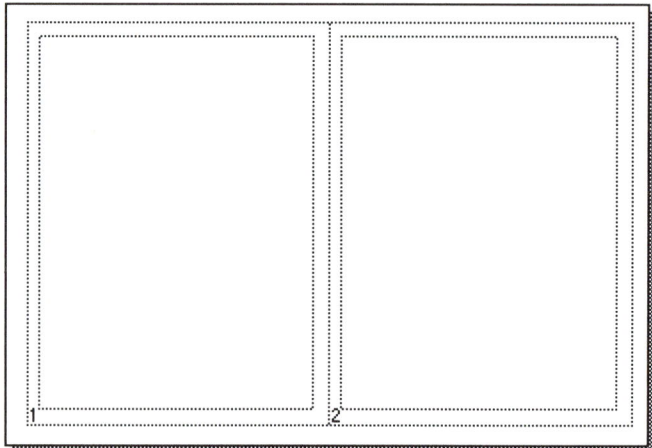

WATCH OUT!

Since there is a half-inch margin bordering each imageable area, it is important to remember that any portion of artwork that falls into the gutter between the two areas will not print. If it is important that you see this area when printing, do not use Tile Full Pages!

Tile Imageable Areas

The Tile Imageable Areas option divides the artboard up into sections (Figure 5.13). While the main imageable area will still be in the center of your artboard, all other areas of the artboard are also designated as separate imageable areas. This means the areas of your design that are positioned across two imageable areas will still tile to print, but you won't lose any portions of the design to the gutter between imageable areas.

5.13

The Tile Imageable Areas option divides the artboard into imageable areas with no margins.

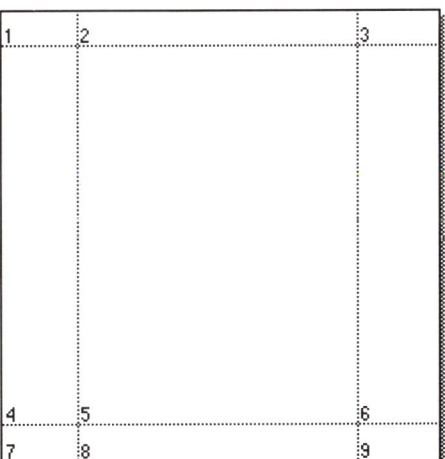

Positioning with the Page Tool

Often when you have completed a design, you'll find that it isn't centered or correctly positioned on your page. Instead of trying to drag the entire design into position, potentially creating a huge disaster, you can position the page *around* the design.

 The Page tool, located in the Toolbox, is an easy way to reposition the page around your design, letting you center the page behind your artwork, instead of vice versa. To use the Page tool, first reduce the size of your view so that you can comfortably see your entire page. Now click on the tool and then click and drag the cursor on your page. The image will remain stationary, but the page will move with your cursor. Position the page over your design as you wish and release the mouse button.

If you obtained some strange results, such as only half of the page border showing, don't be alarmed. This means that the artboard behind your page is not large enough. The Page tool is limited to moving the page around inside the dimensions of the artboard. To remedy the problem, change your artboard dimensions in the Document Setup dialog box (⌘-Shift-D) and then reposition the page again.

Document Information at a Glance

 New in version 5.5, the Document Information dialog box is a smart addition to such a complex and detailed program as Illustrator. This dialog box can give you instant details about the entire document, or just a single selected object in that document (Figure 5.14). Although the Document Information dialog box is really one of the new plug-in filters, it is such a handy device that it seemed appropriate to include it in this chapter. You'll find its concise delivery of document information a big time-saver, especially in complex projects.

To open the Document Information dialog box, choose Other under the Filters menu. The dialog box contains an Info pop-up menu, which lets you choose from the following subjects:

> **General Information**, including document name, file format, and Document Setup specifications.

5.14

The Document Information dialog box contains a gold mine of information about the current document.

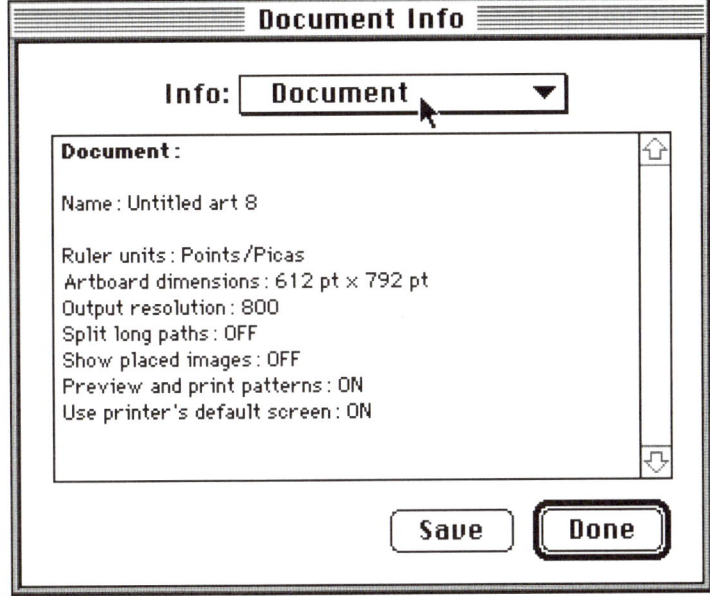

Object Information, including paths and compound paths, masks, custom colors and patterns.

Custom Colors, if any have been created in the document.

Custom Patterns, if any have been created in the document.

Gradients, if any have been created in the document.

Fonts, including both the name and style.

Placed Art, listed by name and location of the original art file on your hard drive or disk.

To save any of these listings, click on the Save button. The listing will be saved as a text file that can be opened and printed in a word processing program. This allows you to send this information with your image file to your printer or service bureau, or save it for future reference when using this image file.

Summary

Adobe Illustrator has several time-saving features that can make your work time more efficient and profitable. By using templates, you can greatly reduce the amount of time you spend designing, as well as incorporate outside elements into your own design. Being able to import artwork into Illustrator, as well as export Illustrator files, is another efficient way to quickly build a design around an existing piece of art.

If you don't have ready access to art or templates, check out the many electronic clip art packages that are available at software stores. These provide a wide variety of both bitmapped and EPS images that can easily be used in Adobe Illustrator. If you have access to a CD-ROM, you'll find compact discs full of photos and images, many of which are in the public domain.

Spend some time brainstorming and researching other ideas to expand your design options. As technology advances, so do the options you'll find available.

Working with Type in Illustrator

One of the hallmarks of a good drawing and design program is how it handles type. After all, unless you're going to use the program solely for drawing pictures, you'll need a way to add type to those designs to help tell the story. For most designers, this doesn't just mean putting words on a page—almost any program can do that. We're talking about the need for virtual *type gymnastics* here.

In version 5.5, Illustrator has taken an already good set of type handling features and made them truly spectacular. With its new abilities to set type in columns, link text boxes, and perform various kinds of numerous text editing, Illustrator seems on its way to becoming a full-featured page layout program. Such comprehensive thinking is truly appealing to designers who want a program that can do "everything."

Let's get in there now and learn what these amazing type features can really do. In this chapter we'll learn type handling from A to Z, including numerous layout, word processing, and styling features, many of which are new to Illustrator 5.5.

Getting Type into Your Design

In this section we'll look at how to insert type, learn how to set up rows and columns, and examine the basic text layout features that Adobe Illustrator offers. Illustrator provides several different options for placing and organizing type, giving you great flexibility in the ways you can use type in a design.

Inserting Type into a Document

There are three type tools in Illustrator: the Type tool, the Area Type tool, and the Path Type tool. Each is used in a different way to insert type into a document.

The Type Tool

The Type tool allows you to enter type in either of two ways. First, you can simply click the Type tool I-beam cursor anywhere on your page to obtain an insertion point. When you see the flashing cursor, you can begin typing or import a text file for placement.

The second method involves using the Type tool to draw a rectangular text box. When you have finished drawing the box, the flashing cursor will appear in the upper-left corner of the box, where text can then be entered or imported. Text entered in this manner will conform to the shape of the box (Figure 6.1). You can also change the shape or size of a box after type has been entered into it. The type will reflow to fit the new dimensions of the box.

While the bounding box will appear when viewing your page in Artwork mode (⌘-E), it disappears both in Preview mode (⌘-Y) as well as when the file is printed.

6.1

The Type tool can be used to draw a rectangular text box. Type entered into this box then takes on the shape of the box.

The flower was yellow and orange, and grew low to the ground. Margaret thought it was a marigold, but she wasn't sure. She opened her mother's big gardening book and found a picture of a marigold.

The Area Type Tool

The Area Type tool converts any graphic area into a text area. For instance, say you have a triangular object drawn on your page. By clicking inside this object with the Area Type tool, you can enter text that will stay within the perimeter of the triangle (Figure 6.2). The type is bounded by the path that is the triangular object.

6.2

The Area Type tool allows you to enter text within the perimeter of any path, regardless of shape.

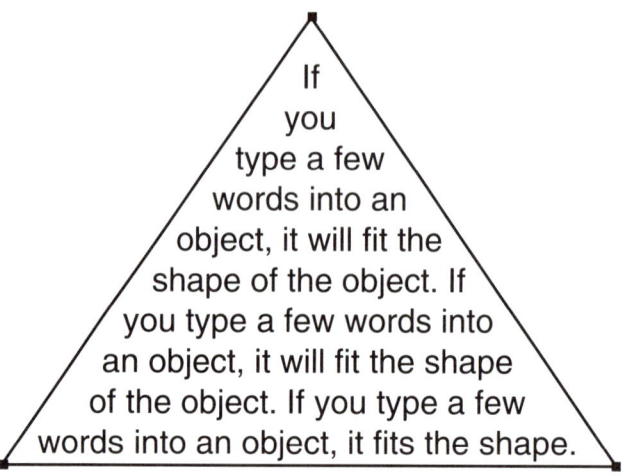

To use the Area Type tool, first use any of the drawing tools to create a closed-path object. Click on the Area Type tool in the Toolbox, then click inside the object. A flashing cursor in the upper-left corner of the object will indicate that the object is now ready to accept your text.

The Path Type Tool

The Path Type tool can use any path, open or closed, as an insertion area for text. It differs from the Area Type tool in that type entered with the Path Type tool follows the path perimeter itself, instead of being bound inside the area enclosed by the path.

This lets you draw any manner of squiggly lines, rounded shapes, or unique objects as paths for your type (Figure 6.3). The type will follow the path as best it can when it is entered—depending on the style and size of type, the result may or may not be attractive.

To use the tool, simply draw your path with any of the creation tools; then use the Path Type tool to click on the path. A flashing cursor will appear, indicating that you can now enter type. As you enter your type,

6.3

The Path Type tool will cause text to follow any open or closed path.

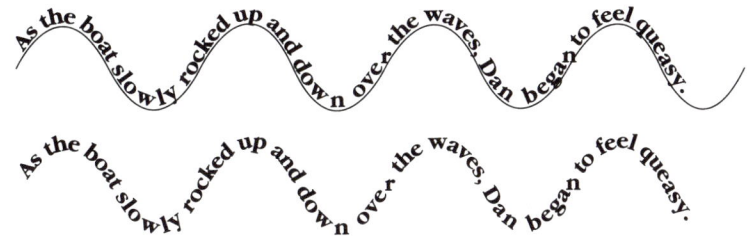

notice the I-beam cursor at the beginning of the line. By clicking and dragging on this cursor, you can reposition the line of type on the path, even to the point of reversing it to print on the opposite side of the path (Figure 6.4).

Converting Text Paths Back to Art Paths

Illustrator 5.5 includes a special filter that makes it possible to change a text path back into an art path. This means you can convert a rectangle text area back into a normal rectangle and apply styling attributes as you would any other object.

6.4

By dragging on the I-beam cursor in front of the type, you can reposition the type along its path, or even position it on the inside of the path.

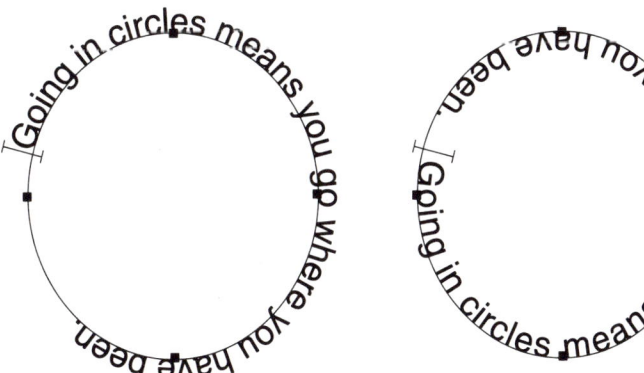

AUTHOR'S NOTE

> The Revert Text Path filter will not automatically load when you install Illustrator. To have access to this feature, move the Revert Text Path filter from the Other Filters folder into the Plug-Ins folder and restart Illustrator.

To revert a text path, first erase all the type from the text path. In the Filters menu, choose Revert Text from the Text pop-up menu. The text path will revert back to its original state, be it a rectangle, oval, or line.

Importing Text

Once you have decided how your type should be placed, the next step is to get it into your document. Of course, you can always type it in directly. This is easiest if you are only entering a sentence or two, or if you have several small bits of type that will need to be placed separately throughout your design.

However, because Illustrator can now act as a layout program, there comes a need for working with larger bodies of type. A large quantity of type can most easily be placed in a document by importing it from an external text file that was created in a word processing application. Adobe Illustrator accepts text files created in the following programs and formats:

Ami Professional

AppleWorks

DBase

FrameMaker

Lotus 1-2-3

MacWrite

Microsoft Word

MultiMate

OfficeWriter

Print Capture

Professional Write

RTF (Rich Text Format)

Symphony

Text (ASCII)

WordPerfect

WordStar

Write Now

Xywrite

To bring text into an Illustrator file, it is best to import it into a rectangle area so that it can be set up into columns and rows, which we'll discuss shortly. Use the Type tool to draw a rectangle and then select Import Text from the File menu. If the text file you choose is longer than space allows, a small plus symbol will appear at the bottom-right corner of the rectangle when the text imports (Figure 6.5).

6.5

When text imported into a rectangle Is longer than space allows, a small plus symbol will indicate there is more text than is displayed.

Lorem ipsum dolor sit amet, consectetuer adipiscing elit, sed diam nonummy nibh euismod tincidunt ut laoreet dolore magna aliquam erat volutpat. Ut wisi enim ad minim veniam, quis nostrud exerci tation ullamcorper suscipit lobortis nisl ut aliquip ex ea commodo consequat.
Duis autem vel eum iriure dolor in hendrerit in vulputate velit esse molestie consequat, vel illum dolore eu feugiat nulla facilisis at vero eros et accumsan et iusto odio dignissim qui blandit praesent luptatum zzril delenit augue duis dolore te feugait nulla facilisi. Lorem ipsum

You can easily add another rectangle of the same size for the overflow text. First, deselect the first rectangle. With the Group Selection tool, click and begin to drag on the edge of the original text rectangle (not on the text itself). Hold down the Option key to make a copy of the rectangle as you drag. Hold down the Shift key to constrain the new rectangle to the same vertical position as the first. Release the mouse button first, and then the Option and Shift keys, when your second rectangle is placed. The text from the first rectangle will now continue into the second, as shown in Figure 6.6.

6.6

When you copy the original rectangle by dragging on it with the Option key pressed, the overflow text will continue into the new rectangle you create.

Lorem ipsum dolor sit amet, consectetuer adipiscing elit, sed diam nonummy nibh euismod tincidunt ut laoreet dolore magna aliquam erat volutpat. Ut wisi enim ad minim veniam, quis nostrud exerci tation ullamcorper suscipit lobortis nisl ut aliquip ex ea commodo consequat.

Duis autem vel eum iriure dolor in hendrerit in vulputate velit esse molestie consequat, vel illum dolore eu feugiat nulla facilisis at vero eros et accumsan et iusto odio dignissim qui blandit praesent luptatum zzril delenit augue duis dolore te feugait nulla facilisi. Lorem ipsum dolor

Linking Text Blocks

Rectangles aren't the only objects that can be used for text. You can link two or more text objects of any shape to get text to flow between them. First create at least two text objects (ovals, squares, and so forth), and import the appropriate text file into the first object using the Area Type tool. With the Selection tool, select all the text objects to be in the chain. Under the Type menu, select Link Blocks (⌘-Shift-G). The text will flow from the first object into the second one and so forth (Figure 6.7). To see which blocks are linked, click on a block with the Selection tool. Illustrator will highlight all the linked blocks.

6.7

With the Link
Blocks command,
you can flow text
between two or
more text objects
of any shape or
size.

orem ipsum
dolor sit amet, cons
ectetuer adipiscing elit, sed
diam nonummy nibh euismod
tincidunt ut laoreet dolore magna
aliquam erat volutpat. Ut wisi enim ad
minim veniam,   quis nostrud exerci tation
ullamcorper suscipit lobortis nisl ut aliquip ex
ea commodo consequat. Duis autem vel eum
iriure dolor in hendrerit in vulputate velit esse
molestie consequat, vel illum dolore eu feugiat
nulla facilisis at vero eros et accumsan et iusto
odio dignissim qui   blandit praesent luptatum
zzril delenit augue duis dolore te feugait nulla
facilisi. Lorem ipsum dolor sit amet, cons
ectetuer adipiscing elit, sed diam nonum
my nibh euismod   tincidunt ut laoreet
dolore magna aliquam erat volut
pat. Ut wisi enim ad minim
veniam, quis

nostrud exe
rci tation ulla mco
rper suscipit lobortis nisl ut
aliquip ex ea commodo consequat.
Duis autem vel eum iriure dolor in
hendrerit in vulputate velit esse molestie
consequat, vel illum dolore eu feugiat nulla
facilisis at vero eros et accumsan et iusto odio
dignissim qui blandit praesent luptatum zzril
delenit augue duis dolore te feugait nulla facilisi.
Nam liber tempor cum soluta nobis eleifend
option congue nihil imperdiet doming id quod
mazim placerat facer possim assum. Lorem
ipsum dolor sit amet, consectetuer adipiscing
elit, sed diam nonummy nibh euismod
tincidunt ut laoreet dolore magna aliquam
erat volutpat. Ut wisi enim ad minim
veniam, quis nostrud exerci tation
ullamcorper suscipit
lobortis nisl ut

Linked blocks are a particularly convenient tool if you're laying out a
newsletter, in which articles that begin on page 1 may continue inside,
on later pages. To create the "jump," you would create one text object on
page 1 and another on the page where the article should continue, and
then link the blocks.

Linked text objects can be unlinked by selecting the objects and then
using the Unlink Blocks command in the Type menu (⌘-Shift-U). You
can also remove or replace an object in the middle of a text chain simply
by selecting the unwanted object and hitting the Delete key. The text
will reflow between the objects.

Setting Up Rows and Columns

A new filter added to version 5.5 of Adobe Illustrator makes it possible
to create rows and columns of text. This works well for setting up a
page layout, such as for a brochure or magazine, as well as for creating
the kinds of rows and columns you might find in a table or spreadsheet.

To use the Rows and Columns filter, first import or type your text into
a rectangular text box. With the text box selected, go to the Text entry
in the Filters menu and select Rows & Columns. The Rows & Columns
dialog box appears (Figure 6.8).

6.8

The Rows & Columns dialog box contains the controls that set up rows, columns, gutters and text flow in your document.

To divide your text into rows and columns, enter the appropriate number in each field. If you turn the Preview option on in the bottom of this dialog box, the changes will be visible in your document immediately. This allows you to try many different styles and make changes without exiting the dialog box each time.

The Columns field separates your text box into the number of columns you specify, separated by a vertical gutter of the width you specify. The Rows field separates your text box into horizontal rows, each separated by a horizontal gutter of the width you specify (Figure 6.9).

You can change the Text Flow option at the bottom of the dialog box just by clicking on its icon. This changes the flow of text between the rows and columns you create, and contains two settings: left to right, or up and down, as shown in Figure 6.10. The Add Guides command adds horizontal and vertical guides to define column and row edges.

As with any other text box, you can link a text object that has been divided into rows and columns to other text objects by using the Link Blocks command discussed earlier.

6.9

A normal text box
(top), separated
into two columns
(middle), and sepa-
rated into two
rows (bottom).

> Mary had a little lamb whose fleece was white as snow, and everywhere that Mary went, the lamb was sure to go.
> Star light, star bright, give me the wish I wish tonight. I wish I may, I wish I might, have the wish I wish tonight.

> Mary had a little lamb whose fleece was white as snow, and everywhere that Mary went, the lamb was sure to go.

> Star light, star bright, give me the wish I wish tonight. I wish I may, I wish I might, have the wish I wish tonight.

> Mary had a little lamb whose fleece was white as snow, and everywhere that Mary went, the lamb was sure to go.

> Star light, star bright, give me the wish I wish tonight. I wish I may, I wish I might, have the wish I wish tonight.

Creating Text Wraps around Graphics

Now that you know how to create columns of text, let's do something fun with them. A text wrap (also called a runaround) is an effective way to combine text and smaller graphic images in one place. In a text wrap, columns of text flow or "wrap" around a graphic object that is placed over them (Figure 6.11). This works best when the graphic straddles the gutter between two columns. You can also use this method to create a drop cap (or pop cap) at the beginning of a paragraph.

6.10

The Text Flow command determines whether text flows from left to right, or from top to bottom through the columns and rows you create.

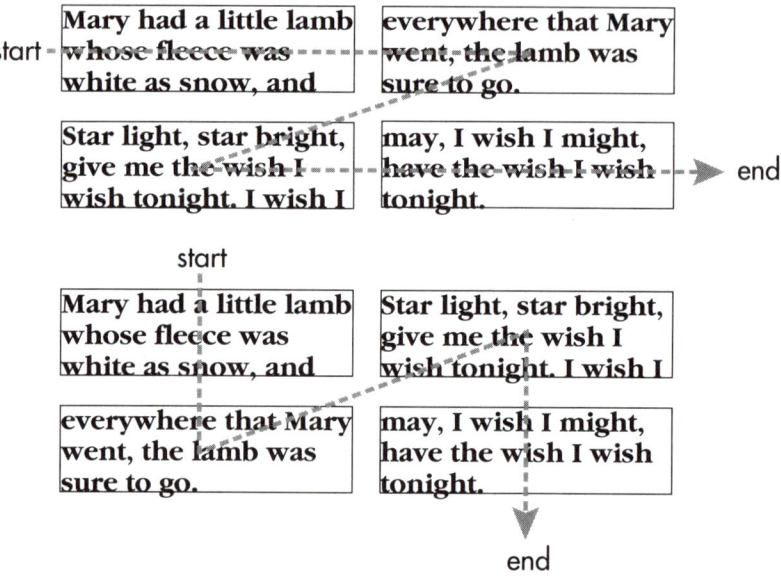

6.11

A text wrap is an effective way to combine smaller graphics within text.

Lorem ipsum dolor sit amet, con sectetuer adipiscing elit, sed diam nonummy nibh euismod tincidunt ut laoreet dolore magna aliquam erat volutpat. Ut wisi enim ad minim veniam quis nostrud exerci tation ullamcorper suscipit lobortis nisl ut aliquip ex ea commodo conseclu quat. Duis autem vel eum iriure dolor in hendrerit in vulputate velit esse molestie con sequat, vel illum dolore eu feugiat nulla facilisis at vero eros et accumsan et iusto odio dig nissim qui blandit praesent luptatum zzril delenit augue duis dolore te feugait nulla facilisi. Lorem ipsum dolor sit amet, consectetuer adi piscing elit, sed diam nonummy nibh euismod tincidunt ut laoreet dolore magna aliqu volutpat. Ut wisi enim ad minim veniam, quis nostrud exerci tation ullamcorper suscipit lobortis nisl ut ali quip ex ea commodo consequat. Duis autem vel eum iriure dolor in hendrerit in vulputate velit esse molestie consequat, vel illum dolore eu feugiat nulla facilisis at vero eros et accumsan et iusto odio dignissim qui blandit praesent lup tatum zzril delenit augue duis dolore te feugait nulla facilisi. Nam liber tempor cum soluta nobis eleifend option congue nihil imperdiet doming id quod mazim placerat facer possim assum. Lorem ipsum dolor sit amet, consectetuer adipiscing elit, sed diam nonummy nibh euismod tinci dunt ut laoreet dolore magna aliquam erat volutpat. Ut wisi enim ad minim veniam, quis nostrud exerci tation ullamcorper

To create a text wrap, first create at least two columns of text. Move your graphic object into place over the columns of text and bring it to the front (⌘-=).

Since you won't want the text to bump directly into your graphic object, use any of the drawing tools to create a closed-path "frame" around the outside of your object. Make sure the frame is slightly larger than the object, and that it contains no fill or stroke.

Bring the graphic object to the front of this frame again (⌘-=). With the Selection tool, click on the text columns and the frame you just created to select them. Under the Type menu, choose Make Wrap. The text will reflow and wrap around the object as you have placed it.

WATCH OUT!

When working with text wraps, make sure that your graphic is placed over the gutter between two columns, or is at least to the side of one column. Graphics placed in the center of one column will cause the text to flow to one side or the other, but the text will not split to create a wrap. It is also important not to make the graphic larger than half the width of the column. As the text wraps, it will have a hard time trying to justify itself in the reduced space that remains. This causes large "rivers" of white space to appear—very distracting and unprofessional, not to mention downright ugly.

You can release a text wrap by selecting the text and frame boxes, and choosing Release Wrap under the Type menu. If you need to change the spacing or size of any of the elements, be sure to release the wrap first, make the changes, and then wrap the text again when finished.

Designing as You Learn:
Wrapping Columns around a Graphic

In this exercise you'll learn firsthand how to create columns and a text wrap. This exercise uses certain text and graphic resources from Illustrator's tutorial files. If you have Adobe Illustrator 5.5 loaded onto your Macintosh, you should also have all of the tutorial files loaded as well.

Look in your Illustrator application folder now for the Tutorial folder. Everything you need for this exercise will be inside the Lesson 4 and 5 folders.

Creating Text Blocks

1. Open a new Illustrator document. Save it and name it Flower Wrap.

2. With the Type tool selected, draw a rectangle. Make the rectangle fairly large, at least 5 inches wide.

3. A cursor will be flashing in the upper-left corner. Select Import Text from the File menu and import the file named On Health Text from the Lesson 5 folder. The text file will flow into your rectangle.

4. Use the Group Selection tool to click on the rectangle. While holding down the Shift and Option keys, drag a copy of the rectangle to the right. Leave about a quarter-inch between the two rectangles for a gutter. Release the mouse button, then the Shift and Option keys. The text from the first rectangle will continue into the second rectangle (Figure 6.12).

Importing and Sizing the Image

1. In the File menu, select Place Art.

2. Choose the file named Flower.template.eps and click on the Place button.

3. A very large image will be imported onto your page. Resize the image to 20 percent using the Scale dialog box and tool.

6.12

The text after two
columns have been
created.

4. Draw another rectangle around the perimeter of the art, making it slightly larger than the image. Bring the image to the front (⌘-=).

5. With the flower image centered over the new rectangle, select both and position them over the middle of the two columns of text (Figure 6.13).

Creating the Text Wrap

1. With the Selection tool, click on one of the columns of text and the extra rectangle behind the image (do not click on the image itself).

2. From the Type menu, select Make Wrap. The text will wrap around the image in both columns (Figure 6.14).

3. Resize your text, change the font, and otherwise style the text and image as you wish.

6.13

The text columns with the flower image placed over them.

6.14

The completed design, showing the text wrap around the image.

orem ipsum dolor sit amet, consectetuer adipiscing elit, sed diam nonummy nibh euismod tincidunt ut laoreet dolore magna aliquam erat volutpat. Ut wisi enim ad minim veniam, quis nostrud exerci tation ullamcorper suscipit lob o rtis nisl u t ali qui lopexea commodo consequat.

Duis autem vel eum iriure dolor in hendrerit in vulputate velit esse molestie consequat, vel illum dolore eu feugiat nulla facilisis at vero eros et accumsan et iusto odio dignissim qui blandit praesent luptatum zzril delenit augue duis dolore te feugait nulla facilisi. Lorem ipsum dolor sit amet, consectetuer adipiscing

elit, sed diam nonummy nibh euismod tincidunt ut laoreet dolore magna aliquam erat volutpat. Ut wisi enim ad minim veniam, quis nostrud exerci tation ullamcorper suscipit lobortis nisl ut aliquip ex ea commodo consequat. Duis autem vel eum iriure dolor in hendrerit in vulputate velit esse molestie consequat, vel illum dolore eu feugiat nulla facilisis at vero eros et accumsan et iusto odio dignissim qui blandit praesent luptatum zzril delenit augue duis dolore te feugait nulla facilisi.

Nam liber tempor cum soluta nobis eleifend option congue nihil imperdiet doming id quod mazim

Word Processing Features in Illustrator

 Illustrator 5.5 has several new word processing features that help you edit text directly in the program. This is a big improvement over past versions, and eliminates the need to use a separate word processing program to perform such tasks as checking spelling and entering "smart" punctuation.

Using the Spelling Checker

The Check Spelling filter reviews the spelling in your document and lists the discrepancies it finds as it matches your words to those in the Adobe Illustrator dictionary. You then have the option of either ignoring the change, choosing a word from a list of suggestions, or adding the word to your own personal dictionary. With this final option, the Check Spelling filter will use your dictionary in addition to its own in the future.

To use the Check Spelling filter, first select a text block to check. (If you want to check the entire document, don't select any text.) In the Filters menu under the Text pop-up menu, select Check Spelling. The filter will immediately check the selected text and display a listing of the misspelled words it finds (Figure 6.15).

- To make no changes to a word, click on the Skip button.
- To skip every instance of the word throughout your document, click on the Skip All button.
- To change a word, select the proper spelling from the list that Illustrator offers, or type in the correct spelling in the field below the list. Click on the Change button.
- To change every instance of the misspelled word throughout your document, click on the Change All button.
- To add your spelling of a word to your personal dictionary, click on the Learn button. The Learned Words dialog box will appear, so that you can add and remove words at will (Figure 6.16).

6.15

The Check Spelling filter offers suggestions for the words it believes to be misspelled.

Here is an example of some spelling for the program to check. I will mispel a few wurdz so it has sumthing to look for.

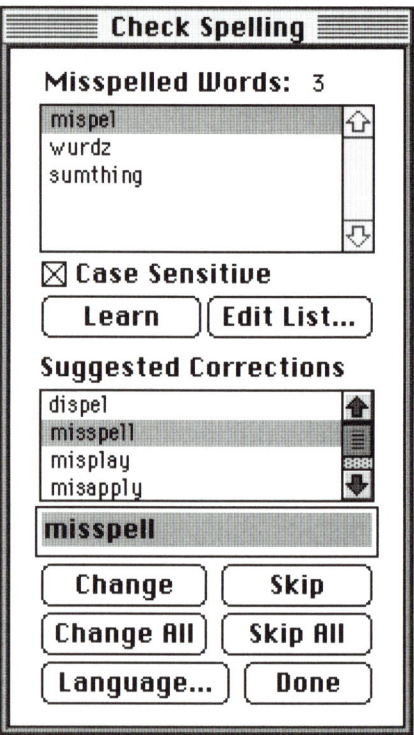

6.16

The Learned Words dialog box lets you add the spelling of new words to your own personal dictionary.

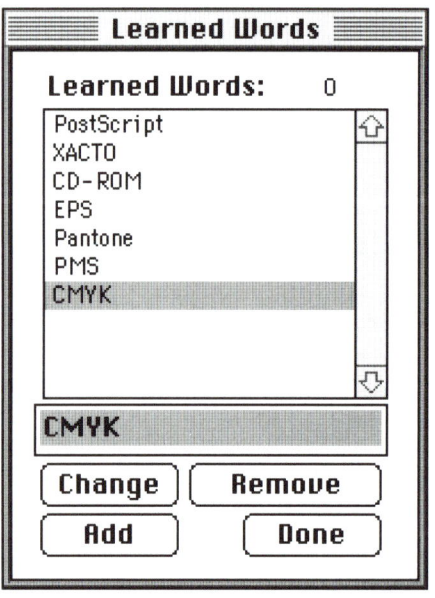

■ To change the language dictionary used by Illustrator (currently there are only two: US English and UK English), click on the Language button and choose the dictionary you prefer from the Plug-Ins folder in the Illustrator application folder.

Auto Hyphenation

The Auto Hyphenation program in Illustrator automatically hyphenates words in text according to the parameters you have entered in the Paragraph palette (⌘-Shift-P). In the Hyphenation area (Figure 6.17) you can specify the number of letters that must occur before and after a hyphen in a word. If dividing a word at a line ending would leave fewer letters before or after the hyphen than the minimum you've specified, Illustrator will adjust spacing to fit the entire word on one line or the other. You can also set the maximum number of hyphenated lines that can occur in a row (three or less is preferred).

6.17

The Hyphenation settings in the Paragraph palette control the way words are automatically hyphenated.

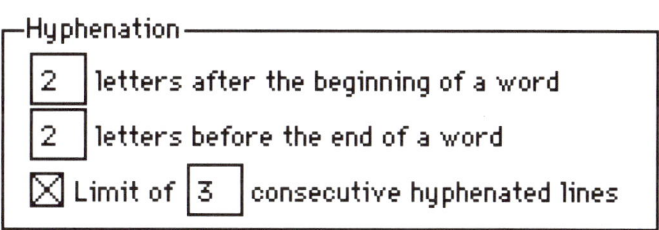

If you don't like the way Illustrator hyphenates words, you can create your own list of hyphenation exceptions. Illustrator will refer to this list in the future to hyphenate words your way. In the Preferences submenu under the File menu, select Hyphenation Options and a dialog box will appear (Figure 6.18). Enter your preferred hyphenation in the Entry field, using one or more hyphens to indicate the correct breaking points. If you enter a word with *no* hyphens, the word will never be hyphenated.

6.18

The Hyphenation Options dialog box lets you enter your preferred way of hyphenating (or not hyphenating) certain words.

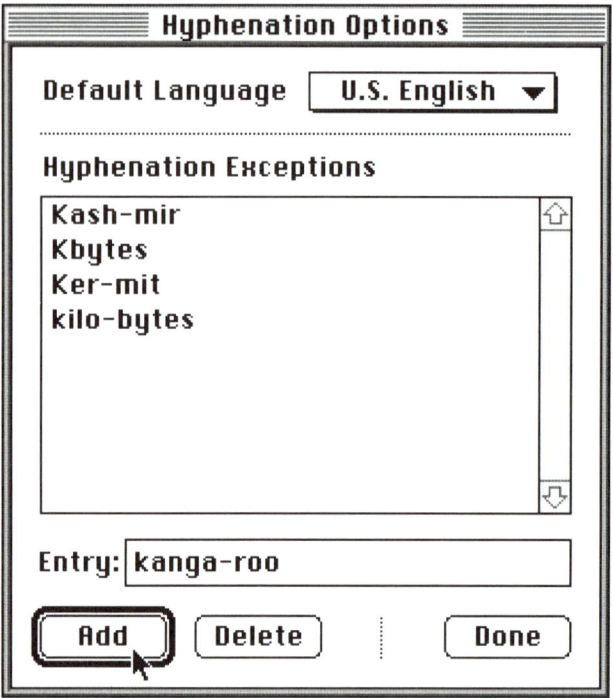

INSIDE INFO

You can insert a discretionary hyphen whenever you want to rebreak a single word by inserting your hyphen at the breaking point and pressing Control-hyphen. Be careful, though. Discretionary hyphens, unlike automatic hyphens, will remain in your text if it reflows, possibly causing a strange hyphenated word in the middle of a line. Thus, it's best to wait until the end of a project before applying discretionary hyphens.

Smart Punctuation

What's so smart about a "smart" punctuation mark? Also called typesetter's punctuation, smart punctuation includes the curly quote marks, apostrophes, and other punctuation marks that are inserted when a manuscript is professionally typeset. Compare the punctuation in Figure 6.19, and see if you can tell the difference.

6.19

Regular punctuation (left) and smart punctuation (right). Can you tell the difference?

"Ethel," asked Lucy, "where's my new coat--in the closet?"

"Ethel," asked Lucy, "where's my new coat—in the closet?"

As you can see, the smart punctuation example has curly opening and closing quotation marks (instead of "inch marks"), a curly apostrophe, and an actual em dash instead of two hyphens. Although your readers might not be able to put their finger on it, text with smart punctuation is easier to read and looks more professional.

Until very recently, only full-fledged desktop publishing programs could automatically replace "typewriter" punctuation marks with smart punctuation. Now many word processors offer this feature, and Adobe Illustrator 5.5 provides the Smart Punctuation filter, located in the Text submenu under the Filters menu. When you open the dialog box, you can pick and choose the type of punctuation to replace, as well as whether to replace punctuation in just a selected area of text or throughout the whole document (Figure 6.20). When you click on the OK button, the changes you choose will be implemented in the area of text you selected.

Since smart punctuation is a visual thing, refer to Table 6.1 to see the differences between each of the punctuation replacements.

6.20

The Smart Punctuation dialog box gives you a choice of replacing several types of punctuation marks in your document.

Smart Punctuation

Replace Punctuation:
- ☒ ff, fi, ffi Ligatures
- ☒ ff, fl, ffl Ligatures
- ☒ Smart Quotes (" ")
- ☒ Smart Spaces (.)
- ☒ En, Em Dashes (--)
- ☒ Ellipses (...)
- ☒ Expert Fractions

Replace In:
- ⦿ Selected Text Only
- ○ Entire Document

☐ Report Results

Cancel   OK

Table 6.1: Smart Punctuation vs. Regular Punctuation

Punctuation	Regular	Smart
Ligatures*	ff, fl, ffl	ff, fl, ffl
	ff, fi, ffi	ff, fi, ffi
Quotes	" ", '	" ", ' '
Spaces	double space after a period	single space after a period
En dash	(none)	–
Em dash	--	—
Ellipses	... or . . .	. . .
Expert Fractions**	1/4, 1/2	$\frac{1}{4}$, $\frac{1}{2}$

*A ligature is a combination of letters that make up a single symbol that is easier to read.
** replaces multiple-character fraction with single character fraction, if one exists in the font character set.

Changing the Case of Letters

The Change Case filter will change text from any case into all upper-case, all lowercase, or mixed (capping just the beginning letter of each word). This can really save you a lot of time that previously would be wasted retyping text or switching back and forth to your word processor.

To change cases, simply select the text with the Type tool by clicking on one end of the text string and dragging the tool over the line of type to highlight it. In the Filter menu, go to the Text submenu and choose Change Case. The Change Case dialog box will appear (Figure 6.21). Select the type of capitalization you prefer: uppercase, lowercase, or mixed case. Click on the OK button to implement your changes (Figure 6.22).

6.21

The Change Case filter dialog box.

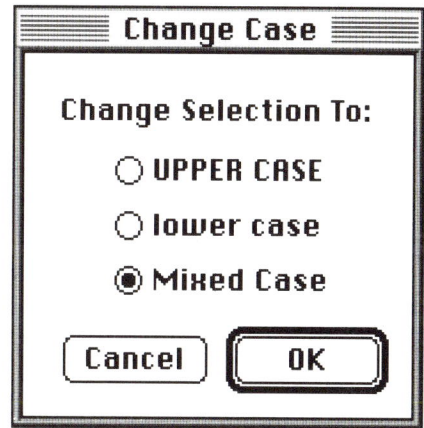

6.22

The Change Case filter can switch the capitalization of a selected area of text.

original   When I grow up I want to be very tall.

lowercase   when i grow up i want to be very tall.

uppercase   WHEN I GROW UP I WANT TO BE VERY TALL.

mixed case   When I Grow Up I Want To Be Very Tall.

Designing as You Learn: Using the Word Processing Features

This exercise is a self-guided tour of the word processing features we just covered. Open a new document and type some text onto the page—if necessary, copy a paragraph or two out of a book so that you get a good mix of words and punctuation.

Now try using each of the text features we just covered. With the exception of one (hyphenation), all of these features are controlled in the Text submenu of the Filters menu.

- check the spelling
- examine the hyphenation
- change the case of the letters
- replace the punctuation with smart punctuation
- find and replace the fonts used

Styling Text in Adobe Illustrator 5.5

Now that your text is entered and edited in your document, let's add some style to the letters themselves to help them make a statement. Of course, the kind of statement they should make depends on the purpose the text serves in your design.

Sometimes type should be large and bold. It should attract the eye and make a definite statement. In other cases, it should be more subdued, giving the necessary information to the reader, but not overpowering the graphic elements of the design. Think about the purpose of your design, and that should give you a pretty good idea of the approach to take with your type.

In this section, we'll talk about the many elements that change the style of type—the physical characteristics that make type take on different visual connotations for the reader. Although a lot of this information is technical, it can also be a lot of fun.

Most of the text-styling features can be applied in any of three ways: with menu commands, with a palette, or with a keyboard shortcut. In most cases, however, the last two methods are easier and faster than the first; so those are the methods you'll find here. It's important that you get used to working with Adobe Illustrator this way. As you use the palettes and shortcuts, you'll find they become second nature. Instead of hunting through a menu for a command, you'll automatically invoke the keyboard shortcut, saving yourself a lot of time.

The Wonderful World of Fonts

A *font* is the generic term for a set of letter forms that can be used to style the text of a design. Also called typefaces, fonts come in families; for instance, Helvetica or Times. Although technically the terms *font* and *typeface* have different meanings, they are often used interchangeably, as they will be in this book.

Changing fonts is a little like putting on a new hat—it can give a whole different look to the same person. Fonts are probably the most *emotional* part of designing with type. A well-chosen font in a design can say as much as the words themselves, if not more.

Take for instance, the differences in the fonts shown in Figure 6.23, compared to the meaning they are trying to express. The first one, Tekton, is a little too informal. The second one, Helvetica, is too bland. Eras is just too futuristic, and Courier reminds me of a form letter you'd receive in the mail. The fifth font, Zapf Chancery, is formal and yet tends to express an emotion more suited to the occasion.

6.23

Different fonts express different emotions.

Tekton You're invited to the Presidential Inauguration…

Helvetica You're invited to the Presidential Inauguration…

Mistral *You're invited to the Presidential Inauguration…*

Courier You're invited to the Presidential Inauguration…

Revue **You're invited to the Presidential Inauguration…**

Each font comes in several weights and styles. Common variations include light, regular, italic, bold, bold italic, and heavy (Figure 6.24). Font families are also classified as being either serif, sans serif, or script (Figure 6.25).

Categories of Fonts

Fonts are also classified according to the way the computer stores and handles them. There are several such categories of fonts on the market today: Type 1, TrueType, and Multiple Master, to name a few. While all of them will work fine on your Macintosh, there are some important points to note about each one.

6.24

Different variations on the Futura typeface.

Futura Light	If wishes were fishes…
Futura Book	If wishes were fishes…
Futura Oblique	*If wishes were fishes…*
Futura Bold	**If wishes were fishes...**
Futura Heavy Oblique	***If wishes were fishes...***
Futura Extra Bold	**If wishes were fishes...**

6.25

Serif fonts have "feet" at the ends of their strokes and are more rounded. Sans serif fonts have no feet and are more angular. Script fonts are fancier and more italic in nature.

serif	**She heard the doorbell ring.**
sans serif	**She heard the doorbell ring.**
script	*She heard the doorbell ring.*

Type 1 fonts are the safest to use if you will be sending your work out to be printed elsewhere. Type 1 fonts are PostScript language fonts, which print cleaner and faster, especially when used with Illustrator EPS files. And being PostScript, they are more compatible with higher resolution output devices. Finally, since Type 1 fonts have been around longer than the other two categories, most print shops have a large variety of Type 1 fonts in stock, meaning less trouble down the road.

TrueType fonts are handy because they can accurately render and print various non-bitmapped sizes of a font from a single screen version (Type 1 requires a separate printer version). Although TrueType fonts are slowly gaining acceptance, many professional printers don't like them. To use them, the printer has to unload his Type 1 version of a font from the output device and load the TrueType font. Warning: they don't like doing this.

Multiple Master typefaces, the latest in font innovation, allow you to create thousands of fonts based on a single typeface. By adjusting the width of characters, line weight, size and style, you can literally design your own personal fonts. I've no word yet on what the professional printers think of this one, or even how easy it is to transfer when printing from somewhere other than your own machine. However, it is an option to consider if you aren't finding the exact look you want in a font.

Changing Fonts in Illustrator

To change a font in your document, use the Selection tool to select the type. If you are only changing a word or two in the midst of a text block, use the Type tool to highlight just those words.

Open the Character palette (⌘-T) and by clicking on the small triangle to the right of the font listed, scroll through your list of fonts to select a new one. The font you choose will immediately take effect.

Searching and Replacing Fonts in a Document

The Find Font filter, another new addition to Illustrator, makes it easy to change fonts on a global scale.

For example, say you want to replace Helvetica Bold throughout your document with Futura Regular. From the Text submenu under the Filters menu, choose Find Font. In the Find Font dialog box, you will see a list of all the fonts currently in use in your document (Figure 6.26). Select Helvetica Bold from the top list of fonts, and then choose Futura Regular from the bottom list.

6.26

The Find Fonts dialog box allows you to search for and replace the fonts in your document.

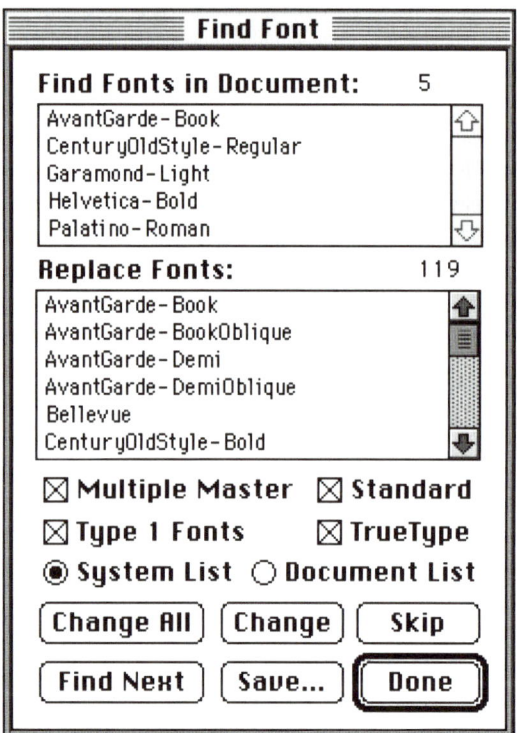

When you have selected the fonts to find and replace, click on one of the standard buttons below:

- **Change All** changes all instances of the font in your document.
- **Change** changes the first instance of the font found.
- **Skip** goes to the next font to be searched for in the document.

- **Find Next** searches for the next instance of the font in the document.
- **Save** saves a list of the fonts used in the document.
- **Done** exits you from the Find Font dialog box.

The Find Fonts dialog box allows you to restrict the fonts shown in the lists to only certain types, such as Multiple Master, Standard, Type 1, or TrueType fonts (you can choose all of them at once, as well). You can also choose whether to list just the fonts already used in the document as replacements, or to list all fonts currently residing in your system. In other words, you can make the search and replace function as narrow or as broad as you need.

Sizing Type: Changing the Point Size

Type is sized in points (72 points are equal to an inch). The most common sizes used are 8, 9, 10, 11, 12, 14, 16, 18, 24, 30, 36, 42, 48, 56, 60, and 72 point type, although Illustrator gives you the option of entering any size above, below or in between. When type is said to be a certain point size, that size reflects the distance from the lowest descender in that particular typeface to the highest ascender. Thus a 24 point character in one typeface may actually look smaller or larger when compared to one of the same size in a different typeface.

To give you an idea of their differences, generally text such as the kind you are reading in this book is set at 10 or 11 point. Newspaper text is set slightly smaller, about 9 point. The headlines in a newspaper are generally about 30 to 48 point, with major headlines reaching sizes of 72 point (Figure 6.27).

You can change the size of type by selecting the text block with the Selection tool, and opening the Character palette (⌘-T). In the Size field you can either click on the black triangle to scroll to a new size, or type in your own number in the field and hit Return to apply the new size.

6.27

**Point sizes vary
from small to large**

12 24 **36 48 72**

Leading Lines of Type

Leading is the vertical space between lines of type, measured from baseline to baseline (the imaginary line on which type sits). Without enough leading, type becomes an unreadable black mess; with too much leading, lines of type seem to lack cohesiveness and are difficult to read (Figure 6.28).

The optimum amount of leading, therefore, is an important factor to consider. Illustrator's Auto-Leading feature sets the leading value at 120 percent of the point size used. (If two or more point sizes are used in the same line, Illustrator will base the leading on the bigger size.) This 120 percent figure is a common standard that works for many purposes, but most often you should visually adjust the leading to find the best match for your font and point size, not to mention your design.

To change the leading for a block of type, first select the type using the Selection tool and then open the Character palette (⌘-T). Like the point size, leading is measured in points. You can either scroll to a new value or enter your own and hit the Return key.

6.28

Optimum leading (top), versus too little (middle), and too much (bottom).

10 point type on 12 point leading

Lorem ipsum dolor sit amet, consectetuer adipiscing elit, sed diam nonummy nibh euismod tincidunt ut laoreet dolore magna aliquam erat volutpat. Ut wisi enim ad minim veniam, quis nostrud exerci tation ullamcorper suscipit lobortis nisl ut aliquip ex ea commodo consequat.

Duis autem vel eum iriure dolor in hendrerit in vulputate velit esse molestie consequat, vel illum dolore eu feugiat nulla facilisis at vero eros et accumsan et iusto odio dignis-

10 point type on 9 point leading

Lorem ipsum dolor sit amet, consectetuer adipiscing elit, sed diam nonummy nibh euismod tincidunt ut laoreet dolore magna aliquam erat volutpat. Ut wisi enim ad minim veniam, quis nostrud exerci tation ullamcorper suscipit lobortis nisl ut aliquip ex ea commodo consequat.
Duis autem vel eum iriure dolor in hendrerit in vulputate velit esse molestie consequat, vel illum dolore eu feugiat nulla facilisis at vero eros et accumsan et iusto odio dignissim qui blandit praesent luptatum zzril delenit augue duis dolore te feugait nulla facilisi. Lorem ipsum dolor sit amet,

10 point type on 18 point leading

Lorem ipsum dolor sit amet, consectetuer adipiscing elit, sed diam nonummy nibh euismod tincidunt ut laoreet dolore magna aliquam erat volutpat. Ut wisi enim ad minim veniam, quis nostrud exerci tation ullamcorper suscipit lobortis nisl ut aliquip ex ea commodo consequat.

Adjusting the Kerning and Tracking

Kerning and *tracking* are two different elements that control the horizontal space between individual letters. Both kerning and tracking are expressed in units of 1/1000th of an em space (the width of one letter "m" in the font and point size currently selected).

Kerning

Kerning controls the space between just two letters. Often, especially in larger point sizes, some letter combinations will look too far apart. By placing your type cursor between the two letters and adjusting the kerning, you can eliminate the white space (Figure 6.29). Most fonts come already kerned, that is, with kerning information included for certain letter combinations. However, you may occasionally need to make adjustments.

To adjust the kerning between two letters, put your Type tool cursor between the two letters and click to get the flashing cursor. In the Character palette, click on the small black flag symbol to the right to open the extended palette (Figure 6.30). Enter a new number in the Kerning field, positive to increase the space or negative to reduce it. Hit Return to implement the changes in your text.

Tracking

Tracking controls the spacing between groups of three or more characters. Most often, tracking is applied to entire lines or paragraphs of text. It is an effective way to pull up widows—small words at an end of a paragraph that sit on their own line (Figure 6.31). It can also help a line

6.29

Kerning adjusts the white space between two letters.

Palomino

Palomino

6.30

The Kerning field is located in the extended Character palette.

Character		
Font: Garamond	Light	▾
Size: 10 pt ▾	Leading: 12 pt ▾	☐ Auto leading
Baseline shift: 0 pt	Kerning: 10 /1000 em	☐ Auto kerning
Horizontal scale: 100 %	Language: U.S. English ▾	

6.3 I

Notice the differ-
ence between the
untracked paragraph
(above) and the one
with tracking added
(below). Not only
does the second one
look tighter, it has
allowed the widow
to be brought back
up on a full line.

Lorem ipsum dolor sit amet, consectetuer adipiscing elit, sed diam nonummy nibh euismod tincidunt ut laoreet dolore magna aliquam erat volutpat. Ut wisi enim ad minim veniam, quis nostrud exerci tation ullamcorper suscipit lobortis nisl ut aliquip ex ea commodo consequat.

Lorem ipsum dolor sit amet, consectetuer adipiscing elit, sed diam nonummy nibh euismod tincidunt ut laoreet dolore magna aliquam erat volutpat. Ut wisi enim ad minim veniam, quis nostrud exerci tation ullamcorper suscipit lobortis nisl ut aliquip ex ea commodo consequat.

or paragraph to look more cohesive by reducing the extra white space left when you try to justify a paragraph (see also "Specifying Word and Letter Spacing," below).

To adjust the tracking for a group of letters, use the Type tool to highlight the letters and open the Character Palette. In the extended version of the palette, the Kerning field will turn into the Tracking field. Enter a new number in this field, positive to increase the space or negative to reduce the space. Hit Return to implement the changes in your text.

INSIDE INFO

Remember, to open the extended version of the palette, click on the small black flag in the right side of the palette (look where the cursor is pointing in Figure 6.30). You can also close the lower portion of the palette by clicking on the black flag.

Specifying Word and Letter Spacing

Word and letter spacing controls the white space between words and letters, primarily in justified text. Unlike the manual adjustments you make in kerning and tracking, word and letter spacing lets you set certain parameters (minimum, maximum, and desired), which the program then takes into account when justifying a block of text. Whenever possible, Illustrator will use the *desired* value to justify the text.

The values in the extended Paragraph palette (⌘-Shift-P) spacing fields are based on percentages of the width of a normal space (Figure 6.32). 100 percent word spacing means that no extra space is added between words; a higher percentage adds space, and a lower percentage subtracts space.

Likewise, zero percent entered in the letter spacing field means that no space will be added between letters. A higher percentage means that percentage of a normal space will be added between letters; a negative value subtracts that percentage of a normal space from between letters.

6.32

The word and letter spacing fields in the extended Paragraph palette are based on percentages of the width of a normal space.

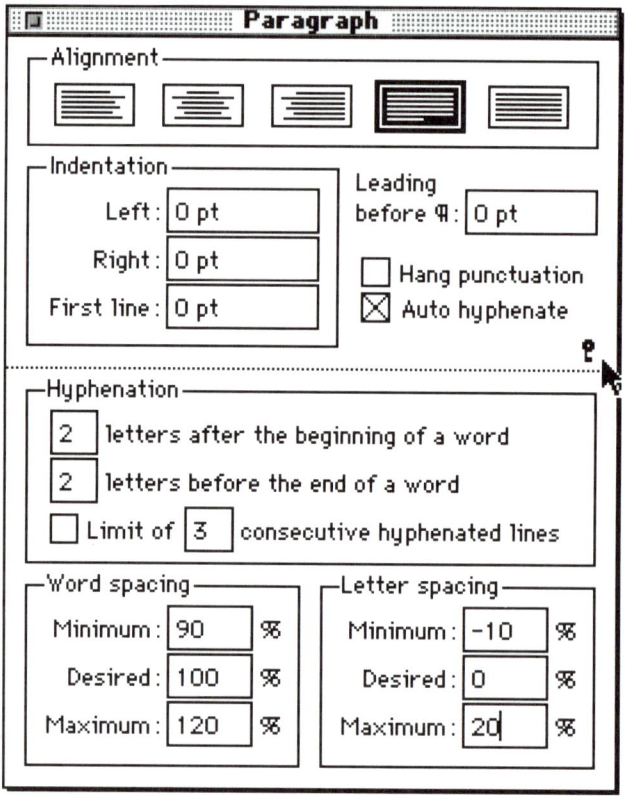

To apply word or letter spacing to a block of text, select the text and open the Paragraph palette (⌘-Shift-P). Enter the new percentages, hitting Return after each one.

Changing the Baseline Shift

It is possible to add or subtract points to the baseline of type, causing the line to move above or below the normal baseline. This is somewhat like the effect you can achieve with superscripting or subscripting, but the point size of the type does not change. Highlight the text with the Type tool and open the extended Character palette. Enter a new value in points in the Baseline Shift field, and hit Return to apply the changes to your text (Figure 6.33).

6.33

Text can be raised above or below the baseline.

You can raise text above the baseline or below the baseline.

Horizontally Scaling Type

One interesting effect you can use with type is to scale it horizontally. By slightly reducing the horizontal scale of large amounts of text, you can fit more text into the same space. Enlarging the horizontal scale of larger display type can create a bolder look (Figure 6.34).

To scale type, highlight the type with the Type tool and open the Character palette (⌘-T). Enter a new value in the Horizontal Scale field and hit Return.

6.34

Horizontally scaled type can create interesting effects.

Horizontal Scale: 100%
YOUR ATTENTION PLEASE.

Horizontal Scale: 150%
YOUR ATTENTION PLEASE.

Type that is scaled down lower than 75 percent of normal begins to lose its readability—this can be disastrous in large blocks of small text. For the most part, save the horizontal scaling effects for larger display type.

Changing the Alignment of Type

Adobe Illustrator has five alignment options for type: Left, Center, Right, Justify, and Justify Last Line. You can see the differences between them in Figure 6.35. To apply an alignment option to text, select the text with the Selection tool and open the Paragraph palette (⌘-Shift-P). Click on one of the alignment options shown in the top of the palette.

If you have only a word or two left at the end of a paragraph, the Justify Last Line alignment option will do horrid things to the spacing of this last line. Be careful when using this alignment option.

Setting Indentation

You can set up both margin and paragraph indents for a block of text using the Paragraph palette (⌘-Shift-P). With your text selected, enter indent values for the margins in the Left and Right fields (in points). To indent the beginning of a paragraph, enter a value in the First Line field.

Setting Tabs in Text

Finally ! If you've used past versions of Illustrator, I'm sure you're breathing a sigh of relief over version 5.5's ability to set tabs in text. Oh, the alignment problems we've endured over the years for lack of this simple device.

6.35

Adobe Illustrator
alignment options
include Left, center,
Right, Justify or Jus-
tify Last Line.

left

Lorem ipsum dolor sit amet,
consectetuer adipiscing elit,
sed diam nonummy nibh euismod tincidunt ut laoreet dolore magna aliquam erat volutpat. Ut wisi enim ad minim
veniam, quis nostrud exerci tation ullamcorper suscipit lobortis nisl ut aliquip ex ea
commodo consequat

center

Lorem ipsum dolor sit amet,
consectetuer adipiscing elit,
sed diam nonummy nibh euismod tincidunt ut laoreet dolore magna aliquam erat volutpat. Ut wisi enim ad minim
veniam, quis nostrud exerci tation ullamcorper suscipit lobortis nisl ut aliquip ex ea
commodo consequat

right

Lorem ipsum dolor sit amet,
consectetuer adipiscing elit,
sed diam nonummy nibh euismod tincidunt ut laoreet dolore magna aliquam erat volutpat. Ut wisi enim ad minim
veniam, quis nostrud exerci tation ullamcorper suscipit lobortis nisl ut aliquip ex ea
commodo consequat

justify

Lorem ipsum dolor sit amet,
consectetuer adipiscing elit,
sed diam nonummy nibh euismod tincidunt ut laoreet dolore magna aliquam erat volutpat. Ut wisi enim ad minim
veniam, quis nostrud exerci tation ullamcorper suscipit lobortis nisl ut aliquip ex ea com
modo consequat

justify last line

Lorem ipsum dolor sit amet,
consectetuer adipiscing elit,
sed diam nonummy nibh euismod tincidunt ut laoreet dolore magna aliquam erat volutpat. Ut wisi enim ad minim
veniam, quis nostrud exerci tation ullamcorper suscipit lobortis nostrud nisl ut aliquip
ex ea commodo consequat

The Tab Ruler palette (⌘-Shift-T), located in the Windows menu, has several features (Figure 6.36). In the top-left corner are style buttons for setting left, right, center, or decimal tab stops. In the upper-right corner of the palette is the Alignment button—click on it to align the ruler with the left margin of the text you have selected. To make the ruler longer, click and drag on the symbol in the lower-right corner. Across the bottom of the palette is the ruler, where you will click to create tabs.

To set a tab, first select the text with the Selection tool. Open the Tab Ruler (⌘-Shift-T). Align the ruler with your text by clicking on the Alignment button. Make the ruler longer if necessary. Now click on the ruler to apply tabs where you need them. If you click the Snap box in the ruler, the tabs will snap to definite ruler increments as you place them.

6.36

The Tab Ruler
palette.

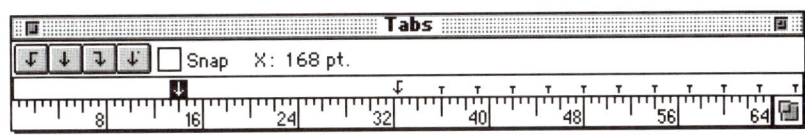

To change the type of tab you use, insert a tab and then click on one of the style buttons in the palette. It will automatically convert the last tab set.

You can move tabs once they are set by clicking and dragging on the tab symbols in the ruler. Release the mouse button to set the tab down in a new place. To delete a tab, click and drag the tab marker off the top or left side of the ruler.

Summary

The text-handling features of Adobe Illustrator have come a long way in the last two versions. The additions to version 5.5 make Illustrator all the more valuable for designers looking for a comprehensive program that can handle type as well as draw.

You may need to review the information in this chapter several times. It may take a while to learn where all the type features are located. Once again, the sooner you get the hang of using the keyboard shortcuts, the faster you'll be able to swing through the Illustrator jungle of commands.

Using Colors, Patterns, and Trapping

S E V E N

When you look at a design, a bright color or two is probably the first thing that catches your eye, enticing you to take a closer look. Color sets the mood for a design—it can scream for attention or subtly set the visual feeling you intend for a viewer. The use of color, therefore, is an important subject for a designer to master.

In this chapter we'll look at color and how to incorporate it into your Adobe Illustrator designs. We'll also look at related subjects such as creating gradients, patterns, and trapping. These will lend even greater designing power to your palette as you search for the proper colors to make a statement.

Working with Colors

Practically all of us associate colors with feelings and memories: blue and green are tranquil and peaceful, red and orange are bold and boisterous. Light blues and pinks are associated with youth, while darker colors tend to reflect maturity and age. When you recall a memory of long ago, often a color is attached to it: how blue was the sky, how green was the grass, and how vivid were the flowers you remember.

It is these associations that make the use of color in a design so important. If you are designing an advertisement, the colors you choose not only attract your readers' attention, they help them remember the advertisement long after it has left their view.

Color, however, can be overused. Too much color on a page confuses the eye and gives it no focal point. Yes, it may be bright or pretty, but it also distracts the viewer from the message of your design. It's far better to use too little color than too much. A single spot of color to attract the eye does much more than a whole circus full of colors competing for your attention.

With these basic guidelines in mind, let's discuss the color options that Adobe Illustrator gives you. Through the use of the process colors (cyan, magenta, yellow, and black), as well as other color systems, Illustrator lets you create literally millions of color combinations for use in your design. What's more, Illustrator makes it easy to create and apply these colors from one location—the Paint Style palette.

Using the Paint Style Palette

The Paint Style palette is the command center for creating and applying colors in Adobe Illustrator. It's a little like the Grand Central Station of palettes—there's so much going on in one place its hard to take it all in. Figure 7.1 shows what each element does.

In the upper-right corner of the palette is the Panel Display pop-up menu. This allows you to choose from four different views of the Paint Style palette, depending on your needs and the room on your screen. You can display the entire palette, the left side, the right side, or just the top half of the palette.

Chapter 3 of this book included a hands-on introduction to the basics of applying color. If you're just joining us, here's a brief review. To fill or stroke an object, you:

1. Select the object,
2. Click on the Fill or Stroke icon in the palette,
3. Click on the appropriate icon in the Color Selector,
4. Click on the color and adjust the tint in the Color Slider area.

Now let's examine each of the sections of the Paint Style palette individually.

Using the Paint Swatches

In the left side of the palette is a large area filled with colored squares called *paint swatches*. This is a handy place where you can store and use specific color combinations you have created in a document. Adobe Illustrator can store up to 225 paint swatches, including gradients and patterns.

7.1

The Paint Style palette.

Fill and Stroke
Click on one of these two icons to specify whether to apply color as a fill or stroke to the selected object.

Color Selector
Click on one of these seven icons to specify the type of color to be used (from left to right): no color, white, black, process, custom, pattern or gradient.

Paint Swatches
The Paint Swatch area has several preset combinations of colors that can be clicked on to choose for fill or stroke. In addition, by clicking on the gradient or pattern swatches, you can automatically open the gradient or pattern list in the Color Sliders area.

Panel Display
To condense or expand the Paint Style palette view, click on the arrow and select a new choice.

Color Sliders
Determine the tint of each color in the mix by sliding the bars or entering a new percentage in the box. This field will change depending on if you are using process or custom colors.

Stroke Weight
Determines the weight (width) of the stroke.

Caps
Sets the style for the endpoints of open paths and dash marks.

Overprint
Click here to cause the fill or stroked object to overprint the objects underneath.

Miter Limit
Switches joins from mitered to beveled when corner points surpass the limit.

Joins
Sets the style for the corners of stroked paths.

Solid or Dashed Line
Click on Dashed and enter dash and gap values in the boxes to create a dotted line pattern out of any stroke. Click on Solid to set a solid stroke line.

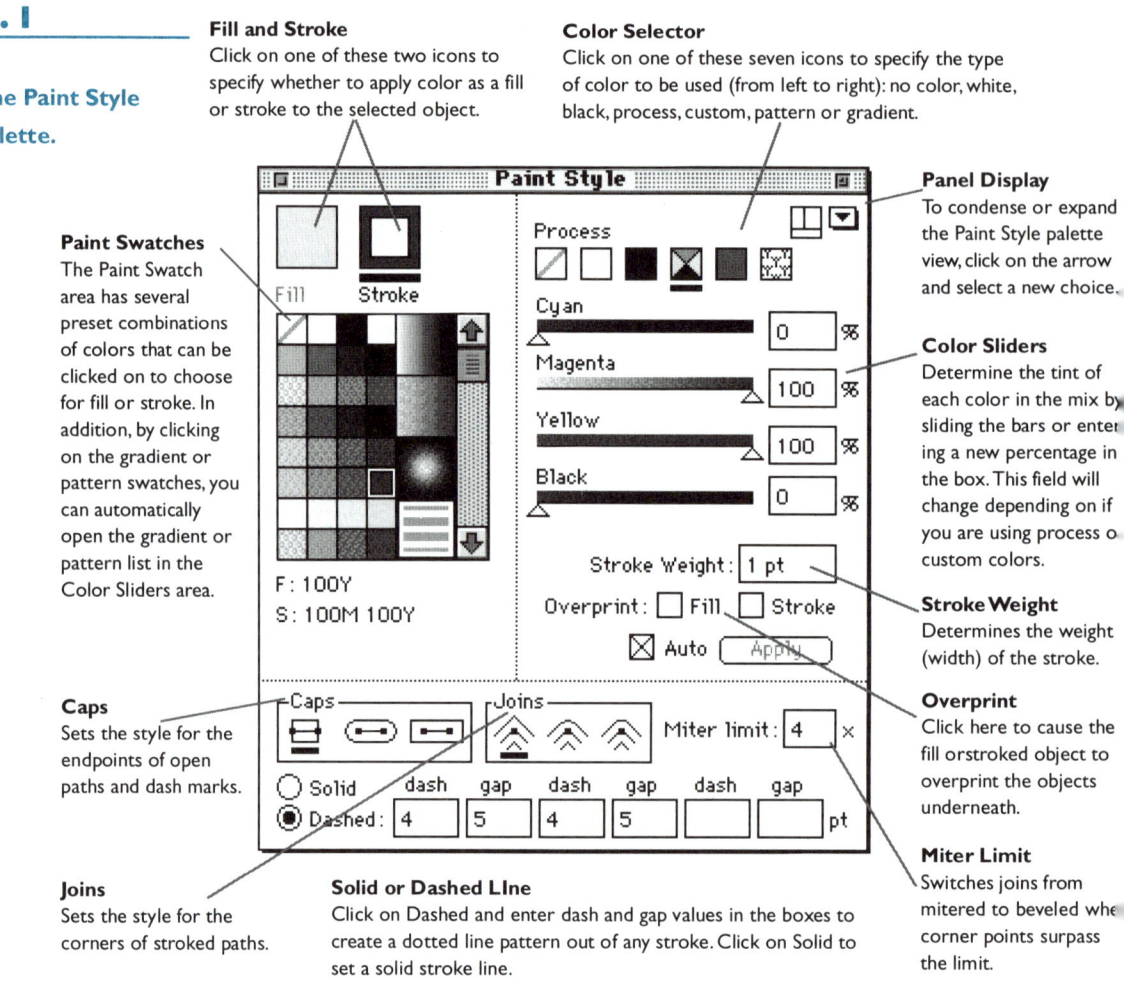

To store a new color in the paint swatch area, first create a fill color using the process or custom color controls, as discussed later in this chapter. It will appear in the Fill box. Next, hold down the Option key and click on an empty paint swatch box. Your new color will now become a paint swatch. If you hold down the Option key while clicking on an existing color in the swatch area, the color in the Fill box will replace the old color. If you want to delete a color from the swatch selection area, hold down the Command key and click on the swatch.

To apply a paint swatch color, first select the object you want to paint or stroke. Then click on the Fill or Stroke button, and click on the swatch.

Using the Color Selector and Slider Tint Bars

The Color Selector buttons in the upper part of the palette control what goes on in the Slider Bar area. If you click on Black or White, a single tint bar will appear with shades from zero to 100%. If you click on the Process button, four tint bars will appear, one for each of the process colors cyan, magenta, yellow, and black.

The Slider Bar area changes, however, if you click on the Custom, Pattern, or Gradient button:

■ The **Custom** button brings up a list of preset colors, with a tint bar under the list (Figure 7.2).

■ The **Pattern** button produces a list of preset patterns that can be used instead of color for filling objects (Figure 7.3).

7.2

The Custom Color list in the Paint Style palette.

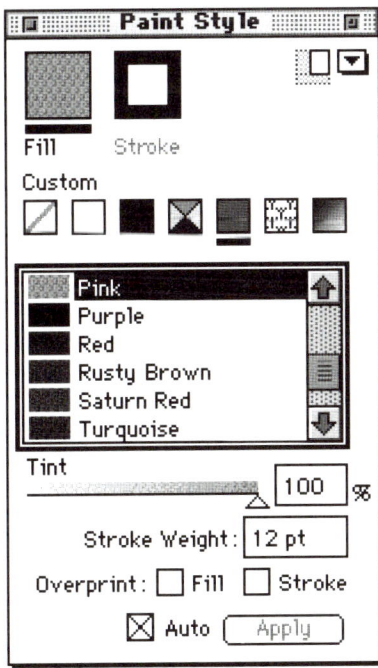

7.3

The Pattern list in the Paint Style palette.

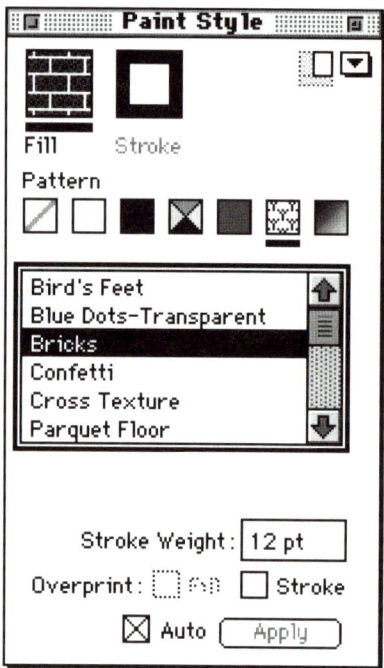

■ The **Gradient** button brings up a list of preset color blends with a field for setting the angle of the gradient within the object (Figure 7.4).

You can use any of these three instead of a fill color in objects. However, only custom colors can be used for strokes. See sections later in this chapter for more information about creating custom colors, patterns, and gradient color blends.

WATCH OUT!

The Pattern button will allow you to specify a pattern for a stroke, but it will not show on your screen, nor will it print unless the path it is applied to is very simple. It is recommended that you save patterns for filling objects only.

7.4

**The Gradient list
in the Paint Style
palette.**

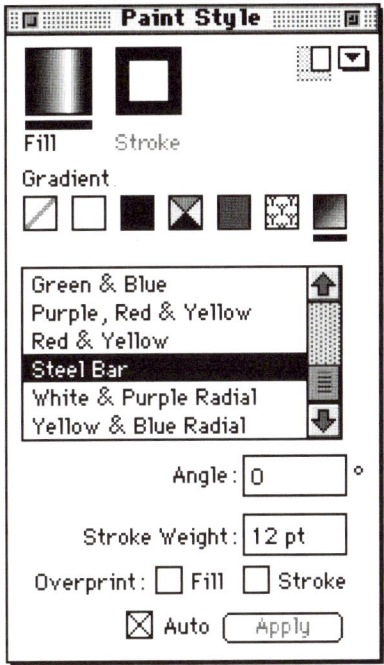

Dashed Lines, Caps, and Joins

At the bottom of the Paint Style palette are the controls for setting solid and dashed lines. By default, the Solid button is selected, but when you want to create a dashed or dotted line, click on the Dashed button. The Dash and Gap boxes will become active. In these boxes enter the length of each dash and the gaps between them in points (Figure 7.5).

Six boxes are provided so that you can create interesting dashed patterns. For a simple dotted line you will only need to fill in the first two boxes, but more intricate designs may require all six boxes. Figure 7.6 illustrates a few possibilities.

7.5

**Enter a Dash and
Gap value in points
to create a dashed
line.**

○ Solid   dash   gap   dash   gap   dash   gap

◉ Dashed: `3`   `3`   ☐   ☐   ☐   ☐ pt

Did you notice that some of the dashed line patterns in Figure 7.6 have rounded dashes instead of the usual blunt rectangular dashes? The Caps field lets you choose the style for the endpoints of an open path, as well as for the individual dashes in a dashed line. To create the rounded look shown in the example, click on the middle icon (Figure 7.7).

7.6

By entering values in the Dash and Gap boxes, you can design your own dashed line patterns.

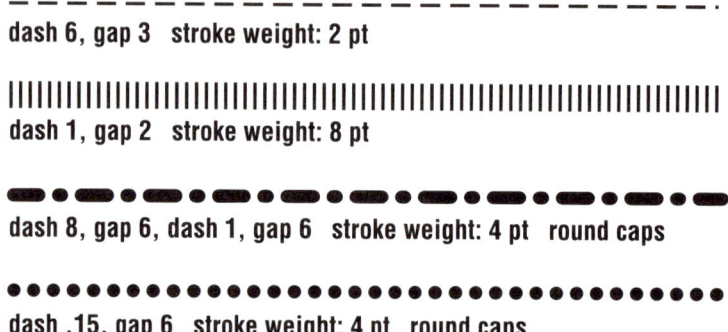

dash 6, gap 3   stroke weight: 2 pt

dash 1, gap 2   stroke weight: 8 pt

dash 8, gap 6, dash 1, gap 6   stroke weight: 4 pt   round caps

dash .15, gap 6   stroke weight: 4 pt   round caps

7.7

The Caps and Joins options available for stroked paths in Adobe Illustrator.

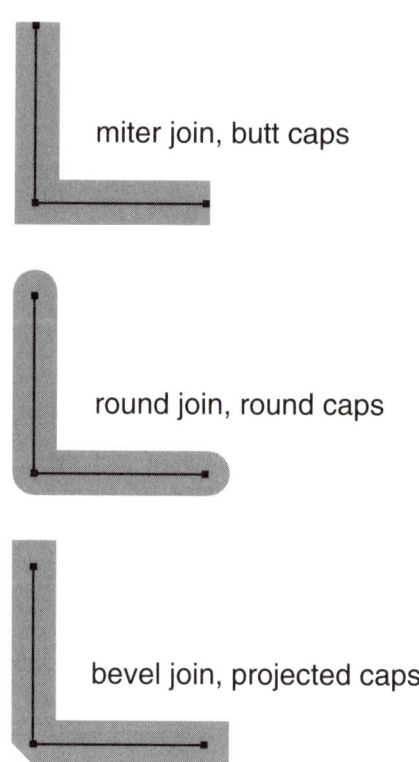

miter join, butt caps

round join, round caps

bevel join, projected caps

Next to the Caps field is the Join field. It contains three icons, each of which sets a different style for the corners of a stroked path. For traditional angular corners, click on the first icon. For rounded corners, click on the second icon, and for beveled corners, click on the third icon.

Next to the Joins field is the Miter Limit field. The value entered in this box is the limit at which the program will automatically switch from a corner join to a beveled join. The default value is 4, which means the program will switch to a beveled join when the length of the corner point becomes four times the line width selected. This prevents corners from being too sharp (Figure 7.8).

Custom Colors

In Chapter 3 you learned how to create combinations of the four process colors using the color sliders in the Paint Style palette. Illustrator also gives you several other options for creating what it calls custom colors. Custom colors are color combinations you can create and give a unique name to for repetitive use in a document. These colors can be created from process (CMYK) colors, or chosen from one of the color matching systems that Illustrator supports: Pantone, Toyo, Focoltone, or Trumatch.

7.8

In the example on the left, a miter limit of 4 points has caused the bevel joins option to take effect on the outside points of the star. In the example to the right, a miter limit of 20 points extends the points of the star to their full length.

mitre limit: 4 pts.   mitre limit: 20 pts.

Illustrator comes with 27 predefined custom colors, created from process colors. When you click on the Custom Color button in the Paint Style palette, the custom colors that have been defined are listed. You can add or delete colors from the list using the Custom Color dialog box.

INSIDE INFO

You can open the Custom Color dialog box by double-clicking on the name of a custom color listed in the Paint Style palette.

Creating a Custom Color

To create a custom color, open the Custom Color dialog box from the Object menu and click on the New button (Figure 7.9). An entry titled "New Color 1" will be added to the list. Adjust the tint bars to the right to create your color and then give it a name. Repeat this process until you have added all the colors you need, then click on the OK button to exit the box.

7.9

The Custom Colors dialog box.

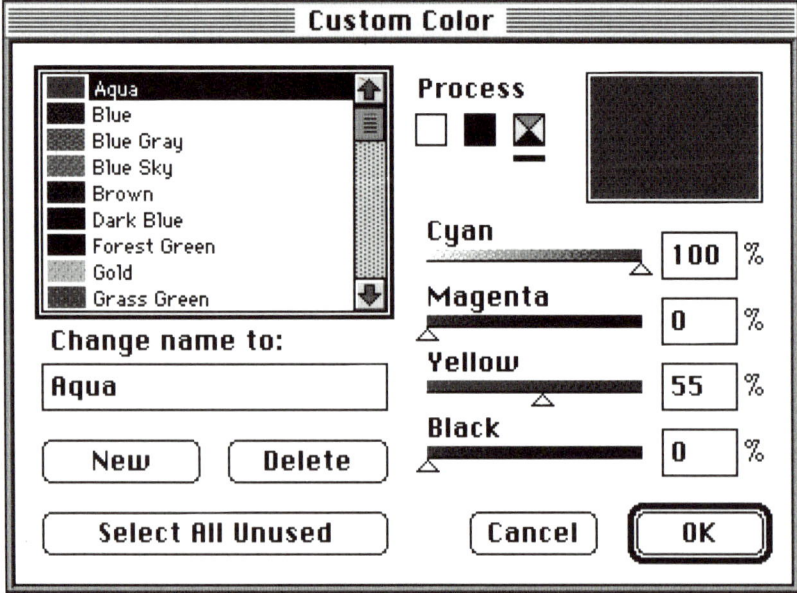

Deleting Custom Colors

To delete a custom color from the list, click on its name in the Custom Colors dialog box and then click on the Delete button. To delete all the colors that are not being used in a document, click on the Select All Unused button and then choose Delete. Click on the OK button to exit the box.

Using Colors from Color Matching Systems

What color do you think of when you hear the word *teal?* Since no two people have the same idea of what a color should look like, color matching systems were invented to maintain a standard for spot color printing. Instead of telling your printer that the new brochure you designed should have a teal logo, you can instead give him a specific color number, chosen from a swatch book that both you and your printer have.

Color matching systems ensure that the color you specify is the color that really gets printed. Unlike process colors, the colors in a color system have been preset to certain values to maintain their integrity. However, color matching systems can only be used for spot color—when you are only using one or two solid colors here and there on a page (as in most of this book). For standard full-color printing (as in this book's color insert), you still must use process colors.

Although it's not obvious when you're working with them in Illustrator, spot colors are printed in a completely different way than process colors. Spot color is also called two-color printing. Each sheet makes two passes through the printing press—once with black ink, and once with an ink mixed to the exact color you've specified. Process color is also called four-color printing. The image is separated into plates for its component colors, and each sheet makes four passes through the press— once for each of the four inks. Needless to say, this is more expensive. Chapter 11 shows how to use Adobe Separator for making "seps."

The color matching systems that are included with Adobe Illustrator are described below. To use one of them you must load it into your document using the Import Styles command in the File menu. To do this:

1. With your file open, select Import Styles from the File menu.

2. Open the Color Systems folder in the Illustrator application folder.

3. Open the file for the color system you have selected. The information will be loaded into your document, where you can access the colors directly from the Paint Style palette using the Custom Color button.

Pantone Matching System (PMS)

The best-known of the color matching systems is the Pantone Matching System (PMS). Printers create PMS colors according to a "recipe," using inks manufactured by Pantone. Designers traditionally select colors by number from a swatch book supplied by Pantone, then tell their printer to use "PMS 341," and so forth. The printer then mixes the ink according to the recipe and the printed results match the original swatch perfectly. PMS colors are used worldwide, but are specifically the standard in the Western Hemisphere.

Pantone also makes the Pantone Process Color System, a listing of over 3000 CMYK equivalents to their original PMS colors. This lets you come close to replicating a PMS color when using standard process colors for printing. Although the result will not look exactly like its PMS equivalent, it does come fairly close.

Both PMS and the Pantone Process Color System are included with Adobe Illustrator.

Toyo Ink Electronic Color Finder 1050

The Toyo Color Finder system is based on colored inks used most commonly in Japan. Like PMS, it consists of a swatch book of numbered colors, each corresponding to an ink mixture created by the printer. The availability of Toyo inks outside Japan is still limited, so if you decide to use the Toyo system, check with your printer or service bureau first.

The Focoltone Colour System

The Focoltone Colour System, from the United Kingdom, puts a new twist on the color matching system idea. The Focoltone system uses 763 mixtures of CMYK colors to provide solid-coverage colors that can be specified using the standard process colors. Like the other systems, Focoltone colors can be chosen from a swatch book.

The Trumatch Color Swatching System

The Trumatch system provides 2000 colors that can be created from process color mixtures. These colors are based on CMYK inks, each hue evenly stepped to cover the visible spectrum available.

Converting Colors to Process

You can use any of the color matching systems as a starting point for specifying color in a document. This can be a fast way to find the color you really want, instead of fiddling with the slider bars until you hit upon the right combination. Once you have selected a color, you can change it to process color to ensure proper process separations.

Custom colors created from process colors also need to be converted to print correctly for process separations. Left as they are, they will print a separate piece of film for each unique custom color name, instead of separating onto the four CMYK plates.

To convert colors to process, first select all objects that need to be converted. If this is everything in your document, just use the Select All (⌘-A) command. In the Filters ➤ Colors menu, select Change Custom to Process. In the Custom to Process box, click on the Retain Tint box and then click OK. All colors will be converted to straight CMYK percentages, retaining the tints that have been specified.

WATCH OUT!

If an Illustrator file is to be imported into a different application, colors must be specified as straight CMYK percentages in order to print process separations correctly.

Using Gradient Fills

What is a gradient fill? It is a blend of color in even steps. A gradient can be created using a single color; for example, blending from 10 percent black to 100 percent black. Or it can be created using two or more different colors, blending evenly through each.

Gradients can create interesting three-dimensional effects in the objects to which they are applied. A radial gradient applied to a circle can suddenly transform it into a sphere. A linear gradient starting with three different shades of black can create a shiny steel bar effect (Figure 7.10).

7.10

Gradient fills can
be used to create
an interesting
three-dimensional
aspect.

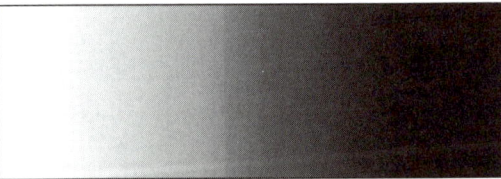

Creating a Gradient

You create gradients using the Gradient command in the Object menu. The Gradient palette (Figure 7.11) offers a list of several preset gradients, along with the tools to create your own.

7.11

The Gradient palette controls the creation of gradient blends between two or more colors.

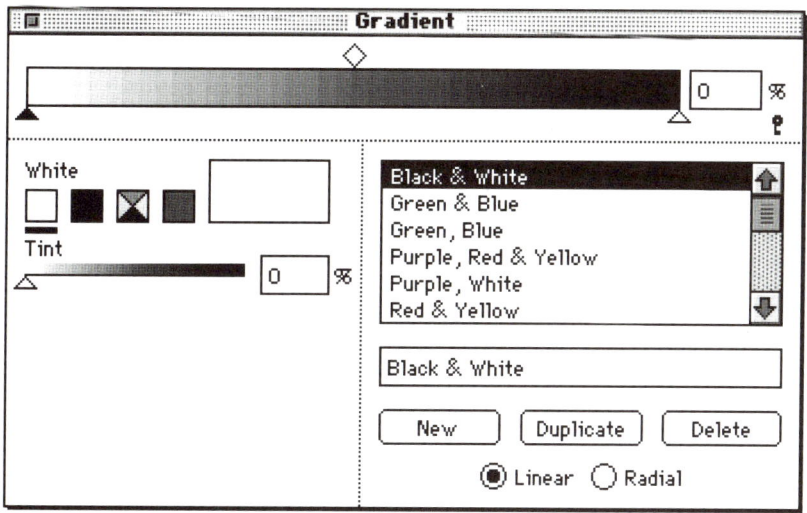

INSIDE INFO

You can easily open the Gradient dialog box by double-clicking on the name of a gradient fill listed in the Paint Style palette.

To create your own gradient, first click on the New button. The name New Gradient will appear listed in the box to the right, and the default gradient (a white-to-black linear gradient) will be displayed in the large slider bar at the top. Now follow these steps:

1. Below the large slider bar are two triangles, representing the starting and ending colors of your gradient. Click on the black one at the left to select it.

2. In the lower-left area of the palette, select the color and tint for the beginning color of the gradient.

3. Click on the white triangle below the left end of the large slider bar now.

4. In the lower-left area of the palette, select the color and tint for the ending color of your gradient.

5. In the lower-right area of the palette, click on either the Linear or Radial button to determine the type of blend. A linear blend travels from one side of an object to the other. A radial blend travels from inside to out, or vice versa. Figure 7.12 illustrates the difference.

7.12

A linear gradient (left) and a radial gradient (right).

6. To adjust the midpoint of the fill, drag the black diamond above the large slider bar. The closer it is to the lighter end of the gradient, the darker the blend will be.

7. Name your gradient.

INSIDE INFO

To reverse the beginning and ending colors of the gradient, simply drag the black arrow to the right end of the large slider bar, and the white arrow to the left end. The colors will trade.

Duplicating an Existing Gradient

You can use an existing gradient as a starting point for further exploration by duplicating and then modifying it within the Gradient palette. Click on the name of the existing gradient in the list and then click on the Duplicate button. A copy of the gradient will appear in the list, which you can then rename and modify.

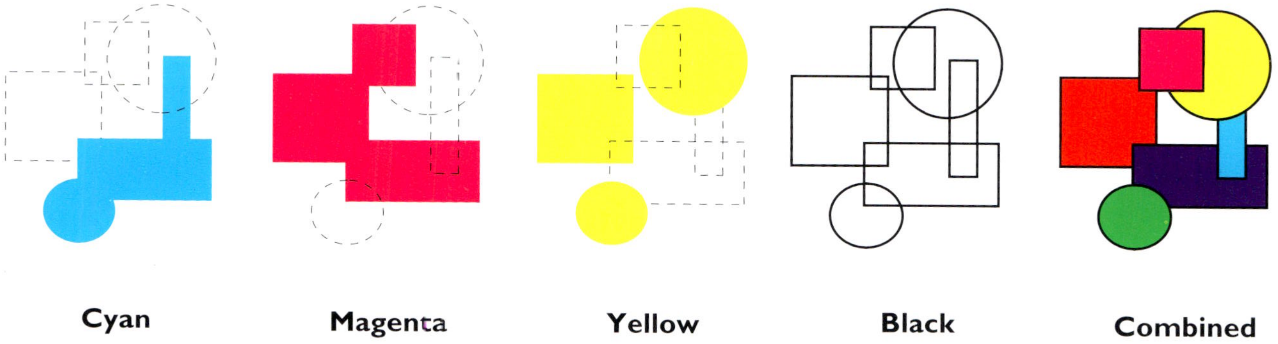

Cyan Magenta Yellow Black Combined

Plate I

Color Separation

The direction and placement of a gradient in an object can be controlled by using the **Gradient** tool

Gradients can help to create a three-dimensional effect when placed correctly in some objects.

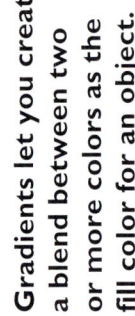

Gradients let you create a blend between two or more colors as the fill color for an object.

Plate 2

Color Gradients

Several preset patterns are included with the Adobe Illustrator application. These can be used instead of a color as the fill for any object.

Plate 3

Preset Patterns

When creating a new pattern, draw the pattern itself within the bounds of a square. The square should be behind all other objects in the stacking order, and the objects in the pattern should be kept within the boundary of the box.

Plate4

Creating Your Own Patterns

When two solid objects overlap in printing, the color of the top object will knock out the color of the area below it. This helps maintain the integrity of the top color.

Since the two colors are printed at different times on the press, misregistration can sometimes cause the knocked out area to show as an unsightly white gap between the two colors.

Trapping solves this potential problem by adding an overlapping safety margin composed of both colors. Although exaggerated in size for this example, a minute area of trapping will eliminate the gap problem.

Plate 5

Color Trapping

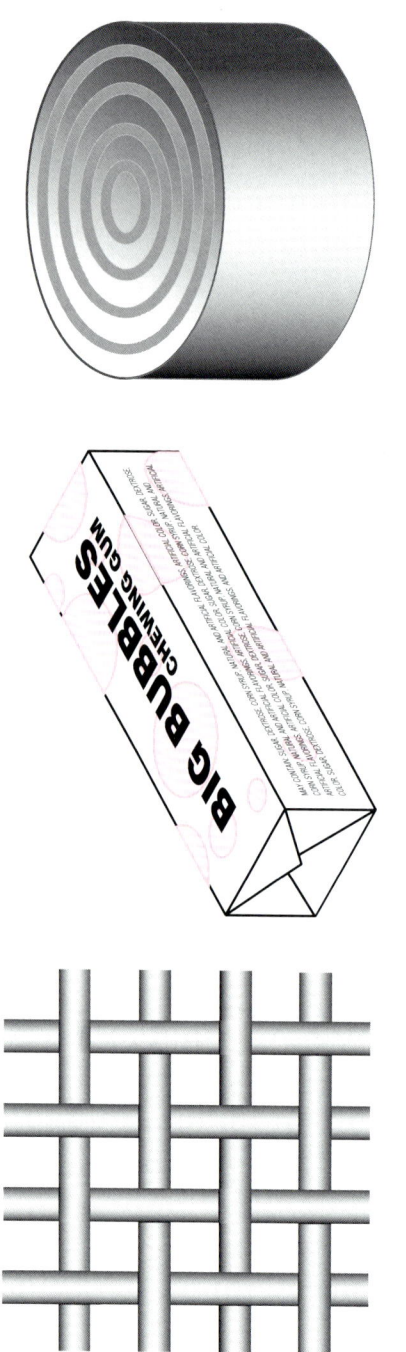

Three-dimensional drawing can be achieved through a combination of angles, rotation, and shading.

BIG BUBBLES
CHEWING GUM

Plate 6

Three-Dimensional Drawing

When drawing in perspective, it's important to use a grid that extends out from a focal point in the design. Blends also give a three-dimensional aspect to the design.

Plate 7

Perspective Drawing

METAL

METAL

STONE

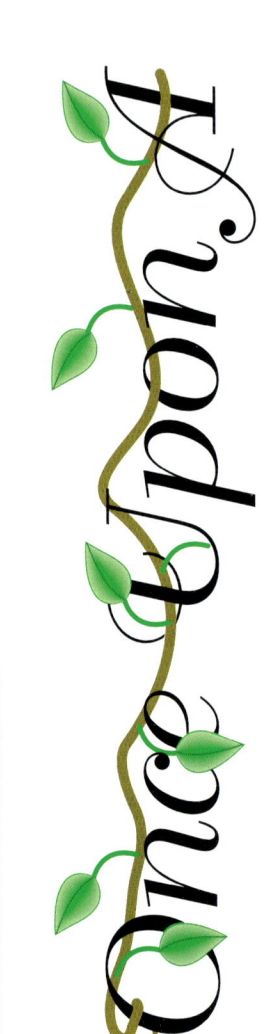

Once Upon A

Plate 8

Layering Elements

Plate9

The Finished Poster from Chapter 12

When the Bees are Buzzing...

Life is sweet for those who know and trust the secrets of the honeybee.

by Cheryl Hindman

L orem ipsumr sit amet, consecteuer adipiscing elit, sed diam nonummy nibh euismod tincidunt ut laoreet dolore magna aliquam erat volutpat. Ut wisi enim ad minim veniam, quis nostrud exerci tation ullamcorper suscipit lobortis nisl ut aliquip ex ea commodo consequat.

Duis autem vel eum iriure dolor in hendrerit in vulputate velit esse molestie consequat, vel illum dolore eu feugiat nulla facilisis at vero eros et accumsan et iusto odio dignissim qui blandit praesent luptatum zzril delenit augue duis dolore te feugait nulla facilisi. Lorem ipsum dolor sit amet, consectetuer adipiscing elit, sed diam nonummy nibh euismod tincidunt ut laoreet dolore magna aliquam erat volutpat.

Ut wisi enim ad minim veniam, quis nostrud exerci tation ullamcorper suscipit lobortis nisl ut aliquip ex ea commodo consequat. Dus autem vel eum iriure dolor in hendrerit in vulputate velit esse molestie consequat, vel illum dolore eu feugiat nulla facilisis at vero eros et accumsan et iusto odio dignissim qui blandit praesent luptatum zzril delenit augue duis dolore te feugait nulla facilisi.

Nam liber tempor cum soluta nobis eleifend option congue nihil imperdiet doming id quod mazim placerat facer possim assum. Lorem ipsum dolor sit amet, consectetuer adipiscing elit, sed diam nonummy nibh euismod tincidunt ut laoreet dolore magna aliquam erat volutpat. Ut wisi enim ad minim veniam, quis nostrud exerci tation ullamcorper suscipit lobortis nisl ut aliquip ex ea commodo conseq.

Duis autem vel eum iriure dolor in hendrerit in vulputate velit esse molestie consequat, vel illum dolore eu feugiat nul-

la facilisis at vero ero.

orem ipsum dolor sit amet, consectetuer adipiscing elit, sed diam nonummy nibh euismod tincidunt ut laoreet dolore magna aliquam erat volutpat Ut wisi enim ad minim veniam, quis nostrud exerci tation ullamcorper suscipit lobortis nisl ut aliquip ex ea commodo consequat.

veniam, quis nostrud exerci tation ullamcorper suscipit lobortis nisl ut aliquip ex ea commodo consequat. Dus autem vel eum iriure dolor in hendrerit in vulputate velit esse molestie consequat, vel illum dolore eu feugiat nulla facilisis at vero eros et accumsan et tusto odio dignissim aliquam erat to odio dignissim aliquam erat volutpatqui blandit praesent luptatum zzril delenit augue duis

Duis autem vel eum iriure dolor in hendrerit in vulputate velit esse molestie consequat, vel illum dolore eu feugiat nulla facilisis at vero eros et accumsan et iusto odio dignissim qui blandit praesent luptatum zzril delenit augue duis dolore te feugait nulla facilisi. Lorem ipsum dolor sit amet, consectetuer adipiscing elit, sed diam nonummy nibh euismod tincidunt ut laoreet dolore magna aliquam erat volutpat.

Ut wisi enim ad minim

dolore te feugait nulla facilisi.

Nam liber tempor cum soluta nobis eleifend option congue nihil imperdiet doming id quod mazim placerat facer possim assum. Lorem ipsum dolor sit amet, consectetuer adipiscing elit, sed diam nonummy nibh euismod tincidunt ut laoreet dolore magna aliquam erat dolore magna aliquam erat volutpat. Ut wisi enim ad minim veniam, quis nostrud exerci tation ullamcorper suscipit lobortis nisl ut aliquip ex ea commodo conseq.

Duis autem vel eum iriure dolor in hendrerit in vuputate velit esse molestie consequat, vel illum dolore eu feugiat nulla facilisis at vero ero.

Lorem ipsum dolor sit amet, consectetuer adipiscing elit, sed diam nonummy nibh euismod tincidunt ut laoreet dolore magna aliquam erat volutpat.

Ut wisi enim ad minim

Plate 10

The Finished Magazine Layout from Chapter 12

Plate 11

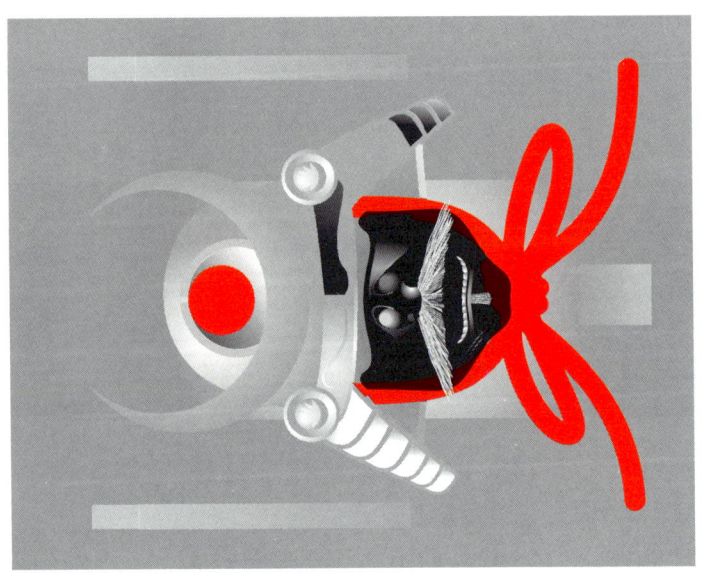

Plate 12

Plate 13

Plate 15

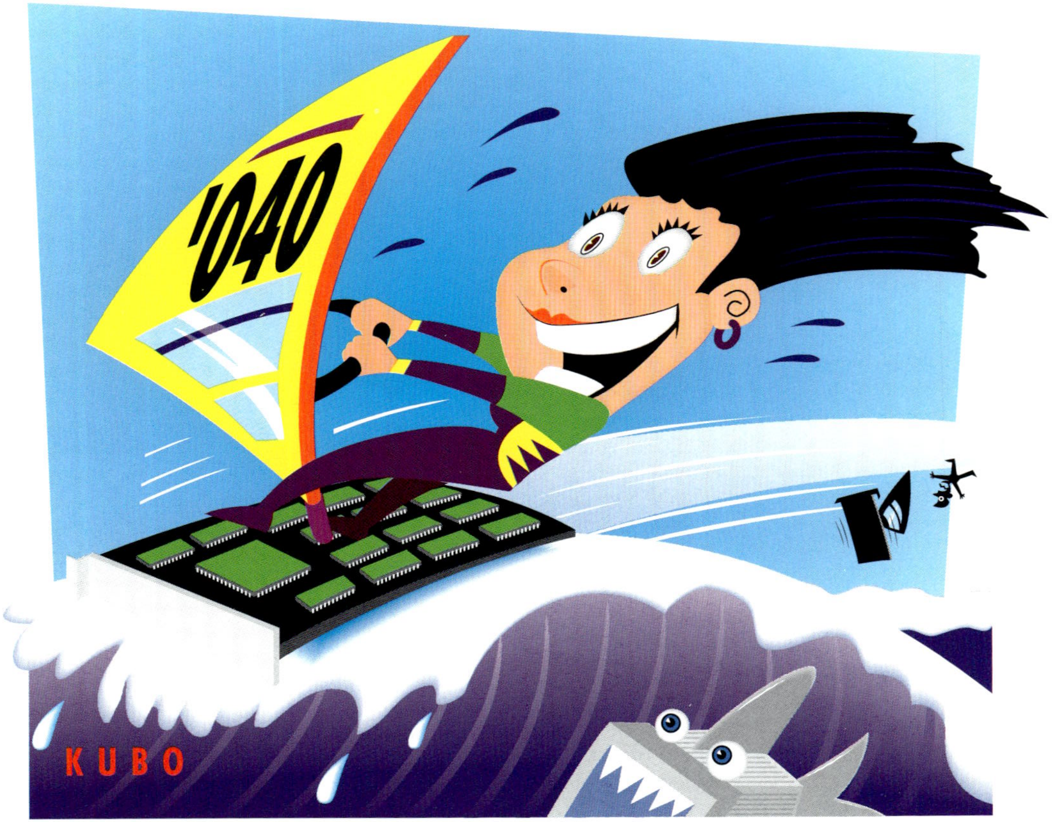

Plate 16

Deleting a Gradient

To delete a gradient from the list in the Gradient palette, simply click on the name and then click on the Delete button.

Creating a Gradient with Three or More Colors

To create a gradient fill with three (or more) colors, create a gradient as directed above. Click anywhere below the slider bar (between the two existing arrows) to create a third arrow. Define this arrow for a third intermediate color and then readjust the diamonds above the bar for the midpoint between colors. Repeat this action for each successive color you wish to include in the blend.

Positioning a Gradient within an Object

 The Gradient Fill tool in the Toolbox gives you the freedom of repositioning a gradient within an object. First select the object with a gradient fill already applied and then click on the Gradient Fill tool in the Toolbox. Click on the object where you want the gradient to begin, and then drag the cursor to the ending point and release the mouse button.

You can use this method to blend a gradient across multiple objects, such as through the letters of a word. Once a gradient has been applied to the objects, select them all (if they're not already grouped), click with the Gradient Fill tool at the left side of the first object, and drag the cursor across to the right side of the last object. The gradient will reposition itself to blend cvenly through all the objects (Figure 7.13). You can also use this method to blend from top to bottom, or vice versa.

Printing and Exporting Gradients

Gradients are a lot of fun to use, but they can cause a lot of headaches when it comes time to print or import them into another application. Here are some guidelines that can help:

■ In the Document Setup dialog box (⌘-Shift-D), using the Compatible Gradient Printing option can improve your success with printing gradients.

7.13

A gradient blend applied to a word (top), and then re-positioned using the Gradient Fill tool in two different ways.

EXCELLENT!
EXCELLENT!
EXCELLENT!

- ■ All colors in a gradient must be created from process colors. Although you can start with a custom color to get the right tint, the color must be converted to process before you print, or the gradient will not work.

- ■ Gradients created in Illustrator 5.5 are not backward-compatible to older versions of Illustrator or other applications. To use a 5.5 file containing a tint in another version of Illustrator, you must save the file as an Illustrator 3.0 file before exporting.

- ■ The integrity of gradients used in graph objects (see Chapter 10) will not remain when you change graph styles. To remedy this, select the objects after changing the graph style and reapply the gradient.

Creating Fill Patterns

Patterns are a unique option to using color as the fill for objects in a design. Adobe Illustrator comes with several predesigned patterns (such as Brick, Confetti, and Stripes) that are ready to be used. You can also easily create and manipulate your own patterns (Figure 7.14).

Using the Preset Patterns

Click on the Pattern button in the Paint Style palette, and you will find a list of the patterns that are currently available on your system. You can use these patterns as you would regular colors to fill the objects in your design.

7.14

Unique fill patterns can be used in place of color to fill objects.

Creating Your Own Patterns

Patterns are generated in Adobe Illustrator from tiles, smaller sections of a whole pattern. In creating your own pattern, you will just be creating one tile for the program to use as the basis for the entire pattern.

To create a pattern, draw a rectangle as the bounding box, or border, of the pattern tile. This border does not need to be filled or stroked, but all the elements of your pattern tile need to fit within the limits of the bounding box. This bounding box must always remain as the bottom element of the pattern tile.

Now create a pattern using any of the tools and colors in Illustrator. Simple geometric patterns are the easiest to create, but let your imagination run wild. When you have completed your creation, use the Selection tool to select all the elements of the tile, including the bounding box.

Under the Objects menu, select Pattern. The Pattern dialog box will appear (Figure 7.15). Click on the New button and your new tile will appear in the preview area. Name the pattern and click on the OK button. Your new pattern will now be listed in the Paint Style palette and can be used as a fill color.

Modifying an Existing Pattern

You can easily modify an existing pattern to create a new effect. In the Pattern dialog box (Object ➤ Pattern), select the name of a pattern from the list and click on the Paste button. A copy of the pattern tile

7.15

**You can create
your own pattern
with the aid of the
Pattern dialog box.**

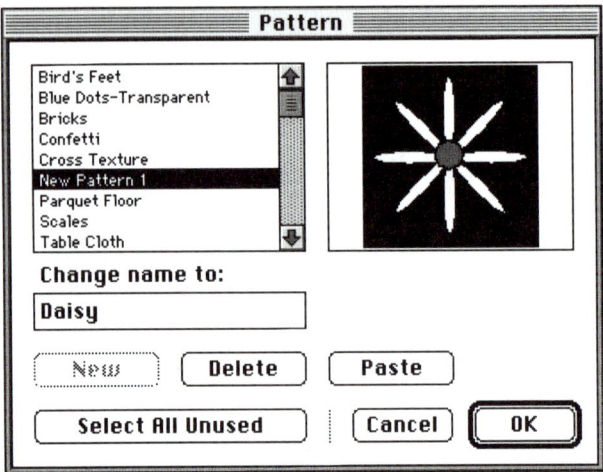

will be pasted into your document. Edit the tile as you wish, select all elements of the tile again, and go back into the Pattern dialog box. Click on the New button and the edited version of the pattern tile will appear in the preview window. Name the new pattern and click OK.

Deleting a Pattern from the List

To delete a pattern from the list, select the pattern name in the Pattern palette and click on the Delete button. To delete all patterns not used in the current document from the list, click on the Select All Unused button and then click on the Delete button. Click on the OK button to exit.

Trapping

Trapping is the slight overlapping of colors between two objects to allow for any misregistration that could occur when printing on a high-speed press (Figure 7.16). If you are creating designs for use in a magazine, book, or other publication that will be printed in such a manner, you should consider using trapping. Without trapping, misregistration of the colors can leave an unsightly white gap, disrupting the continuity of your design.

7.16

Trapping creates a slight overlap between objects of two different colors.

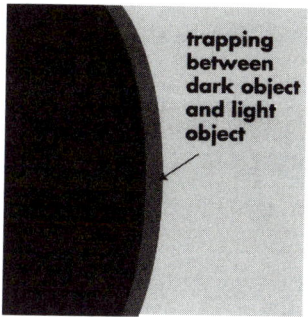

trapping
between
dark object
and light
object

Creating a Trap

You add trapping by selecting two objects and opening the Trap filter dialog box (Filter ➤ Pathfinder ➤ Trap). This filter recognizes the lighter of the two objects selected, and automatically extends the lighter color slightly into the area occupied by the darker color (called *spread*). When you click on the Reverse Trap option, the trap reverses to extend the darker color into the area occupied by the lighter color (called *choke*) (Figure 7.17).

7.17

The Trap filter dialog box.

Pathfinder Trap		
Thickness:	0.25	points
Height/width:	100.0	%
Tint reduction:	40.0	%

OK
Cancel
Defaults

☐ Convert custom colors to process
☒ Reverse traps

Other options in the Trap dialog box include:

■ **Thickness**—the thickness of the trap. Talk with your printer to determine the amount needed. Different presses have different degrees of accuracy when it comes to misregistration.

■ **Height/Width**—a larger value (over 100 percent) increases the width of the trapping applied to horizontal lines. Horizontal lines are more susceptible to misregistration due to the slight stretching of paper as it travels through a press.

■ **Tint Reduction**—applies a lighter tint to the trap area than to the objects. 100 percent means that 100 percent of the CMYK values for both objects being trapped is used to create the trap. This can cause a strange colored tint to show from behind lighter colored objects. To prevent this, use a percentage lower than 100 to create a lighter trap color.

■ **Convert custom colors to process**—creates a CMYK trap when used between two custom colors.

■ **Reverse traps**—changes the spread trap to a choke trap when clicked.

Consult with your printer before creating traps of any kind in your design. Your printer will be able to tell you the amount and kind of trapping to use.

Trapping Text

Text, especially small text, can be hard to read when filled with any other color than black. Likewise, the probability of press misregistration with color-printed text can take what seemed like a cool design and turn it into a nightmare.

Larger display type that has been filled with a color other than black may need to be trapped as an object in order to print correctly. To use the trapping filter, however, you must first convert the text to outlines. This makes the text into an object, rendering it uneditable in the future.

To convert text to outlines, select the text and from the Type menu choose Create Outlines. You can now apply the Trap filter as you would to any other object.

Summary

Illustrator provides a virtually limitless array of options for painting the objects you create. With numerous color options to choose from, as well as gradients and patterns, you can create just about any effect you might want using Adobe Illustrator. And the different methods Illustrator offers for creating colors give you considerable flexibility in adapting to the requirements of particular projects. Designing with color has never been so easy and fun.

CHAPTER

Special Effects

E I G H T

After seven chapters of technical information, it's time we took a break. And what better way to be entertained than to put Illustrator through its paces and see some of the things it can *really* do.

In this chapter we'll take a look at some of the interesting special effects that Illustrator is capable of generating—with a little help from you. Most of the tools, filters, and palettes we'll use here have been introduced in earlier chapters, but you may not have suspected just how powerful they are.

Dividing Paths— Creating That Woven Look

Since all objects in Adobe Illustrator are created out of paths, any design you create stacks these paths one on top of the other. But sometimes a design calls for a path that seemingly winds its way from the front to the back of a stack of objects, such as the braid of a rope, or the weave of a basket or fabric. You may need part of your design to wrap in front of a headline, while another part of the same path needs to stay behind.

In situations like these, you can get the effect you want by dividing the path into two or more sections. This maintains the continuity of the original path, and yet allows the separate pieces to be stacked differently.

Let's take a look at a simple example to illustrate the point. Figure 8.1 shows eight rectangular bars. At the moment, the four vertical bars are placed in front of the four horizontal bars.

8.1

Four vertical bars are placed over four horizontal bars.

The object here is to weave the bars together, like a basket. First select all the objects (⌘-A) and in the Pathfinder submenu of the Filter menu, choose the Divide filter. As illustrated in Figure 8.2, this splits the objects into sections, including a separate piece for each area where the bars cross. These are the areas we will work on next.

8.2

After we apply the Divide filter, the bars are divided into sections, as shown by the corner points around each smaller object.

When you use the Divide filter, the selected objects are joined together as a *compound path*. Clicking on any of the sections with the Selection tool would select all of the objects. Instead, use the Direct Selection tool to click on the intersections where the lighter vertical bars and darker horizontal bars meet (Figure 8.3a).

Change the shade of these areas to match the bars behind them, in this case 80 percent black. Now select the four remaining intersections that need to be changed (Figure 8.3b) and fill them with 40 percent black. The resulting design shows the bars weaving above and below each other (Figure 8.4).

8.3

(a) Use the Direct Selection tool to select certain inter-sections and change the fill. (b) Repeat for the remaining four intersections that need to be changed.

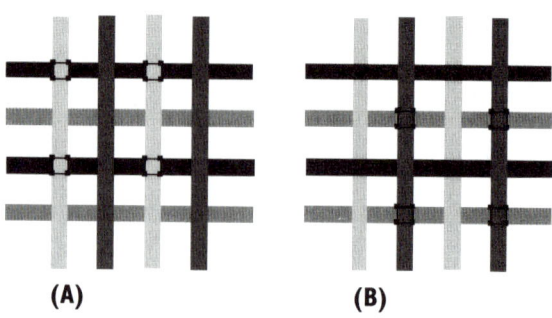

(A) **(B)**

8.4

The finished weave.

This is a simple example of what you can do with splitting paths. For a more three-dimensional look, add a gradient blend such as the steel bar effect shown in Figure 8.5.

8.5

With an added gra-dient, the woven bars take on a more three-dimensional effect.

Drawing in Three Dimensions

No matter what type of designing you do, there will always come a time when you will need to draw three-dimensional objects. Packaging ideas, mechanical parts, and landscape views all call for 3D effects. Using the various techniques available in Illustrator, you can create the effects you need easily and quickly.

Creating a Three-Dimensional Box

For this example, we'll look at the creation of a fictional chewing gum package for promotional purposes. It consists of three main parts: the package front, side, and end.

Figure 8.6 shows our starting point—the package in its 2D form, ready to be transformed. There are three rectangles; the package front is the same width as the package end, and the same length as the package side. Within each rectangle, all the elements are in place at this stage: images, type, and color. This makes it easy to scale, shear, and rotate each section of the package as a whole. Any type you include should be converted to

8.6

All package elements are completely designed before they are assembled into a three-dimensional box. Point A represents the point to click on while performing all manipulations.

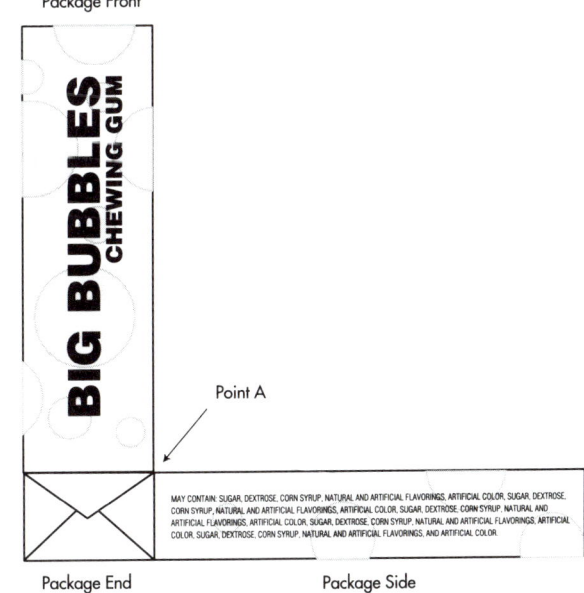

outlines (Type ➤ Outlines); this causes the letters to become independent objects that will shear and scale easily along with the rest of the design.

Point A, as shown in Figure 8.6, is a central point of origin, where you should click when manipulating *any* of the three parts. Manipulating them around a central point keeps the three parts more closely in alignment. Now let's begin assembling the box—starting off with the package front:

1. Use the Selection tool to group all elements added to the package front.

2. Scale the front by holding down the Option key while clicking on Point A with the Scale tool. Using the Non-uniform choice, vertically scale the front to 86.602 percent, maintaining the horizontal scale of 100 percent. This keeps the package front isometrically correct for the next few maneuvers.

3. Click on the Shear tool now, and while holding down the Option key, click on Point A. Shear the front 30 degrees horizontally.

4. Click on the Rotation tool, and while holding down the Option key, click on Point A once again. Rotate the front −30 degrees (Figure 8.7).

8.7

Use this example as a guide for rotating and shearing the different elements of the package.

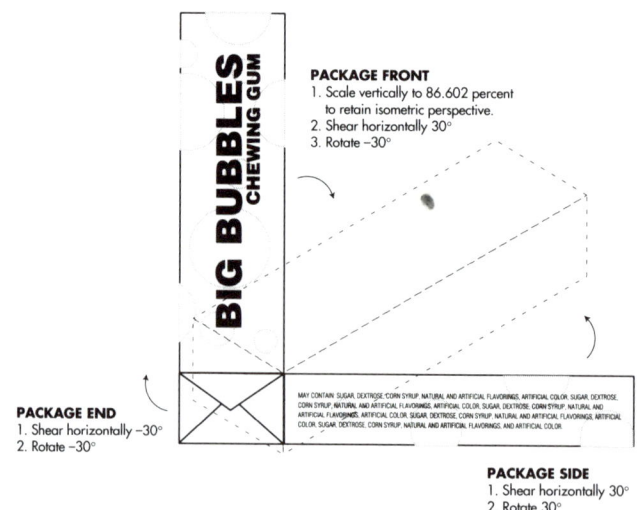

Next up is the package side:

1. Group all of the elements of the package side together first.
2. Click on the Shear tool, and while holding down the Option key, click on Point A. Shear the side panel 30 degrees horizontally.
3. Click on the Rotation tool, and while holding down the Option key, click on Point A once again. Rotate the side 30 degrees.

The final step is to move the package end into place:

1. Group the elements of the end together using the Selection tool.
2. Click on the Shear tool again, and while holding down the Option key, click on Point A. Shear the end panel −30 degrees horizontally.
3. Click on the Rotation tool, and while holding down the Option key, click on Point A once again. Rotate the end panel −30 degrees.

The result is the three-dimensional package shown in Figure 8.8. This method works well for creating three-dimensional "boxes" of any sort.

8.8

The completed package.

Creating a Three-Dimensional Cylinder

Cylinders, whether they are cans, pipes, tubes, or whatever, are another class of three-dimensional objects that often pop up in design work. Fortunately, they are easier to draw than boxes. In this example, we'll go over the construction of a simple can.

First, draw the top of the can as a single circle. Any additional elements should be added on top of the circle at this point. In the example shown in Figure 8.9, gray rings are added to the top. All elements added to the top should be grouped with the original circle. Any text you add should be outlined as well as grouped.

8.9

The top of the can
(cylinder) is cre-
ated and grouped.

Next, scale the top of the can vertically to keep it isometrically in proportion. With the Scale tool selected, hold down the Option key and click anywhere on the grouped circle. In the Non-uniform area of the Scale dialog box, enter a horizontal percentage of 100, and a vertical percentage of 57.735.

Deselect everything by clicking on the artboard. With the Direct Selection tool, click on the two segments that form the lower half of the circle. Copy the lower edge (⌘-C), and use the Paste in Front command (⌘-F) to place the copy back over the lower edge of the circle.

Use the Move command (⌘-Shift-M) to open the Move dialog box. Enter a negative value in the Vertical field and click on the Copy button (the example used -72 points). A copy of the half-circle you created will be pasted below the original.

The lower portion of the cylinder is created by joining the ends of the two half circles.

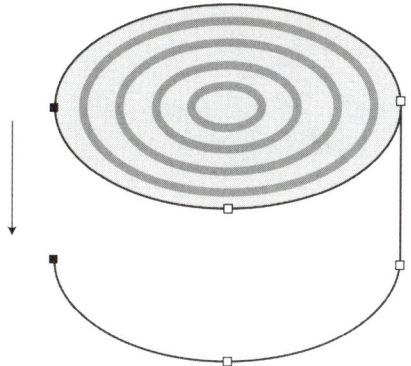

Now use the Direct Selection tool to join the ends of each of the two half-circles you created, as shown in Figure 8.10. This forms the lower portion of the cylinder.

The outline of the can is finished, but the addition of a gradient fill gives the cylinder a three-dimensional touch. Fill the bottom of the can with the steel bar gradient found in the Paint Style palette (⌘-I). Fill the top of the can with the black and white gradient and adjust its position using the Gradient tool. The finished can is shown in Figure 8.11.

8.11

When a gradient is added to the finished cylinder, it takes on the appearance of a tin can.

Creating Spheres

Spheres are perhaps the easiest of objects to make three-dimensional. All you do is draw a circle and let Illustrator do all of the hard work with a gradient fill. How the gradient is positioned within the sphere is up to you, but the results can be quite dramatic.

In Figure 8.12, a regular circle has been filled with a radial black and white gradient. Notice that the gradient is off-center. This adjustment, made using the Gradient Fill tool, brings the sphere to life.

8.12

A circle filled with a radial gradient and adjusted becomes a sphere.

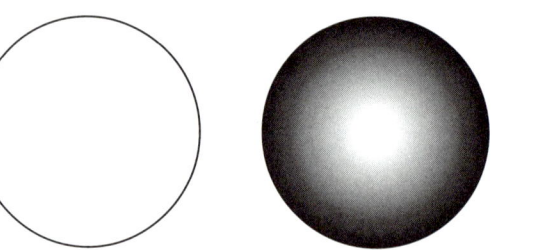

First draw the circle and add the radial gradient. Then select the circle and click the Gradient Fill tool. With this tool, click on the circle wherever you want the center of the radial gradient to start. Move the cursor to the edge of the circle and click again. The gradient will reposition itself within the circle. In Figure 8.12, I clicked where the whitest spot of the sphere now is, then clicked on the lower right edge of the circle. This positioned the beginning of the gradient above and to the left of the center of the circle, which gives a nice 3D effect.

Keeping in Perspective

When you are drawing dimensions on a larger scale, say for a landscape view, two rules of thumb apply:

1. Angle all objects in the design out from a focal point on the horizon.
2. The closer things are to the focal point, the smaller they get.

In Figure 8.13, the focal point is directly behind the locomotive.

When you begin to draw, start with a grid of guidelines, such as the one shown in Figure 8.14. First create a "horizon," a horizontal line that represents the farthest point in your design. Next, assign the focal point by

8 . 1 3

Objects in a dimensional drawing should angle out from a central focal point.

drawing a vertical line. It doesn't have to be directly in the center of your design—placing it to the right or left of center will give you a slightly different perspective.

AUTHOR'S NOTE

For both the horizontal and vertical lines you can use the Ruler Guide feature as discussed in Chapter 5.

Divide up the lower areas between the horizon and the vertical line by drawing lines from each corner up to the focal point. Divide these sections further with more lines as shown.

As you draw, place objects along these lines. (Remember, objects should be scaled smaller as they get closer to the focal point.) By aligning the

Create a grid based on a focal point on the horizon to keep your drawing in perspective.

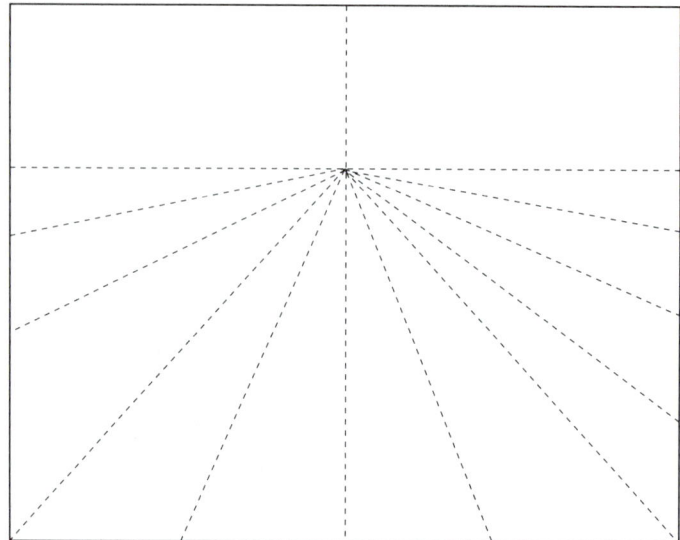

objects on the guidelines you draw, you will keep the correct perspective in your drawing.

Again, adding a gradient fill to objects lends itself very well to a perspective drawing. Experiment with different shade values to achieve the look you want.

Special Effects with Type

What can you do with type? Definitely more than just place the letters on your page and assign them a font and size. With the tools available to you in Illustrator, you can take any ordinary, mild-mannered type and give it superhuman strength—or at least make it *much* more noticeable.

In this section we'll look at several interesting ways to spice up type. Most of these are not recommended for smaller point sizes, but can be very effective when used on 24 point or larger type.

Creating Type Outlines

The first step in creating any special type effect is to convert the type into *outlines*. When you change a word into an outline, each letter becomes an object with anchor points. You can manipulate a type outline in the same ways as any other object.

Select the type to convert. In the Type menu, select Create Outlines. Each letter in the selected type will now become an object.

Masking—Creating "Windows" Out of Type

A mask is a way to make "windows" out of one or more objects in the foreground, letting the background show through. This is particularly effective way to "fill" type with the pattern or texture of an imported object placed behind it. You can use any of the interesting patterns and textures that are available as clip art; in addition, masking makes it possible to use anything you can scan in as a "fill."

In the example shown in Figure 8.15, type has been placed over a rectangle filled with a brick pattern. Although you can fill type outlines with patterns themselves in Illustrator, this will illustrate the point of how to use the masking commands.

To use type as a masking object, first convert the type to outlines, as explained above. Next, the outlined type needs to be made into a compound path. With all the letters selected, go to the Object menu and select Make from the Compound Paths submenu.

8.15

Place type over a pattern to begin the masking process.

The final step in setting up the mask is to move the object with the pattern into the background. Select the object and use the Send to Back command (⌘-hyphen). Now use the Selection tool to select everything—letters and background. In the Object menu under Masks, select Make. The type opens to reveal the background pattern, while the shape of the background object disappears (Figure 8.16).

8.16

The completed mask, with the background pattern showing through the letters.

Creating Drop Shadows

A *drop shadow* is a copy of an object colored differently and placed behind the original object to represent a shadow. The placement of the shadow varies, depending on the effect you want to create and the direction of the imaginary "light source" creating the shadow.

Figure 8.17 shows three examples of drop shadows. All were created by copying the original and placing the duplicate behind using the Paste in Back command (⌘-B). The shadow was then converted to outlines and filled with 30 percent black.

For the top example, the shadow was offset above and to the left of the original by 2 points. This produces more of a three-dimensional block effect on the type.

8.17

Three examples
of drop shadow
effects.

Shadow
SHADOW
Shadow

The other two examples (Figure 8.17, middle and bottom) were created using the Shear tool and the controls in its dialog box. The shadow on the middle example was sheared only slightly (−5 degrees, horizontally). The second example was sheared more (−30 degrees, horizontally). As you can see, the results produce very different looks.

Embossed or Chiseled Type

Using the same technique of layering and offsetting duplicates, as was shown above, you can give type an embossed or chiseled look. In Figure 8.18, I created two copies of the word "stone" and pasted them behind the original. The first one is filled with white and offset above and to the left of the original by 2 points. The second is filled with 60 percent black, and offset below and to the right of the original by 2 points. The original word and the rectangle framing it are filled with 25 percent black.

To create the beveled shadow look on the rectangle, I created two copies of the rectangle and used the Offset Path filter, entering an offset value of 6 points. I filled the first copy with 60 percent black and deleted the upper-left anchor point. The remaining anchor points are adjusted to meet

8.18

A "chiseled out of stone" effect is created using off-set copies of different shades behind type and objects.

the corners of the original rectangle. The second rectangular copy is then filled with 20 percent black.

This creates a chiseled-out-of-stone effect when used with the gray shades as shown in Figure 8.18. For a more embossed paper look, use shades of tan and brown.

Creating Metallic Type

Creating metallic type is a little harder to do than some of the other effects we've discussed, but it is another dramatic effect that can be achieved in Illustrator. Figure 8.19 shows an example. Because of the amount of work involved, the shorter the word used, the better off you'll be.

To begin with, convert the selected type to outlines. Make sure you are working in Artwork mode—what you're about to do may get confusing otherwise.

Select all the letters and, in the Filter menu, choose Offset Path. Enter an offset of 2 points and click OK. A larger copy of each letter will be

8.19

Creating a metallic look is a lot of work, but produces interesting results.

created and placed behind its original. Using the Selection tool, select each letter and its copy and move them over to space the letters properly again.

Move a horizontal guideline into position slightly lower than half of the letter height. Using this line as the cutting point, use the Scissors tool to split each letter (not the copies behind) into two pieces by clicking with the tool at the point to be cut (Figure 8.20). Use the Direct Selection tool to select the ends of each new section, then use the Join command (⌘-J) to close the path.

Now use the Add Anchor Point tool to add an anchor point in the middle of each path area where the letter was cut, as shown. Select this point with the Direct Selection tool and use the arrow keys to move this point down by 2 points on each piece.

8.20

Cut each letter into two pieces and use the Join command to close each path. Add an anchor point and move it down by two points.

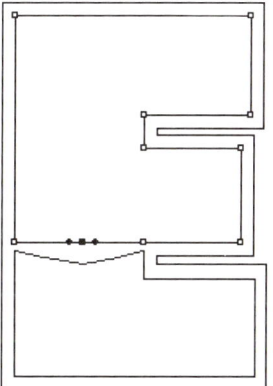

The hard part is over. With the top portion of the letter selected, fill it with a gradient that begins at 0 percent black and blends into 40 percent black, 40 percent cyan. Select the bottom portion of the letter and fill it with a gradient beginning at 5 percent black and blending into 100 percent black and 30 percent cyan. Use the Gradient tool to adjust the position of the gradient so that the lighter part is at the bottom of each section.

Finally, select the larger copy that surrounds the original letter parts and fill it with the steel bar gradient. Adjust the gradient so that it blends from dark at the top, to light in the middle, and back to dark again at the bottom of the letter. If you want, you can add extra light and dark highlights at the area where the two letter parts meet, as I've done in Figure 8.19.

Adding Other Elements to Type

In addition to making type into art itself, you can easily add artwork created separately to regular type. By using the same method used to split the paths of the letters above, you can make the art seem to wind its way around and through the letters of the type. Figure 8.21 illustrates this effect.

8.21

A vine seems to wind its way around and through the letters.

To create this image, first draw the vine separately and place it behind the type. Then convert the type to outlines. At this point, make sure you are working in Preview mode at a very large view, at least 600 percent. This allows you to see the actual width of the vine, so you can accurately cut the type around it.

Using artwork with smaller parts, in this case the leaves and stems, is helpful, because you can use the Bring to Front command (⌘-=) to layer a leaf in front of a letter. With the stem positioned correctly on the vine, it looks as though the leaf is growing out through an opening of the letter.

For areas without leaves, though, it's time to do some surgery. To make the vine wind through the "o" in "Upon," for example, use the Scissors tool to cut both the inside and outside paths of the letter "o" (Figure 8.22). Cut the paths as closely as you can to the vine (this is where working in a very large view helps). Use the Join command (⌘-J) to rejoin the edges of the paths on each side of the vine.

8.22

Cutting and rejoining the paths around the vine.

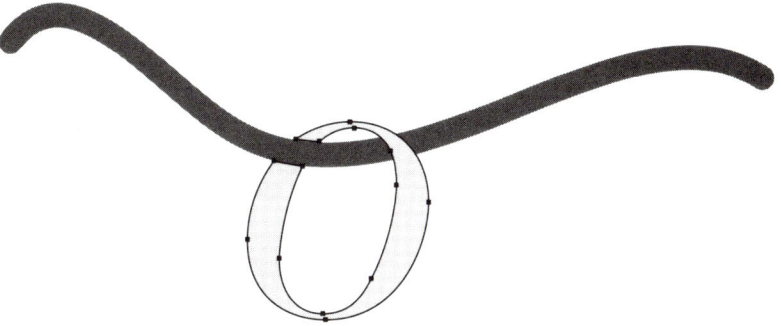

The result looks like the vine is weaving in front and then through the letter "o" in the word. Use this same method on other letters to create the complete effect. Don't forget to layer a few leaves in front of the letters as well for that overgrown look.

Moving Beyond Color with the Blend Tool

We've already explored some of the interesting effects you can achieve using gradient blends of color and the Gradient tool, but we've yet to talk about the Blend tool. The Blend tool, found just to the right of Gradient tool in the Toolbox, creates gradients the old-fashioned way—as Illustrator 3.0 did (Figure 8.23). However, while newer versions of Illustrator have moved on to a better way of blending colors, the Blend tool is still available.

The Blend tool is now more useful for creating shape blends. For example, in a perspective drawing, you may need to create several objects that seem to get smaller as they move into the distance. To do this you could

8.23

Creating a gradient blend the old-fashioned way meant drawing two objects of different shades, clicking on an anchor point of each with the Blend tool, and specifying the number of steps for the blend.

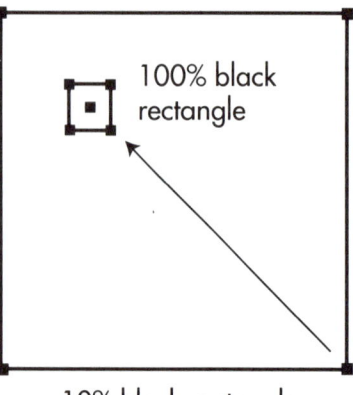

100% black rectangle

10% black rectangle

create one shape, make a very small copy of it to place in the distance, and then use the Blend tool to create the intermediary sizes between the two, as shown in Figure 8.24.

To do this, first use the Selection tool to select each of the objects, then click with the Blend tool *on the same anchor point in each object* (this is important). The Blend dialog box will appear (Figure 8.25). Enter the number of objects you want between your starting and ending objects in the Steps field. The percentage fields in this dialog box are used for shade value differences if you are blending colors as well. Click on the OK button and the new objects will appear between the originals.

8.24

Two objects of different shapes are blended to create several intermediate-sized objects.

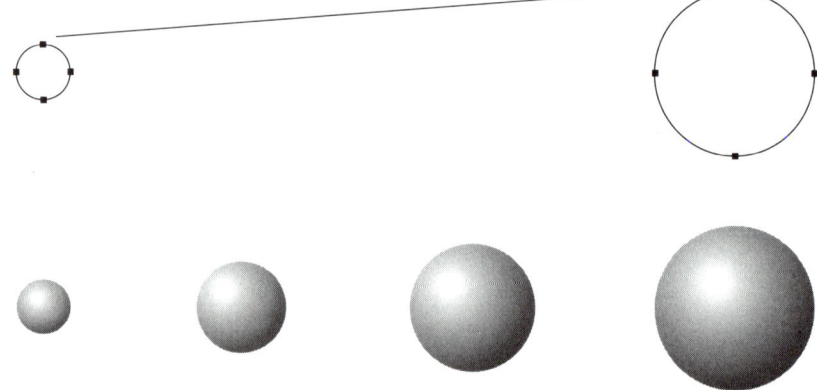

8.25

The Steps field in the Blend dialog box determines the number of objects, or steps, created between the starting and ending objects.

WATCH OUT!

When using the Blend tool on two similarly shaped objects, you must click on the same anchor point in each object. For instance, when blending two squares of different sizes, you would click on the upper-left corner anchor point of each. Clicking on opposing anchor points will cause the shape to rotate as it is blended.

Simulating Motion with the Blend Tool

One interesting application of the Blend tool is to simulate motion using a series of shapes. In Figure 8.26, the first, last, and middle shapes were drawn and placed. Then, using the Blend tool, the first shape was blended to the middle shape, and the middle shape was blended to the last shape. This gives the effect of a bird in flight.

INSIDE INFO

The Blend tool can only be used to blend two single objects; it cannot blend groups of objects. To achieve a blending effect with a group of objects, each individual object must be blended separately.

Morphing with the Blend Tool

Although the effect is not as sophisticated as you can achieve with true morphing software, the Blend tool can be used to transform one shape into another. In Figure 8.27, a dolphin has been changed into a major appliance by blending the basic outline of each shape.

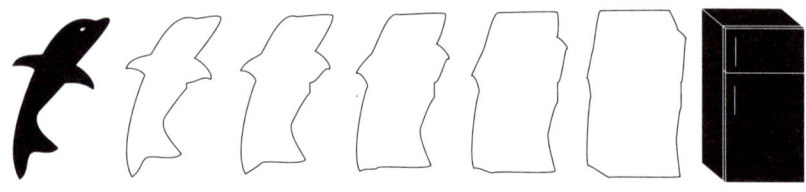

INSIDE INFO

To achieve a good blend between shapes, the starting and ending shapes should have the same number of anchor points. Use the Add Anchor Point tool to add extraneous anchor points to one of the shapes if necessary.

Summary

Adobe Illustrator contains some very powerful tools for creating and transforming objects. Most of the examples shown in this section are easy to replicate—use them as the starting point for your own experimentation. In the next chapter on Illustrator's plug-in filters, you'll be introduced to even more tools to help with your creative process.

CHAPTER

Plug-In Filters

NINE

The plug-in filters in Adobe Illustrator 5.5 are to a designer what the land of Oz was to Dorothy—a whole new world of color and special effects laid at her feet. Although the staggering number of filters provided might make you shy away from investigating them, you'll soon find any time and effort invested in this direction paying off in a hurry.

Some of the filters available for your use are not automatically installed with the Adobe Illustrator application. To gain access to these filters, look in your Illustrator application folder for another folder titled "Other Filters." Move the filters located in this folder into the "Plug-In Filters" folder and restart the application.

Illustrator's filters are varied in their purposes, but most of them automate previously difficult or impossible tasks. In this chapter we'll look at what each filter does and how it works. The filters are divided into nine categories within the Filters menu—we'll start with the first category, Colors.

Colors

The ten filters in the Colors submenu provide a means for adjusting the intensity, blend, and placement of colors in a document.

Adjust Colors

Adjust Colors lets you change the amount of process color (CMYK) in an object by percentage. The dialog box contains percentage fields for each of the process colors (cyan, magenta, yellow, and black), plus radio buttons to Increase or Decrease the percentages you enter (Figure 9.1).

9.1

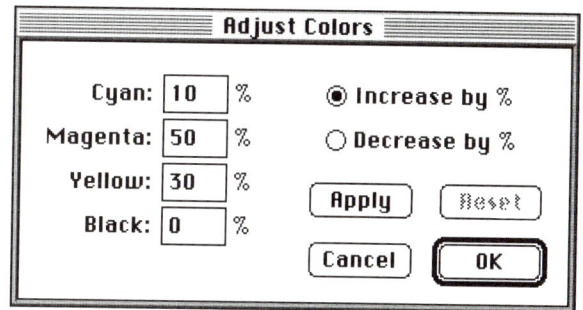

To increase or decrease a color by percentage, select the object with the Selection tool and open the Adjust Colors dialog box (Filter ➤ Colors ➤ Adjust Colors). Enter a percentage in one of the fields provided and click on the Increase or Decrease radio button. To apply the change, but keep the dialog box open, click on the Apply button. To apply the change and exit, click on the OK button. To reset the box for a new change, click on the Reset button and continue.

Blend Front to Back

The Blend Front to Back filter creates a color blend through a series of selected objects, starting with the frontmost selected object in a layer and continuing to the object furthest in back. Each of the selected objects between these two will be filled with gradated percentages of the two colors (Figure 9.2).

To use the Blend Front to Back filter, first select all of the objects you want involved in the blend. Under the Filter ➤ Colors menu, select Blend Front to Back. The selected objects, regardless of color, will now blend in order from the front object to the back.

9.2

**The Blend Front to
Back filter creates
a color blend
through a stack of
selected objects.**

before

after

AUTHOR'S NOTE

When using the Blend Front to Back filter, the color blend will be applied to the selected objects in their stacking order. Regardless of how the objects are positioned on your page, they will be colored based on how they are layered in front of each other (this means the order in which they were created, unless you have manually changed the stacking order).

Blend Horizontally

The Blend Horizontally filter applies a color blend between the two selected objects that are positioned the furthest apart horizontally on your page. The blend is only applied to the objects selected—for example, if you have three circles selected, and the outermost two are 100% black and 100% white, the filter will cause the middle circle to become 50% black.

To apply the Blend Horizontally filter, first select three or more objects on your page. In the Filter ➤ Colors menu, select Blend Horizontally. The blend will be applied to all the selected objects on the page, based on the colors of the two outermost objects selected on the horizontal plane.

Blend Vertically

The Blend Vertically filter is similar to the Blend Horizontally filter, only it blends selected objects along the vertical plane (Figure 9.3).

To apply the Blend Vertically filter, first select three or more objects on your page. In the Filter ➤ Colors menu, select Blend Vertically. The blend will be applied to all the selected objects on the page, based on the colors of the two outermost objects selected on the vertical plane.

9.3

The Blend Vertically filter blends selected objects along the vertical axis.

before   after

Custom to Process

The Custom to Process filter changes a custom color used in an object to its CMYK process color equivalent. The filter also lets you retain the custom color's tint after the conversion, so a 50% "Red" custom color stays the equivalent percentages of that color in CMYK.

This is an important filter to use when you are preparing a file for film output, and need separate negatives for each process color. Using a Custom Color would render a single spot color negative for that color, but after the filter conversion the color will be output in percentages of CMYK.

To use the Custom to Process filter, first select the object to be converted. In the Filter ➤ Color menu, select Custom to Process (Figure 9.4). To retain the same percentage tint after the conversion, check the Retain Tint box. Click on the OK button, and the colors will revert to CMYK percentages.

9.4

The Custom to Process filter dialog box allows you to retain the same tint of a custom color after it is converted to process.

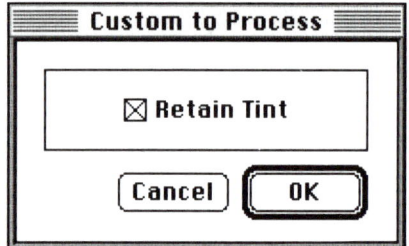

INSIDE INFO

To get a better view of how the Custom to Process filter works, open the Paint Style palette on your desktop. As you use the filter, you will see the palette convert the selected custom color to percentages of CMYK.

Desaturate

The Desaturate filter decreases the intensity of the process color applied to a selected object by reducing the color percentages in 10% increments.

To use the Desaturate filter, first select the object. In the Filter ➤ Colors menu, select Desaturate. If you have your Paint Style palette open at the same time, you will see the percentages drop as you apply the filter. You can reapply the filter again until you reach the shade you desire.

Desaturate More

The Desaturate More filter is similar to the Desaturate filter, but moves in larger increments. This filter decreases the intensity of the process color applied to a selected object by reducing the color percentages in 25% increments.

To use the Desaturate More filter, first select the object. In the Filter ➤ Colors menu, select Desaturate More. If the filter is reapplied repetitively, it will decrease the color intensity until it reaches 0% for each of the CMYK colors.

Invert Colors

The Invert Colors filter inverts the CMYK color percentages currently in use in a selected object to create a color negative. For example, if an object is 30% magenta and 20% cyan, after the filter is applied the object will be 70% magenta and 80% cyan, plus 100% yellow (the opposite of 0% yellow).

To apply the filter, first select an object. In the Filter ➤ Colors menu, select Invert Colors. If your Paint Style palette is open while you use the filter, you will see the color percentages change.

Saturate

The inverse of the Desaturate filter, the Saturate filter increases the intensity of the CMYK color percentages selected for an object. To use the

Saturate filter, select the object and choose Saturate from the Filter ➤ Colors menu. The color will increase in intensity by 10%.

Saturate More

The Saturate More filter works like the Saturate filter, only it increases the intensity of the CMYK colors in an object by 25% each time it is applied, to a maximum of 100%. To use the filter, select an object and choose Saturate More from the Filter ➤ Colors menu.

Create

The six filters in the Create submenu allow you to create certain objects (stars, spirals, and so forth), as well as create mosaic effects in imported PICT images.

Fill & Stroke for Mask

The Fill & Stroke for Mask filter creates two separate fill and stroke objects for a mask, placing the fill behind the mask and the stroke in front of the mask. It is a little tricky to use, but with practice it can render interesting results.

To use the filter on a mask, first click on the mask with the Selection tool. (You can also use the Select Mask filter in the Filter ➤ Select menu.) Open the Paint Style palette and check the Auto Apply box in the lower-right corner of the palette. Choose a fill color and a stroke color and width for the mask. Finally, choose Fill & Stroke for Mask from the Filter ➤ Create menu. The fill and stroke specified in the Paint Style palette will be applied to the masking object.

Mosaic

The Mosaic filter applies a mosaic effect to imported PICT images by clustering similarly-colored pixels into individual tiles. These tiles can be sized, spaced, and the ratio of horizontal to vertical tiles adjusted to create a more artistic rendering of an ordinary image (Figure 9.5).

9.5

The original image (left), and Illustrator's Mosaic rendering of the image (right).

before   after

To use the Mosaic filter, select Mosaic from the Filter ➤ Create menu. From the dialog box that appears, choose the PICT image to use and click on the Open button. The Mosaic dialog box will appear. Here you can enter settings to control different aspects of the image you will create:

- Tile Spacing—the amount of space between each tile both horizontally (width) and vertically (height).
- New Size—the size in points which the image should be after it has been transformed by the filter.
- Number of tiles—the number of tiles across and down that should be created in the mosaic image.
- Lock Width/Height—locks one measurement so conversions will remain dimensionally correct.
- Color/Grayscale—determines whether the mosaic image should be rendered in color or grayscale.

There is also a Use Ratio button. Clicking on this button will automatically size the currently selected setting to stay in proportion with the original image size. When you have entered the settings, click OK. Illustrator will take a moment or two to render the image, and then display it on your page.

WATCH OUT!

It takes a large chunk of memory to use the Mosaic filter. Free up as much memory as possible before using it, or else the filter will stop halfway through rendering the image.

Polygon

The Polygon filter creates a perfectly proportioned polygon, based on the number of sides and radius size entered in the fields in the Polygon dialog box. The radius size determines the distance from the center of the polygon that each endpoint in the image will be placed (Figure 9.6).

To create a polygon using this filter, select Polygon from the Filter ➤ Create menu. In the Polygon dialog box, enter the number of sides and the radius (in points) for your image. A preview image in the dialog box will show a miniature view of the polygon according to the specifications you enter. Click on the OK button when you are finished and the actual polygon will be displayed on your screen.

9.6

Enter your own specifications in the Polygon filter dialog box to create a polygon.

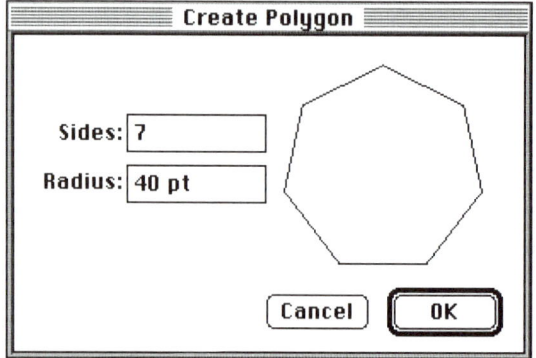

Spiral

The Spiral filter renders a spiral based on the number of winds (rotations around the center point) and the radius that you enter into its dialog box. The spiral itself consists of a single line that can be positioned to swirl clockwise or counter-clockwise (Figure 9.7).

9.7

The Spiral filter creates swirled images.

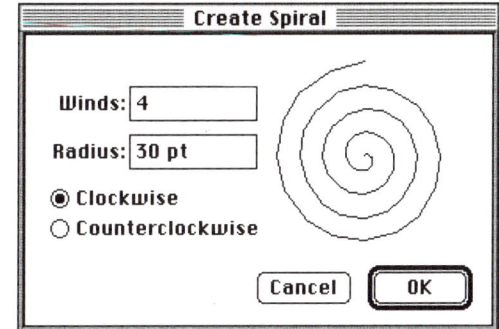

To create a spiral, select Spiral from the Filter ➤ Create menu. Enter the number of winds and the radius of the spiral you want to create. Select whether the spiral should swirl clockwise or counter-clockwise by clicking on one of the radio buttons in the dialog box. A preview of the image will appear in the dialog box as you enter the specifications. Click on the OK button and the spiral will appear on your page.

Star

The Star filter uses the specifications you enter in its dialog box to create a star. To create a star, select Star from the Filter ➤ Create menu. Enter a number (in points) in the first radius field, which specifies the distance from the center point of the star to the end of one of its points. Enter a number in the second radius field to specify the distance from the center point to the inside points of the star. Enter the number of points for the star in the Points field, and click OK. The star will appear on your page (Figure 9.8).

9.8

The Star filter helps you create perfectly proportioned stars.

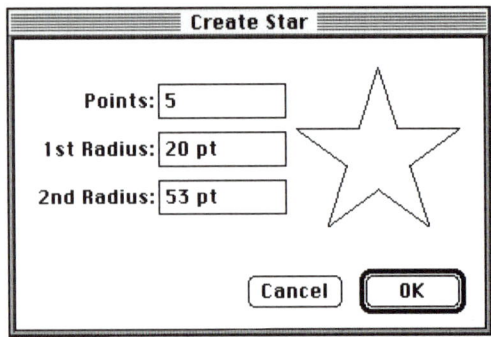

Trim Marks

Trim marks (also called crop marks) are marks that show where an image should be trimmed after being printed. The Trim Marks filter lets you place marks around any object or group of objects on your page. The filter generates the trim marks based on the height and width of the object at its largest points.

To create trim marks, first select the object or objects around which you would like trim marks. In the Filter ➤ Create menu, select Trim Marks. A single set of trim marks will appear around the selected object (Figure 9.9).

9.9

The Trim Marks filter places trim marks in alignment with the edges of a selected object.

Distort

The five filters in the Distort submenu change the shape of selected objects to create interesting effects.

Free Distort

The Free Distort filter allows you to distort the shape of an object by dragging on the corners of a "distort box" that the filter places around the selected object (Figure 9.10).

9.10

The Free Distort filter places a box around an object; you can drag on the box corners to distort the object inside.

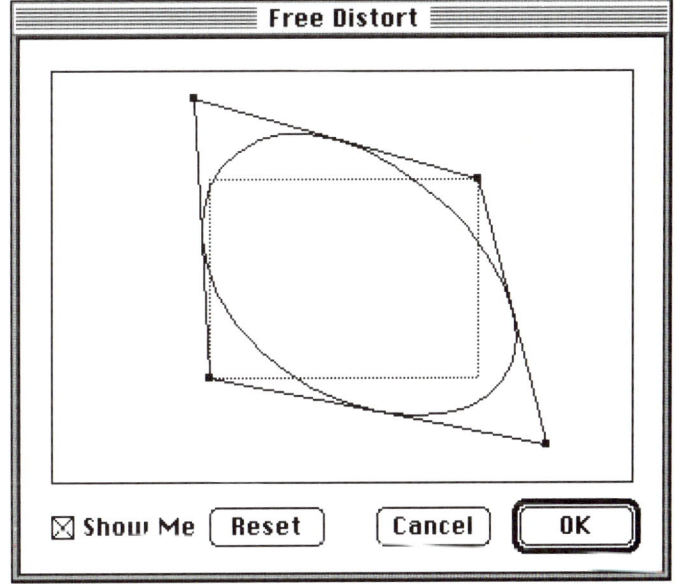

To use the Free Distort filter, first select an object. In the Filter ▶ Distort menu, select Free Distort. The distort box will appear around your object within the Free Distort dialog box. Click and drag on any of the corner points to distort the object while it is in this dialog box, then click on the OK button to exit. The object will stay distorted.

Roughen

The Roughen filter creates a jagged edge around an object by adding extra anchor points and then moving them in different directions away from their original path. This produces a rougher, jaggier look (Figure 9.11).

9.11

The Roughen filter creates a jagged edge around an object.

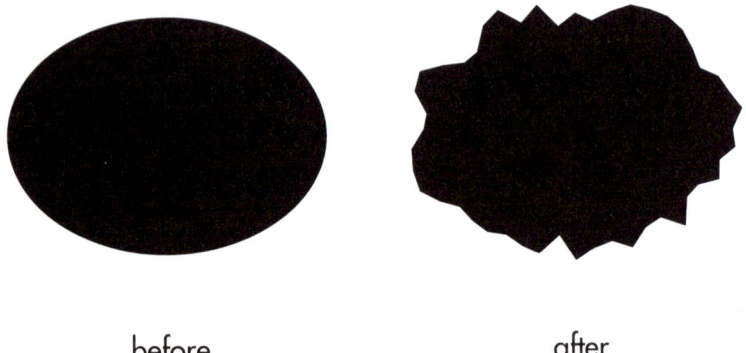

before   after

To roughen an object, first select the object. In the Filter ➤ Distort menu, choose the Roughen filter (Figure 9.12). The Roughen dialog box appears, allowing you to choose how much distortion you want (the lower the percentage, the more the object retains its original shape). You also choose the number of jagged segments per inch to add, and whether the segments should be jagged or rounded. Click on the OK button when you are finished to see your changes take place.

9.12

The Roughen filter dialog box.

Roughen

Size: 5 %

Detail: 10 segments/inch

○ Rounded   ⦿ Jagged

[Cancel] [[OK]]

> **Remember, if you don't like the effect that a certain filter gives you, you can quickly reverse the change by invoking the Undo command (⌘-Z). Your object will revert to its original shape.**

Scribble

The Scribble filter is similar to the Roughen filter. It moves random points in an object away from their original path. However, the Scribble filter does not add extra points; rather it gives you the option of moving the existing anchor points of an object, as well as directional control points (Figure 9.13).

9.13

The Scribble filter changes the shape of an object by moving its existing anchor points.

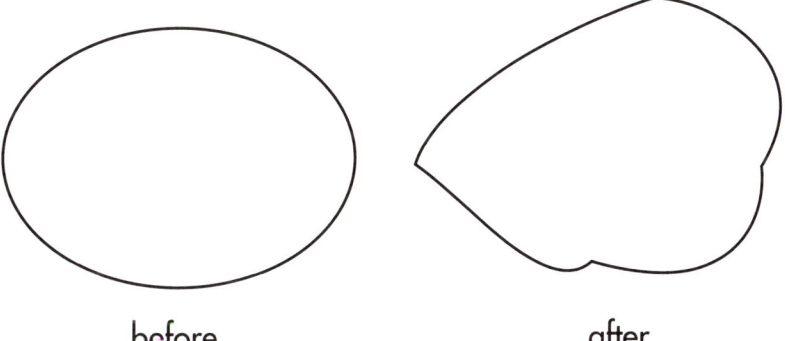

bcfore   after

To apply the Scribble filter to an object, first select the object. In the Filter ➤ Distort menu, select Scribble. In the Scribble dialog box (Figure 9.14), you have the option of changing either the vertical or the horizontal axis of an object (a zero percentage means the sides of the object on that axis will not change). Select the type of points to skew: anchor points, "in" control points, or "out" control points. Click on the OK button when you are finished to see your results.

9.14

The Scribble filter
dialog box.

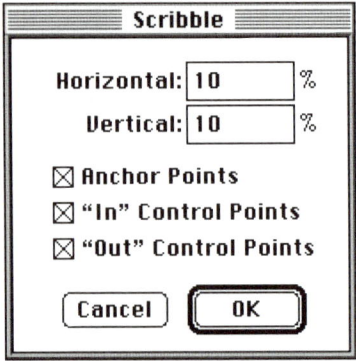

Tweak

The Tweak filter is very similar to the Scribble filter, but lets you specify the horizontal or vertical movement of the points in an object.

To apply the Tweak filter to an object, first select the object. In the Filter ➤ Distort menu, select Tweak. The Tweak dialog box appears (Figure 9.15). Choose the amount of horizontal and vertical change to apply in points. Select the type of points to skew: anchor points, "in" control points, or "out" control points. Click on the OK button when you are finished to see your results.

9.15

The Tweak filter
dialog box.

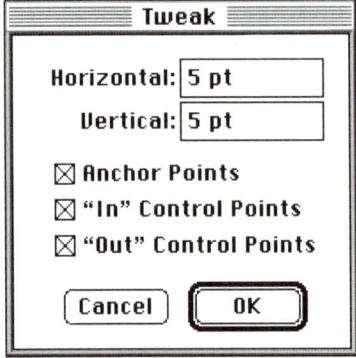

Twirl

The Twirl filter rotates a selected object around a center point, causing a spiral effect. To achieve this, the center is rotated more than the outside edges.

To twirl an object, first select the object. The filter works best when the object you select has several anchor points. In the Filter ➤ Distort menu, choose Twirl. In the Twirl dialog box, enter the rotation of the twirl in degrees and click on the OK button to exit and see the changes (Figure 9.16).

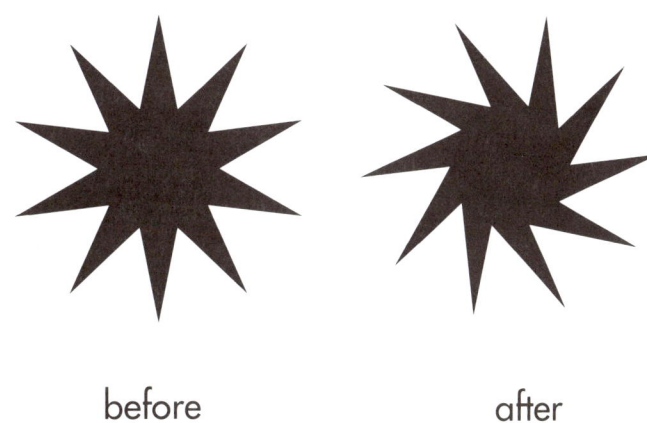

before   after

Objects

The nine filters in the Objects submenu align, scale, and copy selected objects in different ways to create special effects.

Add Anchor Points

The Add Anchor Points filter provides a quick way to add numerous anchor points to a path. When the filter is used on an object, it adds another anchor point between every pair of anchor points in the path. Compared to the Add Anchor Point tool, which adds points one at a time, this filter can really be a time-saver.

To use the Add Anchor Points filter, first select an object. In the Filter ➤ Objects menu, choose Add Anchor Points. The filter will add an anchor point between each pair of anchor points currently in the path (Figure 9.17).

9.17

The Add Anchor Points filter adds numerous anchor points to the currently selected path.

 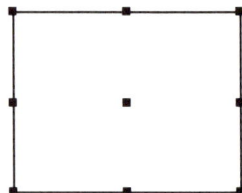

Align Objects

Selected objects can be aligned in numerous ways along either the horizontal or the vertical axis by using the Align Objects filter. The Align Objects dialog box gives you the option of aligning objects according to their top, center, or bottom anchor points for a horizontal alignment, or according to their left, center, or right anchor points for a vertical alignment. You are also given the option of evenly distributing the selected objects along the chosen axis (Figure 9.18).

To use the Align Objects filter, first select the objects to be aligned. In the Filter ➤ Objects menu, choose Align Objects. In the dialog box, choose Horizontal and/or Vertical alignment. Under the alignment you choose, decide which anchor points in the objects should align. If you want the objects evenly distributed along the axis, click on Distribute. As you select different settings, a preview of the settings will appear in a box to the right. When the settings are correct, click on the OK button to make the changes in your document.

9.18

The Align Objects filter aligns selected objects along a chosen axis.

Distribute Horizontally

The Distribute Horizontally filter distributes the selected objects evenly between the two objects furthest apart on the horizontal plane. To use this filter, first select the objects and then choose Distribute Horizontally from the Filter ➤ Objects menu. The selected objects will be distributed accordingly.

Distribute Vertically

The Distribute Vertically filter distributes selected objects evenly between the two objects furthest apart on the vertical plane. To use this filter, first select the objects and then choose Distribute Vertically from the Filter ➤ Objects menu. The selected objects will be distributed accordingly.

Move Each

To move a selected path (or a copy of the path) in a random or set direction, use the Move Each filter to specify the distance and direction. To use the filter, first select the object or objects to be moved. In the Filter ➤ Objects menu, select Move Each. Specify a horizontal and/or vertical movement in points, or click on the Random box to move the objects randomly (Figure 9.19). To move copies of the selected objects, leaving the originals in place, click on the Copy button. Otherwise, click on the OK button to make the changes.

Offset Path

The Offset Path filter creates a copy of a selected path, enlarges it, and places it at a specified distance away from the original. For instance, if you were to draw a circle and use the Offset Path filter, a larger version of the circle would appear surrounding the original, offset all the way around by the amount you specify. To use the Offset Path filter, however, your Macintosh must contain a math coprocessor.

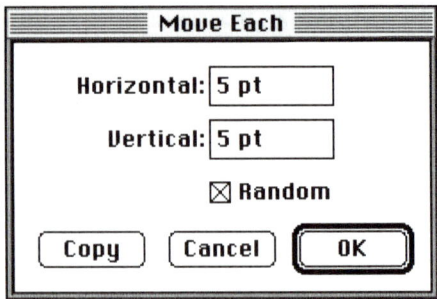

To use the Offset Path filter, select an object and then choose Offset Path from the Filter ➤ Objects menu (Figure 9.20). Enter the Offset amount in points, select Mitre, Round, or Bevel for the type of corners the offset path should have (or ends, if it is an open path), and the mitre limit. Click on the OK button and the offset path will appear outside the original path on your page.

9.20

The Offset Path fil-
ter creates a copy
of a selected path
offset at a specified
distance.

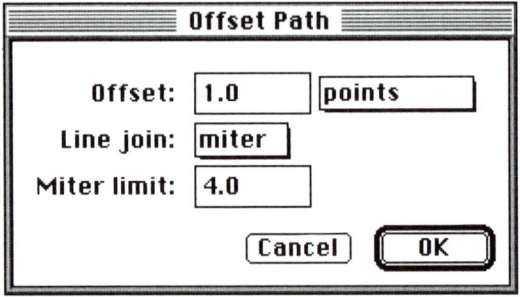

Outline Path

The Outline Path filter traces the outline of a selected stroked object, deletes the original, and substitutes a filled object the same size as the original. The new object can then be used when trapping the object to make color separations. However, since the original object is deleted during this process, you should always make a copy of the artwork before using this filter. Also, this filter requires the presence of a math coprocessor on your Macintosh in order to work.

To use the Outline Path filter, select the stroked object to be outlined. In the Filter ➤ Objects menu, choose Outline Path. A filled copy of the stroked object will replace the original.

Rotate Each

The Rotate Each filter rotates selected objects to a specified angle. If you click on the Random button, the filter will rotate an object to a random angle. If two or more objects are selected, using the Random feature will cause the objects to rotate in different directions as well (Figure 9.21).

9.21

The Rotate Each filter dialog box.

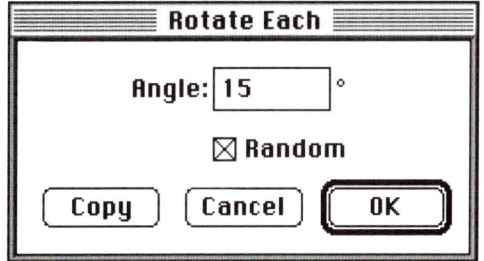

To use this filter, first select the objects to be rotated. In the Filter ➤ Objects menu, choose Rotate Each. In the dialog box that appears, enter the angle for the rotation, or click on the Random box to rotate the object or objects randomly, to any angle. To rotate a copy of the object, leaving the original in place, click on the Copy button. Otherwise, click on the OK button to see the changes take effect in your document.

Scale Each

The Scale Each filter will scale a path or copy of a path to a selected horizontal or vertical percentage. When you use the Random button, the filter will scale all selected objects randomly to different sizes. This filter also contains a Copy button, which scales duplicates while leaving the original intact (Figure 9.22).

9.22

The Scale Each filter dialog box.

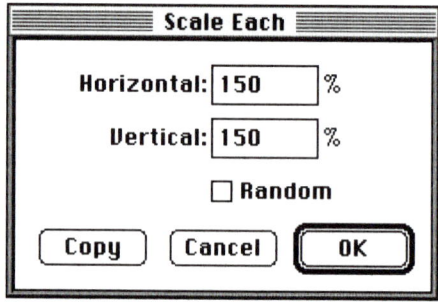

To use the Scale Each filter, first select the object or group of objects to scale. In the Filter ➤ Objects menu, enter a horizontal and vertical percentage for the scale. Click on the Random button if you want to scale the objects to random sizes. Click on the Copy button to scale duplicates of the original, or click on OK to scale the original objects.

Other

The four filters in the Other menu are useful when you are preparing to print. They provide access to information about a file and its many parts and let you specify certain print-related settings.

Document Info

The Document Info filter provides specific details about the currently selected object on your screen or, if no objects are selected, presents information about the document in general. The information is presented in seven categories:

- General information, such as the document name, format, and settings, and the last time the document was modified.

- Object information, such as the number of paths and masks in the selected object, as well as the names of custom colors, fonts, and imported art files used.

- Custom Colors, listing the names of custom colors used in the selected object or document.

- Patterns, listing the names of all patterns used in the selected object or document.
- Gradients, listing the names of gradient color blends used in the selected object or document.
- Fonts, listing the names of fonts used in the selected object or document, as well as font styles.
- Placed Art, listing the name and location on your hard drive of any imported art that has been placed in the document.

To use the Document Info filter, select an object on your screen, or select nothing to find out about *everything* in the document. In the Filter ➤ Other menu, select Document Info. The Document Info box will appear (Figure 9.23). In the top of the box is a pop-up menu—click on it and select one of the seven topic choices. The selected information will appear in the window below.

9.23

The Document Info filter dialog box lists information about a selected object or the entire document.

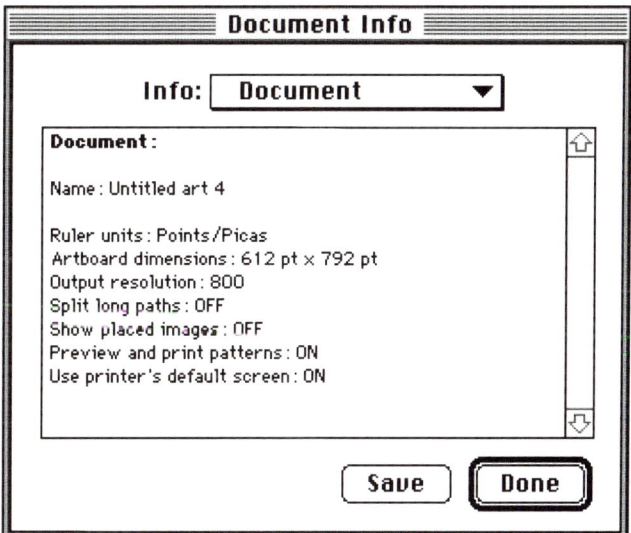

To save a copy of the information in this dialog box to print out later, click on the Save button. This is helpful to give to a print shop, should you send your file out to be printed, since it contains pertinent information they will need to print your file correctly.

Overprint Black

The Overprint Black filter allows the black fill or black stroke of an object to overprint all other colors, based on the settings you enter. The filter can be set to overprint at a certain threshold, for instance, when the black fill or stroke is at a certain percentage or higher. The Overprint Black filter also can be applied to custom colors built with black, or any process color that contains black.

To use the filter, choose Overprint Black in the Filter ➤ Other menu. Then, in the Overprint dialog box (Figure 9.24):

■ check whether to add the overprinting feature, or to remove it,

■ enter the percentage threshold at which black should overprint,

■ select whether just the fill, just the stroke, or both instances of black should overprint,

■ choose whether just the currently selected object or all instances of black in the document should overprint,

■ if you want custom colors and process colors containing black to overprint, click on those choices as well.

9.24

The Overprint Black filter dialog box.

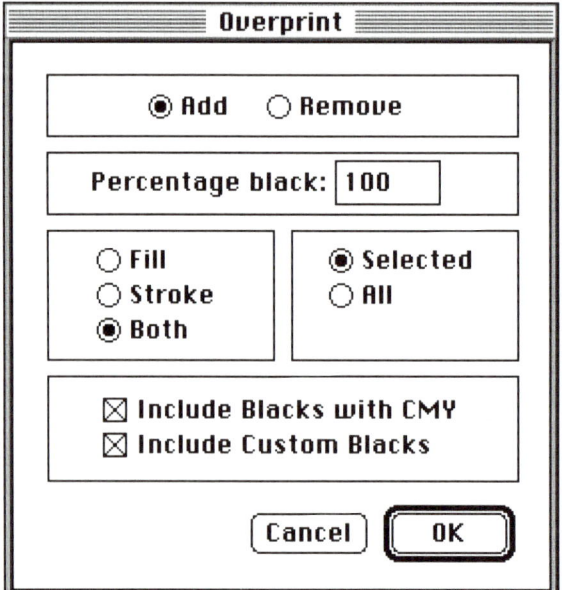

Make Riders

A *rider* is a PostScript-coded file, added to a document to provide printing information: the screen frequency, angle, halftone dot shape and flatness of the document. It also provides a way to add an annotation to the printed file. The settings you specify in a Riders file override the settings entered using Adobe Separator (see Chapter 11 for information about Adobe Separator).

The Make Riders and Delete Riders filters are not automatically added to the Filters folder when you install Illustrator. You must manually move them into your Plug-Ins folder in order for them to load when you start Illustrator. Once the Make Riders filter has been loaded, a rider will be added to all files you create until you remove the filter from the Plug-Ins folder or use the Delete Riders filter to disable the rider.

To enter settings for the rider, select Make Riders from the Filters ➤ Other menu. In the Make Riders dialog box (Figure 9.25), choose from the following pop-up menus:

- Screen Frequency—sets the line screen value used when printing the file in *lines per inch* (lpi). The higher the number, the smaller the dots used in each line, creating a higher resolution and better quality output. This setting can range from 1 to 999.

- Screen Angle—determines the angle for printing the line screen to make the lines of dots less conspicuous. The default setting for black is 45 degrees. Each successive color uses a different angle to avoid a dot pattern called a moiré that can appear when the angles are incorrect.

- Spot Function—provides a listing of dot shapes that can be used instead of a standard round dot when printing halftones. Different shaped dots provide different effects when used in a halftone.

- Flatness—determines how the PostScript interpreter draws curves within a document. The interpreter divides curves into smaller line segments to create more accurate curves. However, curves that become too complex can generate a PostScript error, and your file will fail to print. The higher the flatness number is set, the less complicated the curve will be and the file will print faster. The setting must be between 0.2 and 200.

- Annotation—allows you to add an annotation of up to 256 characters to your file. The annotation will print in the bottom-left corner of the page.

- Error Handler—prints error information on the page, should a PostScript error occur while printing the file.

9.25

The Make Riders filter dialog box.

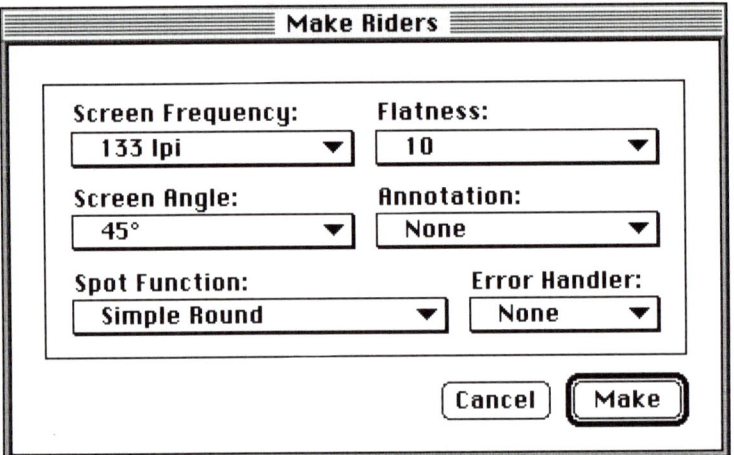

Click on the Make button when you are finished. A Save dialog box will appear, letting you save your changes as the official Adobe Illustrator EPSF Riders file.

Delete Riders

The Delete Riders filter lets you delete a rider. To use the filter, select it from the Filters ➤ Other menu. In the Delete Riders dialog box, find the rider's file name and click Delete.

Pathfinder

The 14 filters in the Pathfinder submenu manipulate (add, divide, merge, and so forth) the paths between combinations of overlapping objects.

Unite

The Unite filter combines multiple overlapping objects into one by tracing around the outside of all the objects to create a new object. The original objects used in the tracing are deleted when the new object is formed (Figure 9.26).

To use the filter, first select the objects to be merged. In the Filter ➤ Pathfinder menu, select Unite. The new object will appear on your screen.

9.26

The Unite filter joins multiple objects into one.

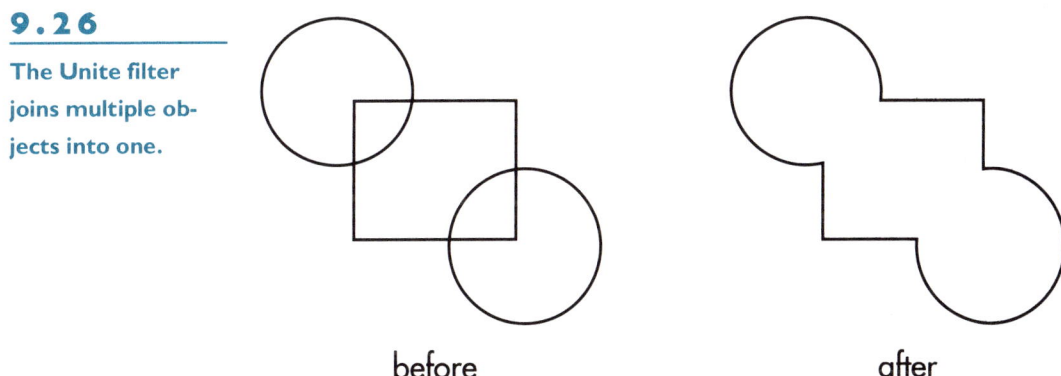

before   after

Intersect

The Intersect filter traces over the intersecting area of two objects, deleting the originals and creating a new shape based on the overlapped area. To use the filter, first select two overlapping objects. From the Filter ➤ Pathfinder menu, select Intersect. The new object, in the shape of the overlapping area, will appear (Figure 9.27).

9.27

The Intersect filter traces the inter-secting area of two objects.

 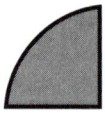

before   after

Exclude

The Exclude filter is the opposite of the Intersect filter. It traces over the areas of intersecting objects that do not overlap, leaving open spaces where the overlap was. To use the filter, select two or more overlapping objects. In the Filter ➤ Pathfinder menu, select Exclude. The filter will drop out the overlapping areas, creating a merged object out of the re-maining parts (Figure 9.28).

9.28

The Exclude filter traces over the ar-eas that do not intersect in two overlapping objects.

before   after

Minus Front

The Minus Front filter traces around the area of the backmost object that is visible, deleting all the objects stacked on top of it but retaining the shape of where they overlapped the bottom object. To use the filter, select several overlapping objects. In the Filter ➤ Pathfinder menu, choose Minus Front. The new object will appear (Figure 9.29).

9.29

The Minus Front filter traces the visible portions of the backmost object in a stack.

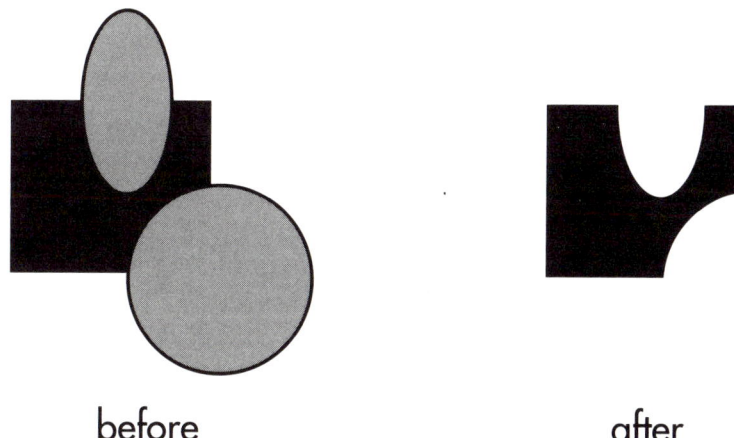

before   after

Minus Back

Similar to the Minus Front filter, the Minus Back filter traces around objects underneath the top object in a stack, keeping the top object but cutting it away where it overlapped other objects. To use the filter, select all the objects in a stack. In the Filter ➤ Pathfinder menu, select Minus Back (Figure 9.30).

Divide

The Divide filter divides overlapping objects into sections. Each area where an object overlaps another object becomes a separate object, which can be filled and stroked separately from its original object. To use the filter, select a group of stacked objects. In the Filter ➤ Pathfinder menu, choose Divide.

9.30

The Minus Back filter traces the invisible portions of objects layered under the top object, cutting away the object where it overlaps.

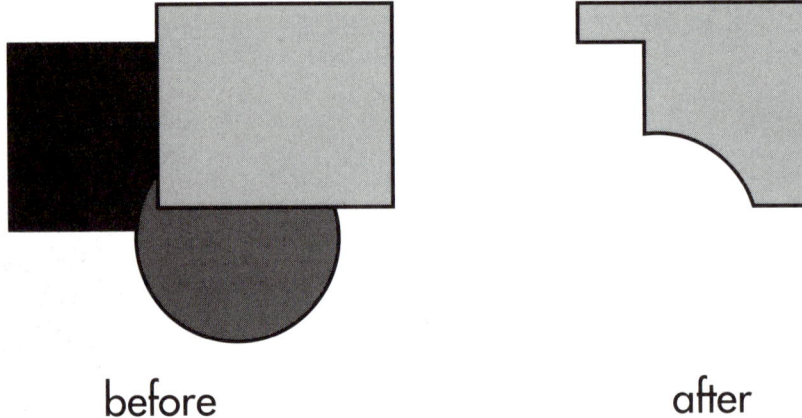

before   after

To style the parts separately now, click on the artboard to deselect the grouped object, then use the Direct Selection tool to click on each area and style it differently (Figure 9.31).

9.31

The Divide filter divides overlapping objects into sections.

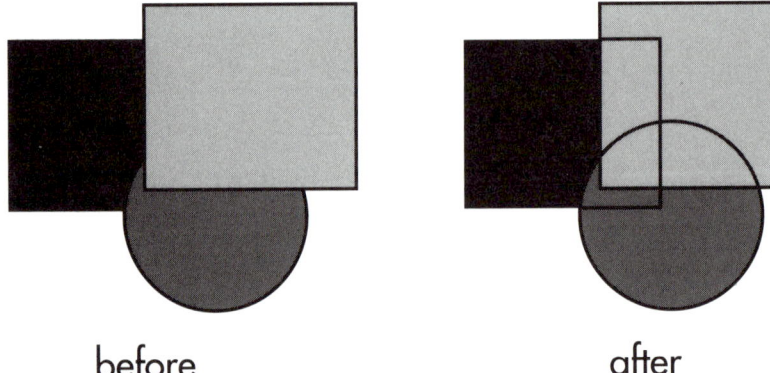

before   after

Outline

The Outline filter separates a stack of grouped objects into separate open paths, based on the areas where the objects intersect. If the objects are filled with color when the Outline filter is applied, the visible areas of each object will retain that color as an outline. To use the Outline filter, select a group of objects and in the Filter ➤ Pathfinder menu, choose Outline (Figure 9.32).

9.32

The Outline filter separates a stack of grouped objects into separate open paths.

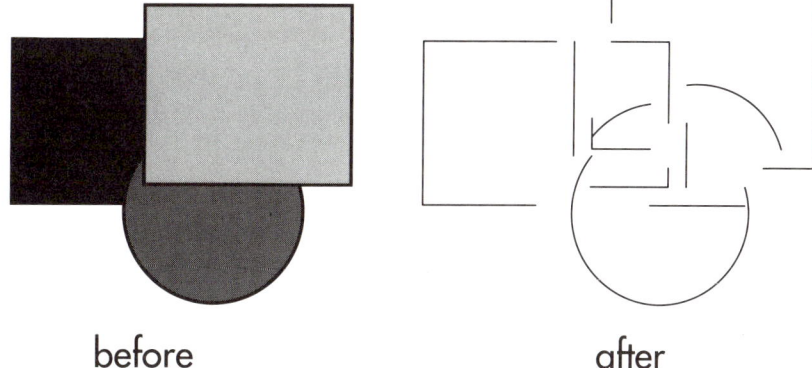

before   after

Trim

The Trim filter trims the path of each underlying object in a stack to follow only the visible areas of each object. To use this filter, first select all the overlapping objects. In the Filter ➤ Pathfinder menu, select Trim. The objects will be trimmed so that their paths follow only the visible areas on your page (Figure 9.33).

9.33

The Trim filter trims the paths of overlapping objects so that they conform to the visible areas.

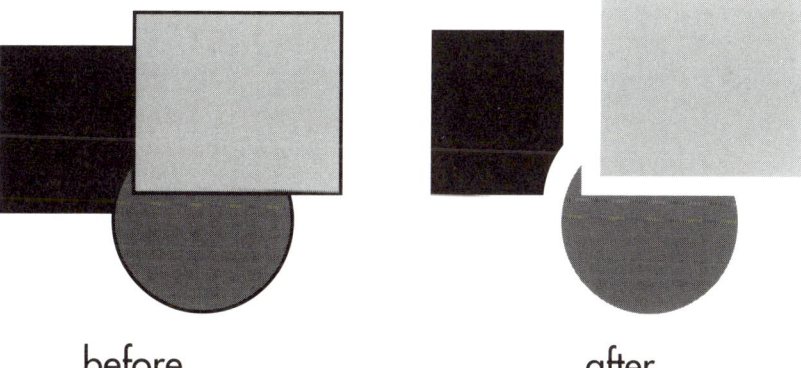

before   after

Merge

The Merge filter performs the same functions as the Trim filter, and also merges overlapping objects of the same fill color to become one object.

To use this filter, select the objects and then choose Merge from the Filter ➤ Pathfinder menu. The selected objects will be trimmed so that their paths follow only the visible areas on your page, and any objects of the same fill color that overlap will be merged (Figure 9.34).

9.34

The Merge filter trims while merging objects of the same fill color.

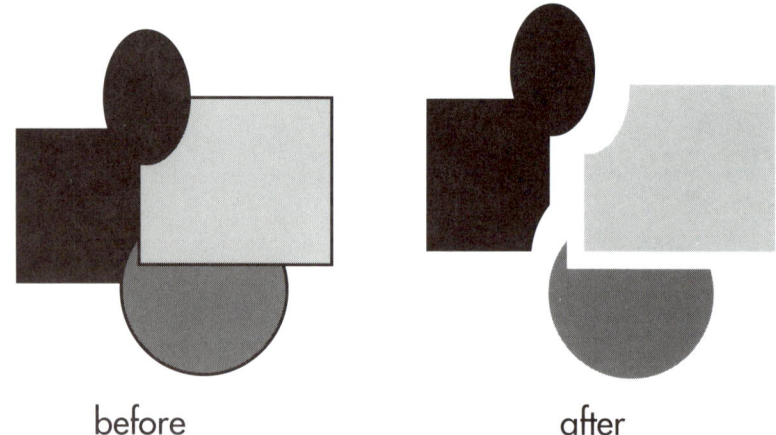

before   after

Crop

The Crop filter deletes everything in a stack of selected objects *except* what is hidden under the overlap of the topmost object. The remaining segments are trimmed according to their stacking order (Figure 9.35).

9.35

The Crop filter deletes everything in a stack of objects except what is hidden under the topmost layer.

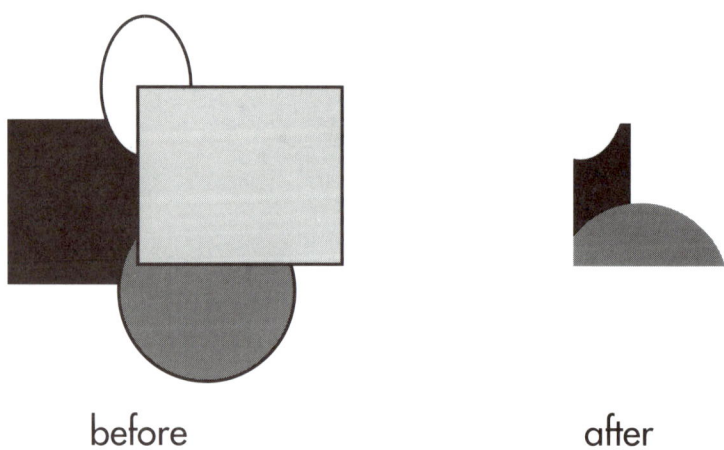

before   after

To use the Crop filter, first select the objects to be cropped. In the Filter ➤ Pathfinder menu, select Crop. The cropped area will remain on your page.

Hard

The Hard filter (formerly called the Mix Hard filter) mixes the colors of two (or more) overlapping objects to create a transparent effect in the overlap area. The resulting color combines the highest CMYK value from each of the two objects to show how the objects will overprint. This is usually a very dark color.

To use the Hard filter, select the objects and in the Filter ➤ Pathfinder menu, choose Hard. The overlapping areas of the two objects will now have their own paths, filled with the representative color (Figure 9.36).

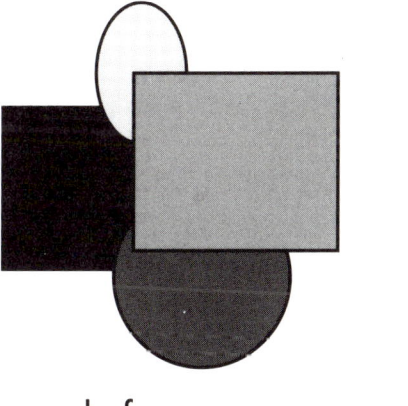

before   after

Soft

Like the Hard filter, the Soft filter mixes the colors of two (or more) overlapping objects to create a transparent effect in the overlap area. However, with the Soft filter you can choose the *mixing rate*, a percentage that determines the transparency level. This allows you to create a more visible, transparent effect than the Hard filter produces.

To use the Soft filter, choose two or more objects that overlap. From the Filter ➤ Pathfinder menu, select Soft. The Soft dialog box will appear, allowing you to change the mixing rate (the lower the number, the more transparent the color), as well as determine whether to change custom colors to process (Figure 9.37).

9.37

The Soft filter creates a user-defined transparent effect between the colors of overlapping objects.

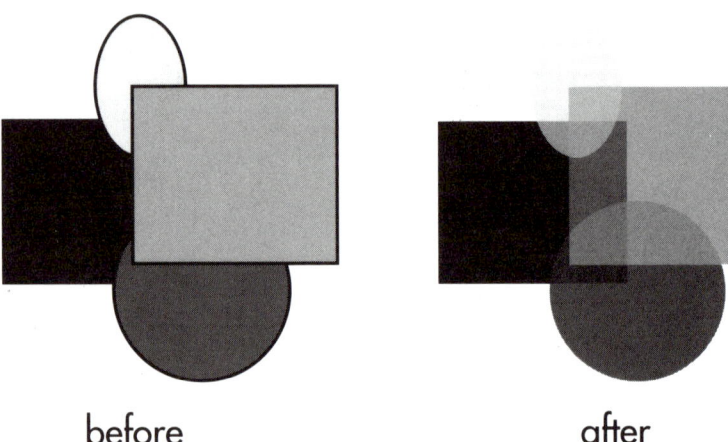

before   after

Trap

The Trap filter allows you to create customized color traps between objects. *Trapping* is the addition of a small amount of overlap between colors to allow for any misregistration that could occur during printing on a high-speed press.

In the Trap dialog box you can specify the thickness of the overlap (in fractions of a point), a smaller or larger percentage of trap for horizontal lines (since they are more apt to need more trapping if the paper stretches on the press), and a tint reduction to change the tint of the trap itself (Figure 9.38).

For more on trapping and using this filter, see the section on trapping in Chapter 7.

9.38

The Trap filter dialog box.

```
╔══════════════ Pathfinder Trap ══════════════╗
║                                              ║
║  Thickness:      │ 0.25 │ points   ┌─────────┐║
║                                    │   OK    │║
║  Height/width:   │ 100.0 │ %       └─────────┘║
║                                    ┌─────────┐║
║  Tint reduction: │ 40.0 │ %        │ Cancel  │║
║                                    └─────────┘║
║  ☐ Convert custom colors to process┌─────────┐║
║                                    │Defaults │║
║  ☐ Reverse traps                   └─────────┘║
╚══════════════════════════════════════════════╝
```

Options

The Options filter sets certain preferences for the rest of the tools in the Pathfinder menu. In the Options dialog box you can enter a value that controls the precision used by the other filters in this menu when they are applied. The smaller the number used, the more closely each filter will render its change (and the longer it will take). Besides the precision value, the dialog box also provides options for removing redundant points rendered by the other filters, as well as removing unfilled objects when the Divide and Outline filters are used (Figure 9.39). To change the options, select Options from the Filter ➤ Pathfinder menu.

9.39

The Options filter dialog box controls the precision with which the other Pathfinder filters are applied.

```
╔══════════════ Pathfinder Options ══════════════╗
║                                                 ║
║  Calculate results to a precision of │0.028│ points  ┌──────┐║
║                                                       │  OK  │║
║  ☒ Remove redundant points                            └──────┘║
║                                                       ┌──────┐║
║  ☒ Divide and Outline will extract unpainted artwork  │Cancel│║
║                                                       └──────┘║
║                                                       ┌──────┐║
║                                                       │Defaults│║
║                                                       └──────┘║
╚═════════════════════════════════════════════════╝
```

Select

The seven filters in the Select submenu let you select objects with matching styles throughout a document, making global changes quick and easy.

Same Fill Color

The Same Fill Color filter selects all objects in a document that are filled with the same color as the originally selected object. To use the filter, select one object and choose Same Fill Color from the Filter ➤ Select menu. All other matching objects in the document will become selected.

Same Paint Style

The Same Paint Style filter selects all objects in a document that have the same paint style commands as a selected object, including fill, stroke, and line weight. To use the filter, select one object and choose Same Paint Style from the Filter ➤ Select menu. All other matching objects in the document will become selected.

Same Stroke Color

The Same Stroke Color filter selects all objects in a document that match the stroke color applied to the object originally selected. To use the filter, select one object and then choose Same Stroke Color from the Filter ➤ Select menu. All other matching objects in the document will become selected.

Same Stroke Weight

The Same Stroke Weight filter will select all the objects in a document that match the stroke weight of the object originally selected. To use the filter, select one object and in the Filter ➤ Select menu choose Same Stroke Weight. All other matching objects in the document will become selected.

Select Inverse

The Select Inverse filter selects the opposite of what is currently selected when the filter is applied. For instance, if you have three objects on a page and only one of them is currently selected, after you apply the Select Inverse filter the other two objects will be selected and the original object will be deselected.

To use the Select Inverse filter, choose Select Inverse from the Filter ➤ Select menu. All objects that weren't selected before applying the filter will now become selected.

Select Masks

To find masks in a document, use the Select Masks filter. When nothing is selected in a document, the filter will select all masks that have been created. When you apply the Select Masks filter with objects already selected, the filter will deselect any objects that aren't masks, leaving only the masks selected.

To apply the filter, choose Select Masks from the Filter ➤ Select menu. The filter will search out and highlight all masks found in the document.

Select Stray Points

When you are drawing, often single points will be left here and there throughout a design. Whenever you click any of the drawing tools on your page without actually drawing a rectangle or line, a point will be left. The Select Stray Points filter is a good way to round up and delete the extra points that may be left lying around.

To use the filter, choose Select Stray Points from the Filter ➤ Select menu. All single points found in the document will become selected, at which point you can easily delete them all at once.

Stylize

The six filters in the Stylize submenu provide styling options for the objects in your design, such as arrowheads and drop shadows.

Add Arrowheads

The Add Arrowheads filter gives you 27 different arrowheads and ends that can be added to either end of a currently selected line. In addition, the size of each arrowhead can be scaled larger or smaller.

To use the filter, first draw or select a line. In the Filter ➤ Stylize menu, choose Add Arrowheads. In the dialog box that appears, you can scroll through the different styles of arrowheads by clicking on either of the pointing hands (Figure 9.40).

9.40

The Add Arrow-
heads dialog box
gives you 27 differ-
ent choices of
arrowheads you
can add to the
ends of open paths.

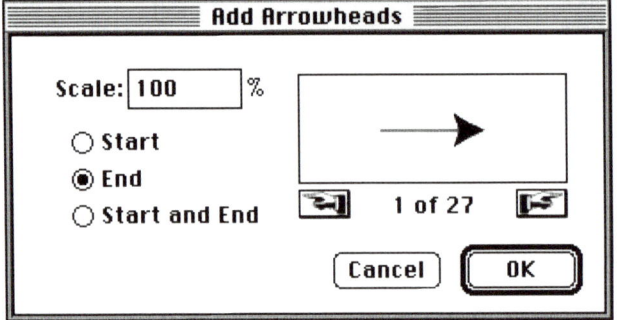

When you find the one you like best, click on the Start, End, or Start and End buttons to apply the arrowhead to the correct end of the line. If you want to scale the arrowhead, enter a new percentage in the Scale field and click OK.

Bloat

The Bloat filter curves all paths in an object outward, giving an object a bloated look. The Amount value entered in the Bloat dialog box deter-mines the angle of the curve from each anchor point. As the percentage grows higher, the curve becomes more pronounced and the anchor points begin to draw in closer to the center (Figure 9.41).

To apply the Bloat filter, first select an object. In the Filter ➤ Stylize menu, select Bloat. Enter a percentage in the Amount field—the larger the value, the greater the curve. Click on the OK button to apply the changes.

9.41

The **Bloat** filter curves the paths in an object outward, based on the percentage you enter in the dialog box.

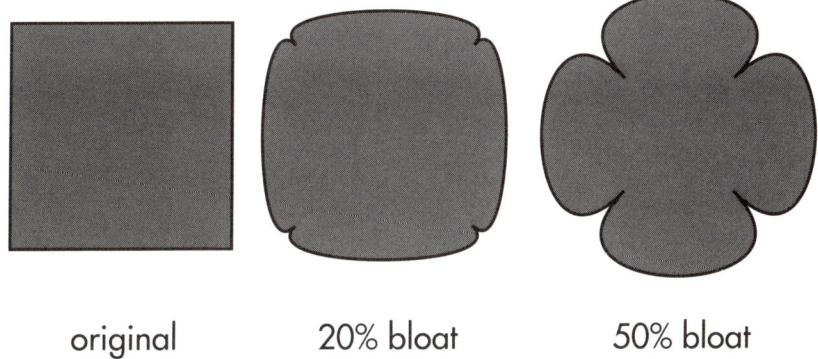

original   20% bloat   50% bloat

Calligraphy

The Calligraphy filter makes a regular stroked path look as though it were drawn with a calligraphic nibbed pen (Figure 9.42). To apply the filter, first select a path (open or closed). In the Filter ➤ Stylize menu, choose Calligraphy. Enter a pen width and angle in the dialog box and click on the OK button to apply the changes to your selected object (Figure 9.43).

9.42

The **Calligraphy** filter gives a calligraphic effect to any stroked path.

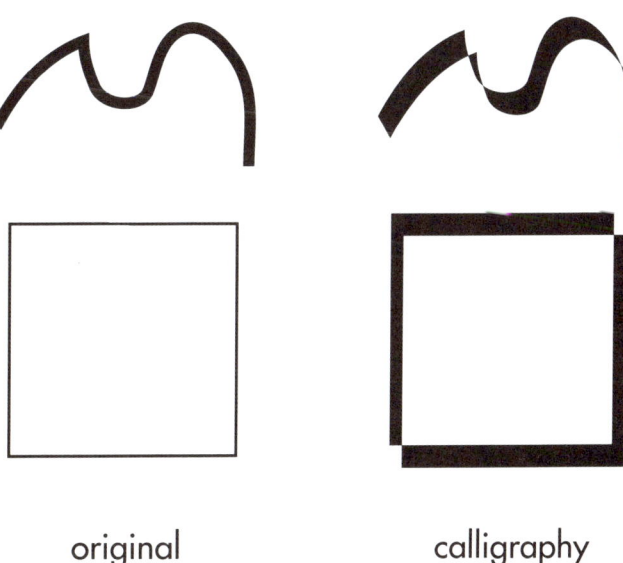

original   calligraphy

9.43

The settings in the
Calligraphy dialog
box affect the way
the filter is applied
to a stroked path.

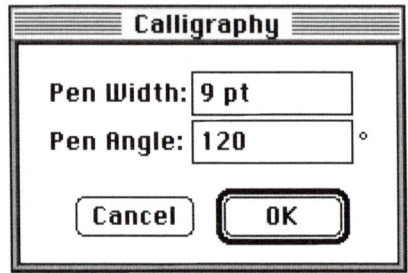

Drop Shadow

The Drop Shadow filter adds a "shadow" the same size and shape as the selected object directly behind it. In the Drop Shadow dialog box (Filter ➤ Stylize ➤ Drop Shadow), enter horizontal (X) and vertical (Y) offset values, as well as a darkness value for the drop shadow. Click OK to apply the drop shadow, or click on the Reset button to enter new settings. As you enter new values, a preview of the drop shadow will be shown in a window to the right (Figure 9.44).

9.44

The Drop Shadow
filter creates a
drop shadow be-
hind a selected
object.

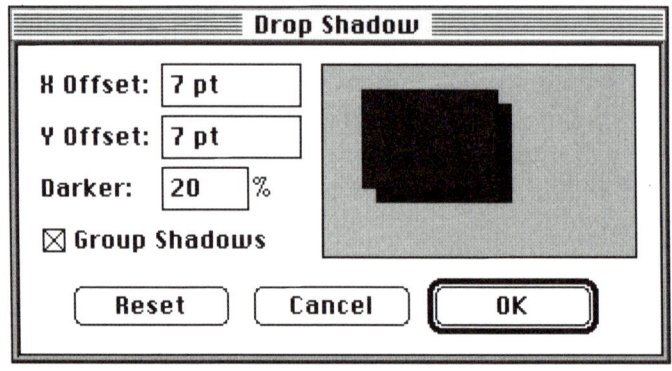

Punk

The Punk filter randomly moves the anchor points of an object to create a different look. To use the filter, first select an object. In the Filter ➤ Stylize menu, choose Punk. Enter an amount in the Punk dialog box to determine the amount of jaggedness to be applied (the higher the percentage, the jaggier it gets). Click OK to apply the Punk value to your selected object (Figure 9.45).

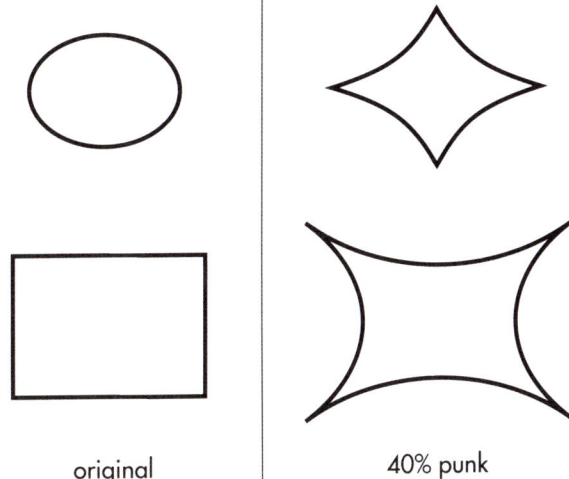

9.45

The Punk filter randomly moves the anchor points of an object.

original   40% punk

Round Corners

The Round Corners filter converts the corner points of the selected object into smooth corners. To use the filter, select Round Corners from the Filter ➤ Stylize menu. Enter a radius value for the corner roundness (the larger the value, the bigger the curve). Click on the OK button to apply the filter to a selected object.

Text

The eight filters in the Text submenu add several word processing and layout features to Adobe Illustrator. All of the Text filters are discussed at length in Chapter 6, *Working with Type in Illustrator*. To avoid repetition here, refer to Chapter 6 for a complete explanation of the Text filters and how to apply them to your text.

Summary

The plug-in filters we've discussed in this chapter greatly expand the design options that Illustrator provides. Many of them are great time savers, doing the hard work of searching, replacing, cutting, deleting, and adding different elements to a design for you. Others simply add special effects just for the fun of it.

As you become more familiar with each of the filters, you'll discover new ways to use them to improve your productivity. Most of them can do in a few seconds what previously would take several minutes to do—or longer. Enjoy them as much as possible.

CHAPTER

10

Creating Graphs

T E N

Graphs are a design element often overlooked until the yearly sales report is due. Then you go crazy trying to draw an informative graph by hand at the last minute, usually ending up with an average, nondescript graph. It gets the job done, but it could have been so much better if you'd only had the time…

Informative and attention-grabbing graphs are easy to create in Adobe Illustrator. Not only does it incorporate a graph feature directly in the drawing program, but as you will see, it allows you to add creative touches that other programs can only dream of. The software automates the tedious sizing and drawing stages of the process, leaving you with just the creative decisions to make. Information is entered or imported into a spreadsheet format and generated into the graph styles of your choice. Illustrator also offers the option of adding your own design elements into the graph, giving you a slick, customized result.

In this chapter we'll look at Adobe Illustrator's graph functions. We'll discuss how to set up a basic graph and how to enter and edit the data. We'll also delve into customizing a graph—how to make it a unique and individual statement about you, your company or client, and the information you are presenting.

Using the Graph Style Dialog Box

The first step in creating a graph is to open the Graph Style dialog box. This is where you will enter most of the graph preferences, such as the type of graph you want and the axis on which the graph should be placed.

To open the Graph Style dialog box, double-click on the Graph tool in the Toolbox, or in the Object ➤ Graphs menu choose Style. The Graph Style dialog box will open, presenting you with the choices outlined below (Figure 10.1).

The Graph Style
dialog box contains
preference settings
for the type of
graph you want
to create.

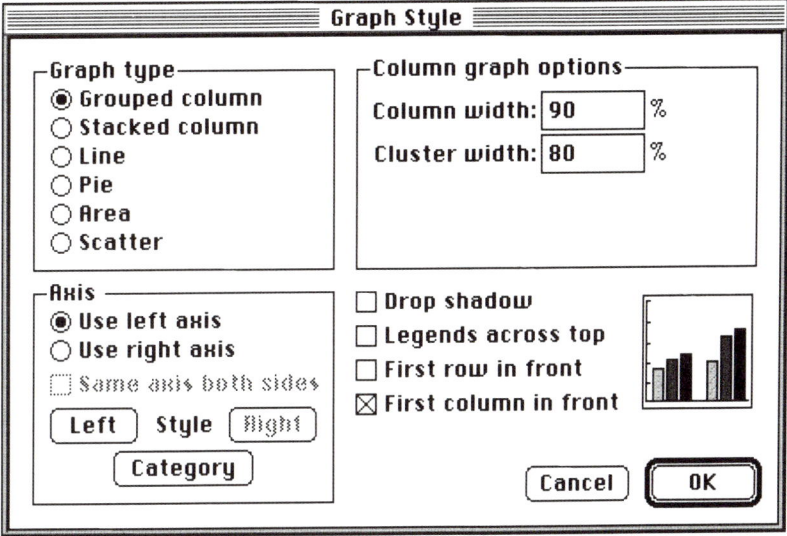

Graph Type

Illustrator lets you create graphs of any of the following types (the
Graph Style dialog box icons are shown in Figure 10.2):

- **Grouped column**   Side-by-side columns that compare two or
  more items over a period of time (Figure 10.2a).
- **Stacked column**   Stacked columns (one behind the other) that
  compare the progress of two or more items over a period of time
  (Figure 10.2b).
- **Line**   One or more lines that track the progress of one or more
  items over a period of time (Figure 10.2c).
- **Pie**   A circle showing divisions in percentages of a total item
  (Figure 10.2d).
- **Area**   Similar to the line graph, showing the progress of two or
  more items over a period of time. The area below each line is
  filled in an area graph (Figure 10.2e).
- **Scatter**   Items on a scatter graph are plotted on the X (horizontal) and Y (vertical) axes. Points can be placed at any coordinate,
  showing the concentration of data in different areas on the
  graph (Figure 10.2f).

10.2

The graph types
available in
Illustrator.

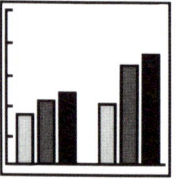

(A) A grouped column graph.

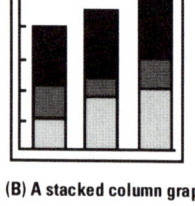

(B) A stacked column graph.

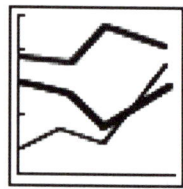

(C) A line graph.

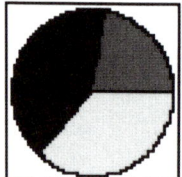

(D) A pie graph.

(E) An area graph.

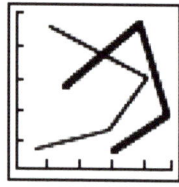

(F) A scatter graph.

Selecting the Axis

The Axis settings in the Graph Style dialog box let you choose how to place the Y (vertical) axis in your graph:

- **Use Left Axis** Places the Y axis along the left side of your graph.
- **Use Right Axis** Places the Y axis along the right side of your graph.
- **Same Axis Both Sides** Places the Y axis on both sides of your graph.

Once you have selected where the Y axis should be displayed, you can set the preferences for how that axis will look by clicking on the Left or Right button. If you have selected Same Axis Both Sides, you can set different preferences for each side by entering separate information in the Left and Right settings.

When you click on either the Left or Right buttons, the Graph Axis Style dialog box will appear (Figure 10.3). Here you can enter values for the way the axes are divided up, as well as specify the type of tick marks and number of divisions between each one (*tick marks* are lines along the axes that show the division of the graph values).

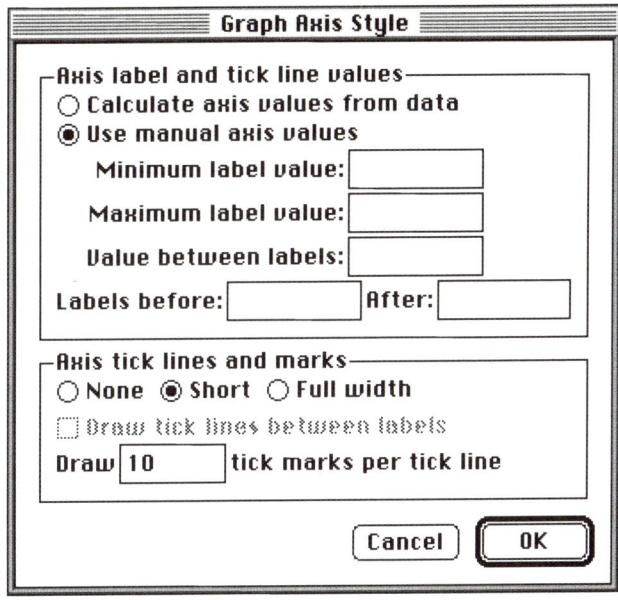

10.3

The Graph Axis
Style dialog box
contains settings
for the axis values
and how the tick
marks are
displayed.

Graph Options

Depending on the type of graph you have selected, the Graph Options
area of the Graph Style dialog box may present you with more choices
to make, as outlined below.

Column Graph Options

If you have chosen either of the column graphs, you can enter values in
the Options area that determine the width of each column and cluster
of columns (Figure 10.4). A column width value of 100 percent would
mean that the columns are flush against each other; the default of 90
percent means that some space will be left between each column. The
default of 80 percent for cluster width means that a little more space
will be left between each cluster of columns.

10.4

Column Graph options.

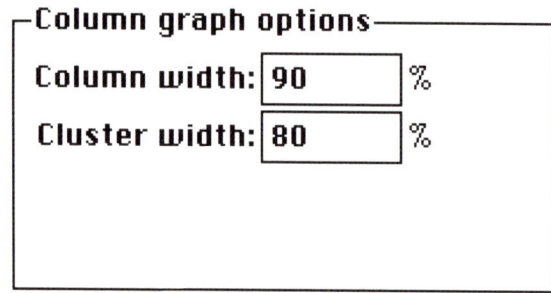

Line Graph Options

The Line Graph Options give you the following choices (Figure 10.5):

- **Mark Data Points** Places a square at each data point charted.
- **Connect Data Point** Joins the data points on the graphs with a line.
- **Fill Lines** Lets you specify the width of line created in the Connect Data Points option.
- **Edge-to-Edge Lines** Draws lines across the horizontal axis to make reading the data easier.

10.5

The Line Graph options.

```
┌─Line graph options────────
│ ⊠ Mark data points
│ ⊠ Connect data points
│     ☐ Fill lines
│        fill line width:[          ]
│ ☐ Edge-to-edge lines
```

Pie Graph Options

When you create a pie graph you will be given a choice (shown in Figure 10.6) of how to place the *legends*, the information that explains what each "slice" of the pie represents.

10.6

The Pie Graph options.

┌─**Pie graph options**─────────┐
│ ⦿ **Standard legends**   │
│ ○ **Legends in wedges**   │
│ ○ **No legends**   │
│   │
│   │
└──────────────────────────────┘

■ **Standard Legends**   Places the legends in a key format outside the pie, with a colored box next to each legend that matches the color of the corresponding pie slice.

■ **Legends in Wedges**   Places the information inside the pie slice to which it corresponds.

■ **No Legends**   Keeps legends from appearing anywhere.

Scatter Graph Options

The scatter graph options (Figure 10.7) are the same as for line graphs, except that there is no Edge-to-Edge Lines option.

10.7

The Scatter Graph options.

┌─**Scatter graph options**─────────┐
│ ☒ **Mark data points**   │
│ ☒ **Connect data points**   │
│   ☒ **Fill lines**   │
│   **Fill line width:** │6 pt│ │
│   │
└───────────────────────────────────┘

Other Graph Style Preferences

There are four other preferences in the Graph Style dialog box that stand alone (Figure 10.8):

- **Drop Shadow**   Creates a three-dimensional effect by putting a drop shadow behind the bars of a column graph, or behind an entire pie graph.
- **Legends Across Top**   Displays the graph legends across the top of the graph, instead of to the right.
- **First Row in Front**   Places the first row of data from the worksheet in front of other data in the graph.
- **First Column in Front**   Places the first column of data from the worksheet in front of other data in the graph.

10.8

The remaining preferences in the Graph Style dialog box refer to positioning information.

☐ Drop shadow
☐ Legends across top
☐ First row in front
☒ First column in front

WATCH OUT!

You must select **First Column in Front** whenever creating an area graph to prevent columns (that is, plotted areas) from disappearing behind each other.

Drawing a Graph

In order for the program to generate the graph you want, you have to feed it the dimensions for creating the graph. This can be done in one of two ways: by manually drawing an outline on your page, or by specifying the exact dimensions.

Manually Drawing a Graph Outline

You do not have to draw the graph to its exact size when using the manual method to specify the outline. What you draw can always be resized later to the correct proportions.

To draw the outline, click on the Graph tool. Click on your page where you want the upper-left corner of the graph to be and drag the mouse down and to the right, creating a rectangular outline. Release the mouse button when you are finished. Your preliminary graph and the Graph Data dialog box will automatically appear, ready to take you on to the next step.

You can also draw the outline from the center out. With the Graph tool selected, hold down the Option key and then click and drag with your mouse down and to the right. A rectangular outline will appear on your page. Release the mouse button when you are finished. Your preliminary graph and the Graph Data dialog box will automatically appear.

Drawing a Graph Outline
with Predetermined Dimensions

If you know the size your graph needs to be before you start, you can enter those dimensions in the Graph dialog box. The program will then generate a graph of that size.

To open the Graph dialog box, select the Graph tool and click and release on your page. The Graph dialog box will appear (Figure 10.9). Enter the Width and Height of your graph in the appropriate fields and click OK. Your preliminary graph and the Graph Data dialog box will automatically appear, ready to take you on to the next step.

10.9

Enter precise dimensions for your graph in the Graph dialog box.

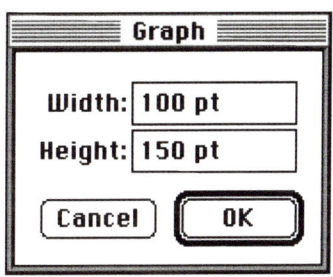

Entering Graph Data

The Graph Data dialog box (Figure 10.10) is a spreadsheet of rows and columns, into which you can enter the data for your graph. The dialog box can handle up to 32,767 rows by 32,767 columns worth of data—however, the memory on your Macintosh may not be quite so flexible.

10.10

The Graph Data dialog box contains rows and columns of cells, ready for your graph information to be entered.

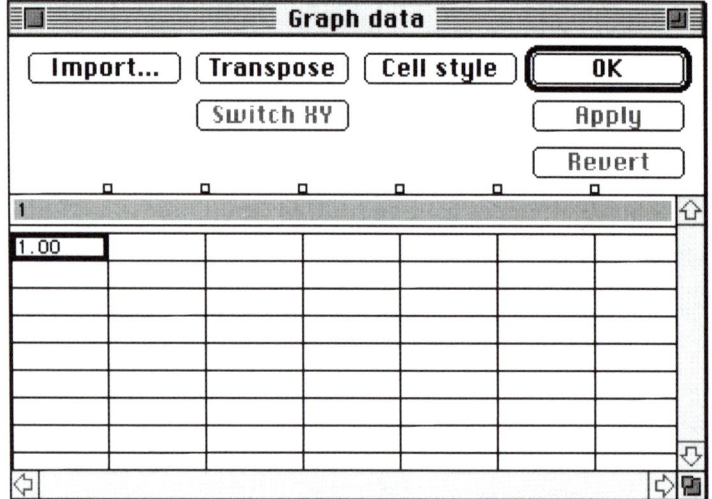

The worksheet area of the Graph Data dialog box is broken down into cells, the small boxes into which data will be entered. When you move your cursor from cell to cell with the arrow keys, a dark line will appear around the currently selected cell.

The cells are grouped into horizontal rows and vertical columns. The first row and column in the worksheet will contain the labels for the type of information you enter. Category labels, which will be positioned along the horizontal axis of the graph, go in the first column of the worksheet. Category labels signify the different categories of information that are compared in the graph. Legend labels, which will be positioned along the vertical axis of the graph, go in the first row of the worksheet. Legend labels show the differences in data between the categories.

At the top of the Graph Data worksheet area is a long horizontal row called the *entry line*. This is where all the data will be entered, one cell at a time.

AUTHOR'S NOTE

If your label consists solely of numbers, place quotation marks around them, for example, "1994". If you need to have quotation marks around the numerical information, enter two sets of quotation marks, for example, " "1994" ". This rule applies only to labels that consist strictly of numbers.

You can enter information into the cells in three ways: by manually entering it, by importing it from another file, or by pasting it in from another graph. Let's look at each of these options individually.

Manually Entering Information

With the Graph Data dialog box on your screen, enter the category and legend in the first column and row (Figure 10.11). Using the Tab key to

10.11

Information is entered in the entry line. When you hit the Tab or Return key, it is placed in the selected cell.

	Brown	Smith	McBride	Floyd		
Cows	6	10	2	5		
Horses	3	5	6	2		
Pigs	2	0	3	5		
Ducks	0	0	5	3		
Dogs	2	3	4	2		
Cats	3	2	1	5		

Graph data

Import... Transpose Cell style OK

Switch XY Apply Revert

10

move horizontally and the Return key to move vertically, enter the information cell by cell. (You can also move between cells using the arrow keys or by clicking the mouse.)

Remember, you move the black rectangle to select the proper cell, but the information itself must be entered on the entry line above. When you hit the Tab or Return key, the information will be entered into the currently selected cell, and the black rectangle will move on to the next cell.

Click OK when you are done. A graph created according to your specifications will appear (Figure 10.12).

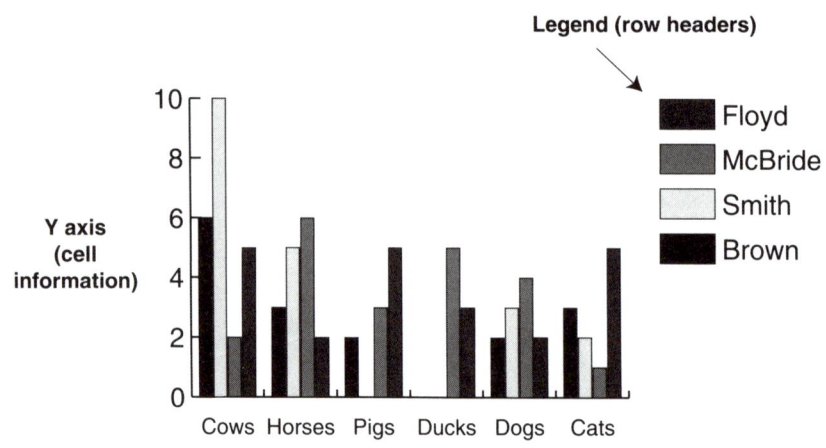

10.12

An example of an Illustrator graph, showing the type and number of animals owned by each farmer.

Importing Data into the Worksheet

A text file containing data created in another application can be imported into the worksheet if it has been set up correctly. In order for the file to import correctly, each cell must be separated by a tab (to create the columns), and there must be a carriage return at the end of each row. Note that the file must be saved as a *text* (ASCII) file—a file saved in a format such as *Normal* in MS Word won't work.

To import a data file into the worksheet, first click on the first cell in the top-left corner of the worksheet where data should appear. This selects it as the entry point for the imported file. Click on the Import button at the top of the dialog box, select the name of the text file, and click on the Open button. The data will flow, across and then down, into the cells. Click on the OK button to see the graph.

Pasting Data into the Worksheet

You can also bring data into the worksheet from another application via the Clipboard. Again, the data must be set up properly in order for it to work, with one tab between columns and a return at the end of each row.

Open the application and the file containing the data. Select and copy the data to the Clipboard. Go back into Illustrator and click on the cell in the upper-left corner of the worksheet. Paste (⌘-V) the information from the Clipboard into the worksheet. Click OK to see the graph.

Editing Graph Data

You can edit the data in a graph after creating the graph. To do this, open the graph file if it isn't already opened, and under the Object ➤ Graphs menu, choose Data. The Graph Data worksheet will appear. Use the arrow keys to move to the cells that need to be changed. The cell will become highlighted. Enter the new information on the entry line to replace the incorrect entry. Remember, you must hit the Tab or Return key in order for the information to be placed in the currently selected cell.

WATCH OUT!

If you ungroup the graph elements on your page, they will cease to be recognized as part of the graph and they cannot be edited with any of the graph editing tools. Although you may eventually need to ungroup the elements to change some of the graph styling, make sure the correct data has been entered before ungrouping the graph. Ungrouped graphs can still be edited using the tools in the Toolbox, but you will not have access to the Graph Data and Graph Style tools.

Manipulating Graph Data Elements

The Graph Data dialog box can also be used to manipulate the data in your graph. Changes that you can make include transposing the information in rows and columns, adjusting the column width and number of decimals for numerals entered in the worksheet, and switching the X and Y axes for scatter graphs.

Transposing Data in Rows and Columns

The Transpose command in the Graph Data dialog box will automatically switch rows to columns, and vice versa. This is helpful if you have all the information entered in the worksheet, only to discover, on viewing the graph, that you've entered (or imported) the information on the wrong axes.

To use the Transpose command, select the entire graph and in the Object ➤ Graphs menu, select Data. The Graph Data dialog box will appear, showing the data as you originally entered it into the worksheet. Click on the Transpose button, and the information will switch automatically, placing what was in rows into columns and vice versa. Click on Apply to see the changes take place in your graph, and on the OK button to keep the changes.

Transposing the Axes in a Scatter Graph

With the Switch XY button in the Graph Data dialog box, you can switch the X and Y axes on a scatter graph. This button works *only* with scatter graphs—use the Transpose button to switch data around on other types of graphs.

To switch the X and Y axes of a scatter graph, select the graph and in the Object ➤ Graphs menu choose Graph Data. In the Graph Data dialog box, click on the Switch XY button. Click OK to exit the dialog box and see the changes in your graph.

Customizing the Cells

Often the information you need to enter into the worksheet may be longer than the default cell size of seven characters. You can change the size of the cell by clicking on the Cell Style button at the top of the Graph Data dialog box. In the Cell Style box, enter a new cell width, from 3 to 20 characters (Figure 10.13).

10.13

The Cell Style dialog box changes the width of and number of decimal places in each cell.

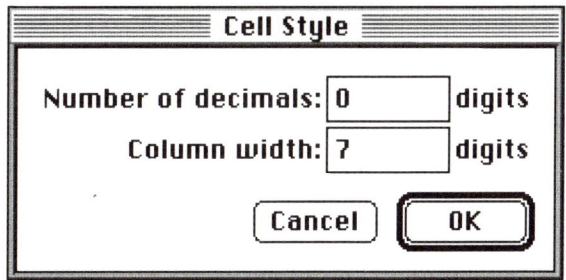

You can also change the number of digits that can be entered after a decimal in each cell. In the Cell Style box, enter the number of digits you want after a decimal, from 0 to 10 digits. Click on the OK button to return to the Graph Data dialog box. The cells in the worksheet will change accordingly.

Customizing Graphs

Once the data has been entered and you have a preliminary graph visible on your page, there are still many ways you can customize the graph to make it more eye-catching. However, it is important to remember that ungrouping the graph in any way will make it impossible to use the Graph Data features to change the graph in the future. Still, by using the Direct or Group Selection tools, you can make several changes to a graph while retaining its connections.

Selecting and Changing Elements

Illustrator automatically groups together related elements of a graph. For instance, in a graph that compares quarterly results for different divisions of a company, all the bars for a particular division are grouped together and filled with the same color. This makes it easy to select groups of elements and change them globally throughout the graph. The same holds true for the text elements of a graph.

The elements of a graph can be styled in a variety of ways. You can change the color, shade, font, and size of the different elements using the Paint Style and Character palettes. You can also use any of the transformation tools to scale, shear, rotate, or reflect graph parts (or the graph as a whole) to create new looks.

INSIDE INFO

Always remember to use the Group or Direct Selection tools when editing the elements of a graph. Not only does this help the graph retain its connections to the Graph Data worksheet, it also allows you to make changes globally to connected elements.

Changing the Fill Color and Shade

Using the Group Selection tool, you can easily change the color of the bars, lines, or markers in a graph. For example, to change the color of the bars in a column graph, click twice on a bar with the Group Selection tool. All the related bars that should be colored the same way will become selected. Use the Paint Style palette (⌘-I) to change the shade or color of the bars. Repeat this for each of the elements you wish to change.

To select the legend box along with the bars, double-click with the Group Selection tool on a legend box. The box and its associated bars will become selected and ready for changes.

Changing the Font
and Type Size of Graph Text

Like the other elements of the graph, text in a graph can be selected in groups with the Group Selection tool. Click with the tool once to select one text entry, or twice to select all of the type in an area. The text in the legend area is grouped into one section, the text along the X axis forms another group, and the text along the Y axis is another group.

Once you have selected a group of text items, use the Character palette (⌘-T) to change the font and point size of the type.

Using and Creating Specialized Graph Designs

To make a graph even more attractive, you can use specialized graph designs to represent the bars or markers in a graph. For example, a graph representing the monthly sales for an oil company might use barrels to represent each of the bars in a column graph. A report on the yearly snowfall at different ski resorts might use snowflake markers on a line graph.

You can create these designs yourself, or select a design from the collection included in Illustrator's Sample Files folder. To open these for your use, use the Import Styles command under the File menu. Locate the Sample Files folder and open the Column & Marker and Graph Styles files. This loads them into the file you currently have open, making them accessible.

Creating Your Own Graph Design

If you prefer to create your own design for use in a graph, simply draw the design on a page. Since you will need to keep the design close to the same width as the existing bars in your graph, make a copy of a bar from your graph and paste it down on the page to use as a guide as you draw the new design.

Once your design is complete, place a rectangle around the design and send it to the back. You do not need to fill or stroke the rectangle—it just needs to be placed behind the entire design.

Use the Group Selection tool to select the entire design and the rectangle behind it. In the Object ➤ Graph menu choose Design, and the Design dialog box will appear (Figure 10.14). Click on the New button to

The Design dialog box, showing the list of designs available for use in customizing your graph.

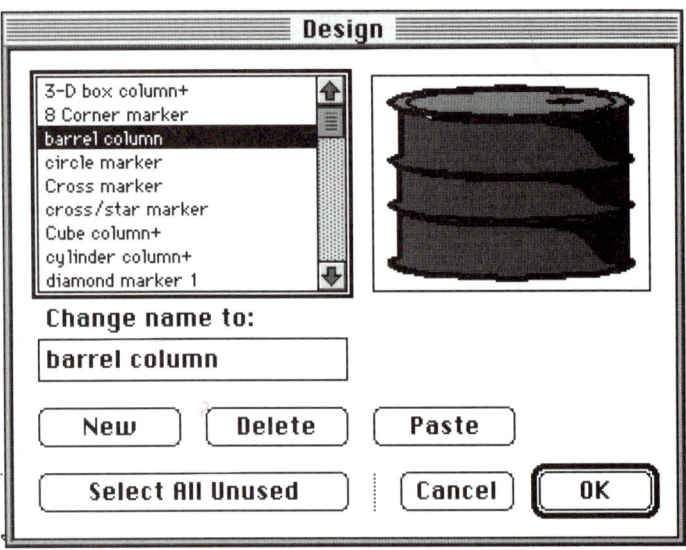

see a preview of the selected items in the box to the right. Give your design a name and click on the OK button. Your design will now be added to the list of designs available for use in your graph.

Applying a Design to a Bar Graph

When you are ready to add designs to your graph, open the graph and use the Group Selection tool to select the bars to be replaced with the new design.

In the Object ➤ Graphs menu, select Column. The Graph Column Design dialog box will appear (Figure 10.15). First choose the design name from the scrolling list in the bottom-left corner of the dialog box. A preview of the design will appear to the right.

In the upper-left corner, choose how you want the design to be displayed from the Column Design Type list:

- ■ **Vertically Scaled** Scales the design to fill the vertical height of the column.
- ■ **Uniformly Scaled** Scales both the height and width of the design until it reaches the appropriate vertical height.

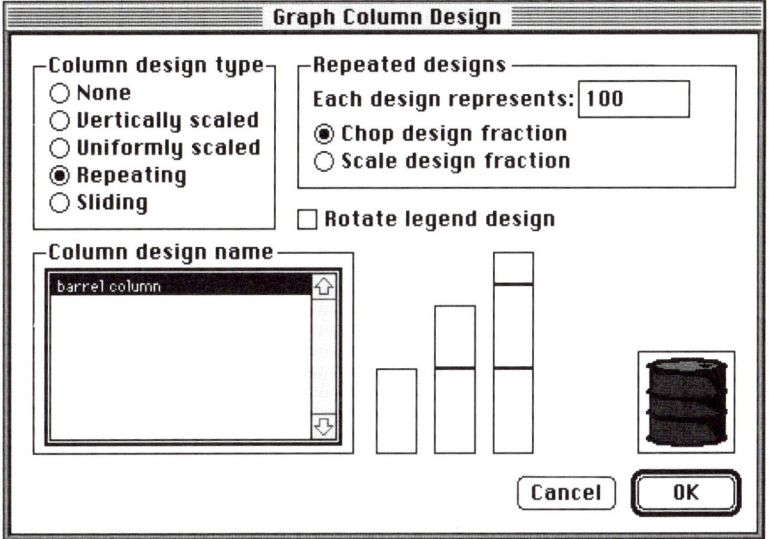

- **Repeating** Stacks small uniform copies of the design upon each other to reach the appropriate vertical height. You can define the value that each copy of the design represents.

- **Sliding** Is similar to Vertically Scaled, only you can choose the parts of the design that should be scaled, leaving other parts unscaled.

In the Repeated Designs area (only available if you have chosen Repeating from the Column Design Type list), you can choose the value of each repeated design—for example, how much oil each barrel symbol on the graph represents. You can also choose whether fractions of the value should be scaled or represented by a chopped version of the design. For instance, if you decide that each barrel represents 10 units, the number 15 would be represented by one barrel, plus half of another.

Finally, if you want to rotate the way the design is presented in the legend listing, click on Rotate Legend Design. This will cause a design such as a pencil to rotate and be placed horizontally instead of vertically next to each legend entry.

Click on the OK button when you are finished to see the changes take place in your graph (Figure 10.16). Add a heading or extra explanatory type to your graph if needed, or go back to the Graph Style dialog box to adjust the tick marks or axis values if necessary. When you are satisfied with the results, your graph is finished.

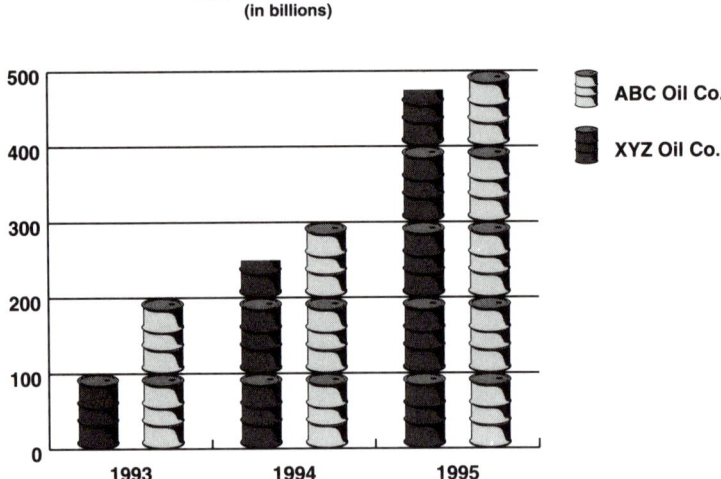

10.16

A finished graph using the barrel design.

Placing Markers on a Line or Scatter Graph

If you want to use specialized graphic designs in a Line or Scatter graph, choose Marker from the Object ➤ Graphs menu instead of Column. This brings up the Graph Marker Design dialog box, which is similar to the Graph Column Design dialog box (Figure 10.17). Click the On Data Point button and then choose a design name from the list below. Click on the OK button to apply the design to your graph. Figure 10.18 shows a line graph with different markers for each of its three data series.

10.17

The Graph Marker Design dialog box.

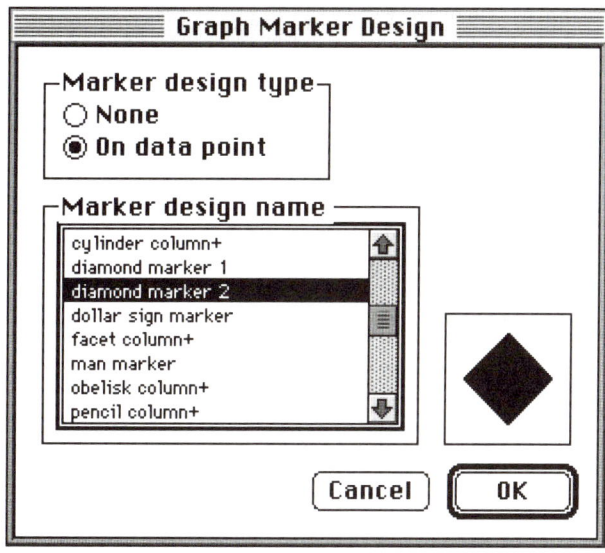

10.18

A line graph using markers from the Graph Marker Design dialog box.

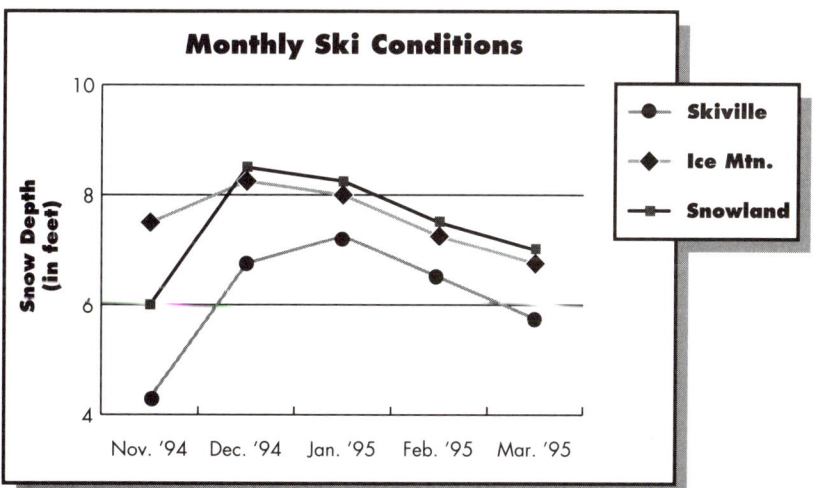

WATCH OUT!

You may need to go into the design and fill the markers with different colors. Unfortunately, once you apply the markers you no longer can select them by group to make a global change. This means you need to select each appropriate marker with the Group Selection tool and apply a new fill color individually.

Summary

Attractive and informative graphs are easy to create using the Graph function in Adobe Illustrator. The Graph tools and commands automate much of the hard work, leaving the designing aspects up to you. Invest a little time to practice using the different graph styles. When you become familiar with them, you'll soon be creating your own graph designs with ease.

CHAPTER

11

Adobe Acrobat, Adobe Separator, and Adobe Type Manager

E L E V E N

In this chapter, we'll look at the peripheral programs included with your Adobe Illustrator package: Adobe Acrobat, Adobe Separator, and Adobe Type Manager. Each of these programs can play an important part in the way you use Adobe Illustrator. We'll begin with Adobe Type Manager.

Adobe Type Manager

Adobe Type Manager (ATM) is a font utility package that can render sharp versions of any size PostScript font on your screen. Traditionally, each point size of a PostScript font requires a separate font file to be loaded into your system. With ATM, only the outline fonts and one bitmapped font of any size are installed. ATM will use this information to create the other sizes as needed.

ATM is automatically loaded onto your machine when you install Adobe Illustrator. You don't work directly with the program; it does its thing behind the scenes. However, you can manually turn ATM off and on in the ATM control panel, as well as set different options for its use.

The ATM Control Panel

The ATM control panel device allows you to turn the ATM program off and on, as well as change the font cache, line spacing, and character shapes. To open the ATM control panel, go to the Apple menu and choose Control Panels. Double-click on ATM, and the ATM control panel will open (Figure 11.1).

You can also temporarily disable ATM by holding down the mouse button while restarting your Mac. This will turn ATM off until the next time you restart your Mac.

I I . I

**The ATM
control panel.**

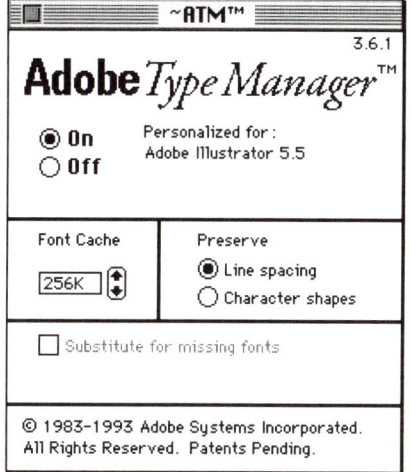

Increasing the Font Cache

The *font cache* is a portion of your Mac's memory set aside to store the font data that ATM produces. The default font cache is 256K, although you may need to make it larger. If your program seems to slow down when you scroll through a font menu, or if the font on your screen defaults to Courier, you need to increase your font cache. The setting in the control panel increases or decreases by 32K each time you click on an arrow next to the field. After you select a new font cache value, you will need to restart your Macintosh before the cache is actually increased.

Line Spacing and Character Shapes

The Line Spacing and Character Shape options are included in the control panel because ATM can affect the automatic leading, as well as compress or clip characters, when used with certain fonts. It is recommended that you leave the Line Spacing option on unless you actually see characters being clipped or compressed unacceptably. This will keep your line and page breaks uniform.

Adobe Acrobat

Adobe Acrobat is a program that lets you view a document even if you don't have the associated fonts or the program used to create it. You can use Acrobat to send files to others who may not have Adobe Illustrator loaded on their systems. There are several components to Acrobat: the Exchange program lets you share files with other users; the Distiller program lets you convert files to PDF (portable document format); and the Reader program can be distributed with your PDF file to a client who doesn't have Illustrator.

Illustrator PDF files can be imported and opened in any program that supports PDF, such as the most recent versions of QuarkXPress and MacDraw. PDF files created in any other program can also be imported, edited, and printed in Illustrator.

Saving a File as PDF

PDF files can be created directly in Illustrator, or within the Acrobat Distiller application, which is included with Illustrator 5.5. (It is also sold separately, as are all the components of Acrobat.) If you have the file open in Illustrator, simply select Save As from the File menu. In the Save As dialog box, choose PDF from the Format pop-up menu. Name the file as you normally would and click on the Save button.

The Acrobat Distiller application can create a PDF file out of *any* Post-Script file, even if it was not originally created in Illustrator. To use this method, open the Adobe Distiller application from the Adobe Illustrator folder. From within the Distiller, open the PostScript file by using the keyboard shortcut ⌘-O. In the Open dialog box, select the file to be converted and click on the Open button. If you need to rename and relocate the file, do so in the next dialog box that appears. Then click on the Save button. The file will be converted and saved.

Opening a PDF File in Illustrator

Opening a PDF file in Illustrator is as easy as opening any other file. In the Open dialog box (⌘-O), select the name of the PDF file and click on the Open button. The file will open in a new Illustrator window. If the file is more than one page long, a dialog box will give you the option of which page to view.

You can now edit the document. When you are finished, you can save it as a regular Illustrator file or a new PDF file, or you can save it back to the original PDF file. However, if you choose the latter, Illustrator will not be able to re-embed any fonts that might be used into the old PDF file.

Adobe Separator

The Adobe Separator program is an individual application found in the Adobe Illustrator application folder. Adobe Separator prepares Illustrator EPS files so that when printed, the colors will separate onto different pieces of film (known as *color separations*). Adobe Separator also lets you specify information such as line screen values, resolution, orientation, emulsion and so forth to the file you separate.

Opening a File in Adobe Separator

First, open Adobe Separator from the Adobe Illustrator application folder. Using the Open command (⌘-O), select the file to be separated and click on the Open button.

If you haven't run the Adobe Separator application before, you will have to select a PPD (PostScript Printer Definition) file before you can continue. If you switch printers, you need to reselect a PPD file. A PPD file provides the program with information about the output device you will use. Since different devices require different setup information, Adobe Illustrator includes an exhaustive list of PPD files.

Choose the PPD file that matches the printer you will be using. If you are sending your files out to a service bureau to be printed, contact them before going any further. They will be able to tell you which PPD to use. Click on the Open button when you have made your choice.

Setting the Specifications

Now that your file is open, you can begin to select the proper specifications. Your file is displayed in the Separator Setup window (Figure 11.2). This shows a preview of what the film separations will look like.

11.2

The Adobe Separator Setup window.

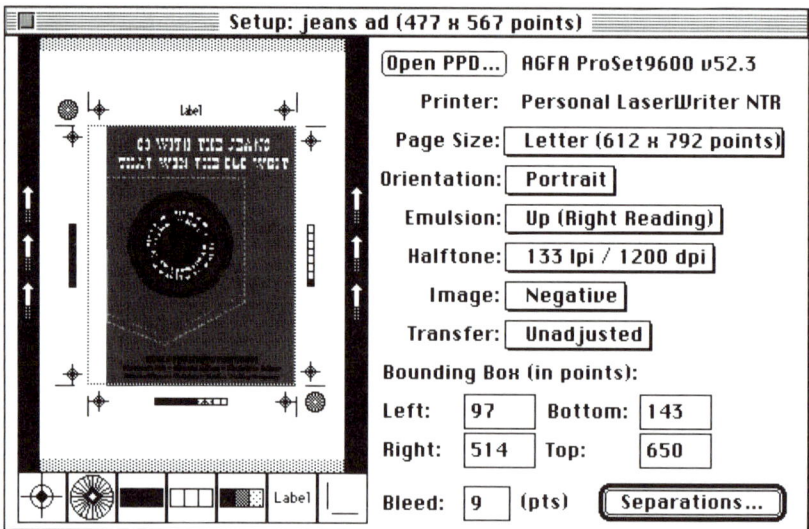

The right side of the Setup window shows the default settings for the PPD file you selected:

- **Page Size**   The size of the page that the image will require to completely print all areas of the design, including crop marks and registration marks.

- **Orientation**   The positioning of the page, either portrait (vertical) or landscape (horizontal). Depending on the width of the film you use, you may be able to conserve film by printing an image landscaped.

- **Emulsion**   The dull side of film, coated with a silver halide emulsion. Film is either right-reading emulsion up, or right-reading emulsion down.

- **Halftone**   The line screen, or lines per inch (lpi), and resolution, or dots per inch (dpi), determine the quality of the printed image. Higher values for each will usually result in finer image; lower values will result in a coarser image. The optimum value for any image depends on both on the ability of the output device you will use and the quality of the image itself.

- **Image**   Negative or positive. Negative (the US standard) produces reversed negative images on film. Positive (the European and Japanese standard) produces a positive image.

- **Transfer**   Adjusts the output of Separator based on densitometer readings taken from your image setter to compensate for differences in tint values between your image and the machine.

- **Bounding Box**   Sets the boundary around your image where crop marks will print.

- **Bleed**   The area outside of the bounding box where colors must extend if they are to cover the entire page. A bleed of at least 9 points (1/8") is an industry standard. This ensures that the color of your page will print correctly even if a page isn't trimmed exactly perfect after printing.

As you can see, the specifications for setting up color separations are complex and highly technical; and a book of this scope cannot explain them in depth. Fortunately, you won't usually need to change the default settings once you have the correct PPD file selected. If you are a novice to the prepress and printing world, take the time now to find out more about how to properly set up your film for color separation output. Trial-and-error is an expensive way to learn about this field. Contact your service bureau or press for more information about their film requirements, or their requirements for files that they will output to film. A customer service representative will be more than happy to explain their requirements to you.

WATCH OUT!

> You should ALWAYS consult with your printing vendor before setting the specifications in Adobe Separator. They will be able to give you a list of their output requirements. If you are preparing your own film for a client, be sure to check with them as well. They may have different requirements than what you would normally use to produce film. Checking in advance will save you the time and money of having to output the same film over again.

Adding Printer Marks

When you open a file in Adobe Separator, numerous marks are automatically added around the edges of the image, as shown in the preview window. These are the various printer marks used to ensure the proper alignment, screen angle, and film quality of color separations.

Crop marks, as you probably know, are used to show where an image will be trimmed after printing. Star and crosshair *register marks* are used to align properly the different pieces of film generated for each color on a page. *Color bars* show how consistently color is being printing during different stages of printing. *Gradient tint bars* show the consistency of tint values throughout a print run. *Labels* are used to show the file name, separation color, line screen and angle on each piece of film.

While Adobe Separator places all of these printer marks on your film automatically, you can add or delete any of the marks directly on the page preview in the Separator Setup window.

Making Separations

When the settings and printer marks are complete, click on the Separations button. The Separations dialog box will appear (Figure 11.3). Here you can choose which colors to output, as well as the frequency and screen angle of each. If you are printing custom colors, you can choose to convert them to process colors in the Convert to Process field.

11.3

The Separations dialog box.

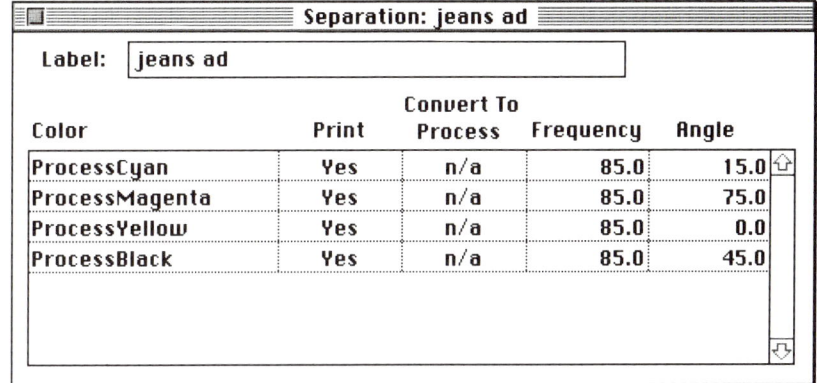

To make changes in any field, click directly on the field itself.

When you are finished, close the Separations dialog box by clicking in the upper-left corner.

Saving the Separations

To save your color-separated document, use the Save Separations command (⌘-S). When you do, you will actually be saving *a separate file for each of the four colors.* You must save a separation in this way in order to properly print it on an image setter. The Save Separations command handles this process automatically. The dialog box will automatically return to your screen each time you click Save, until all the color separations have been saved. Each separation file will have a different extension added onto its name—.C for the cyan file, .Y for the yellow file, and so forth.

Printing the Separations

To print your separations, select Print All Separations from the File menu (⌘-S). Each separation will queue up and print in order to the output device you have selected in your Chooser.

If you are sending the file out to a service bureau to be printed, send the original art file along with the four separation files. You can also print a laser composite to send along to the service bureau for use as a gray-scale proof:

- With the file open in Adobe Separator, set the Emulsion field to Up (Right Reading). Set the Image field to Positive.

- In the File menu, choose Print Composite. Make sure your Chooser is set to print to a laser printer before invoking the Print command.

Summary

The peripheral programs included with Illustrator are handy utilities that you will use often for viewing, exchanging, and printing the designs you create. To further enhance your skills, let's move on now to the final chapter of this book, Special Projects. Here you will find three design projects that you can create—or use as the starting point for expanding on your own ideas.

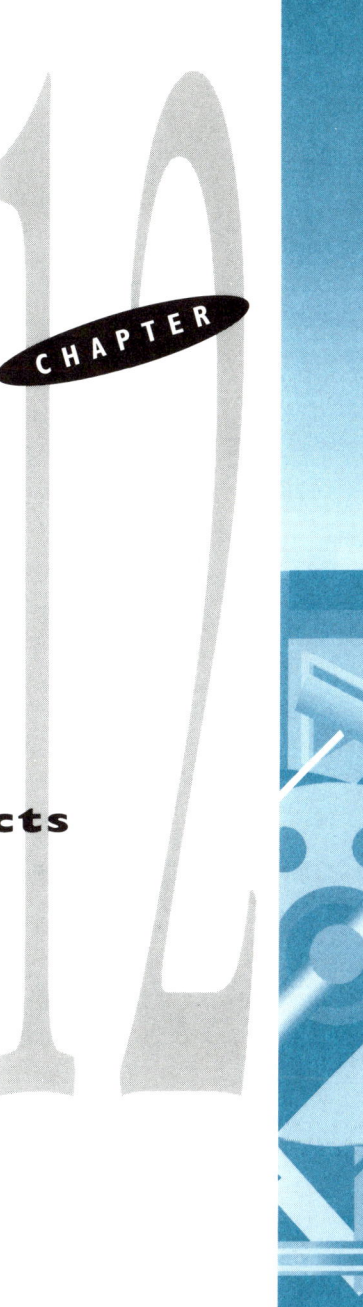

Special Projects

CHAPTER

12

T W E L V E

This chapter is a chance for you to take what you've learned about Adobe Illustrator and put it to practical use. The three projects you'll tackle here range from very easy to advanced. Not only will they provide you with practical Illustrator experience, but they can also provide a starting point for similar projects that you may encounter in the future.

The smallest and easiest project is designing a business card. From there, you'll proceed to designing an artistic poster for an advertisement. The final project will take you into the world of publishing, where you'll compile a two-page layout for a magazine.

Designing a Business Card

Business cards should be a direct reflection of the company they represent. Is the company "solid and respectable," like a law firm? Or are they a youthful group of clothing designers who want their card to reflect today's fashion trends? While the main purpose of a business card is to give information—the company name, address, and phone number—the fonts and design you choose in your design will convey a wealth of information about the company's image to their clients.

For this project, you will create a business card for a fictional ski resort (Figure 12.1). To begin, open a new document (⌘-N) and enlarge the view to 100 percent.

INSIDE INFO

To quickly zoom in or out to a 100 percent screen size, double click on the Zoom tool in the Toolbox.

12.1

**The finished
business card.**

Drawing the Card Outline

Using the Rectangle tool, draw the outline of the card itself. A standard business card is 21 picas wide by 12 picas high (3.5" × 2"). Click on the Rectangle tool and hold down the Option key while clicking on your page. The Rectangle dialog box will appear. Enter the width and height in points (252 points wide by 144 points high) and click on the OK button.

Change the rectangle that appears into a guide using the Make Guides command (⌘-5). If you don't already have the rulers open in your document, open them now (⌘-R) and make the top left corner of the rectangle the 0,0 point for the rulers. Your project should now look like Figure 12.2.

12.2

**The outline of the
business card is
made into a guide.**

Adding the Rules

The design of the business card includes two vertical rules and one horizontal rule. The first vertical rule is a 0.5-point rule approximately 100 points long. It is placed 1.5 picas from the left edge of the card, and 1.5 picas up from the bottom of the card.

The second vertical rule is placed to the right of the first. It is a 2-pt rule, approximately 125 points long. It is placed 6 points to the right of the first rule (2 picas from the left edge of the card) and 9 points up from the bottom of the card.

The horizontal rule is a 0.5-point rule, approximately 228 points long. It is placed 2.5 picas up from the bottom of the card and 1.5 picas from the left edge. With the rules placed, the card should now look like Figure 12.3.

1 2.3

The business card outline with rules in place.

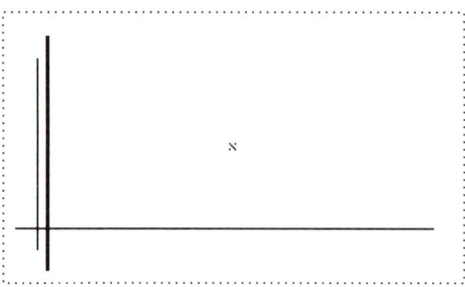

Adding the Business Name and Address

The logo for this fictional business is the name itself, or rather a version of it in a certain font. With your Adobe Illustrator 5.5 package came numerous fonts, among them one called Pepita MT. This is the font used in the name of the business.

With the Type tool selected, click your cursor approximately 3.5 picas in from both the bottom and the left side of the card. Type the words **Snowland Ski Resort** and then open the Character palette. Change the size of the type to 24 point, and the font to Pepita MT.

Select the Type tool again and click on the point that is approximately 1.5 picas from the bottom and 3.5 picas from the left side of the card. Before you begin typing, change the font and size in the Character palette to 8 point Helvetica Regular. Now on your page, type in **P.O. Box 1348, Alpine Valley, CO 75600 800-555-5555**, adding a little extra space between the address and the telephone number. The business card should now look like Figure 12.4.

12.4

The business card with the company name and address in place.

Adding the Employee Name

The final step in creating the card is to add the employee name. Regardless of how fancy the company logo is, the employee name is traditionally in a fairly simple typeface to ensure readability. For our card, the employee name is in Helvetica Bold, with the employee's title underneath in Helvetica Regular.

Using the Type tool, click on the card and type in the employee name and title. Now click on the Selection tool, and in the Type ➤ Alignment menu, choose Center (⌘-Shift-C). Click and drag the type into the proper position, centered over the company name. The top of the employee's name should be approximately 2 picas from the top of the card, and the center anchor point of the type should be about 11 picas from the left side of the card.

Click on the card outline now. If it does not become selected, you may need to unlock it first (⌘-7). Release the guide (⌘-6), and make sure the rectangle is stroked with a 0.5-point black rule, and has no fill. Glance back at Figure 12.1 to see the completed business card.

Creating a Poster Advertisement

Your next assignment, should you choose to accept it, is to create an artsy poster/advertisement. Often you'll see advertisements such as these being sold as frameable art in poster galleries. The emphasis for this assignment is definitely creativity—use your imagination and add to this design if you like.

For a poster such as this, there's generally a twist that lures the reader in. Our mythical advertiser is a culinary academy that is promoting a cooking contest for its students. Our poster, therefore, uniquely illustrates a particular dish, Duck à l'Orange, as shown in Figure 12.5.

Setting Up the Design

Before we get started drawing, let's set up the gradients that will be used in this design. Open a new document (⌘-N) and then open the Gradient palette by selecting Gradient from either the Object menu or the Window menu (both commands work the same), or by double clicking on the Gradient tool in the Toolbox.

The first gradient you need to create is the one used in the oranges. Click on the New button in the Gradient palette, and then click on the white arrow under the right side of the large gradient slider bar above. In the lower-left area of the palette, click on the Process Color button and make this first color 67 percent magenta, 90 percent yellow.

Click on the arrow under the left end of the large slider bar now. Make this color 20 percent magenta, 40 percent yellow. Move the midpoint diamond above the slider bar down (left) until the field to the right of the bar says 30 percent. Make sure the Radial button in the lower-right is selected. Name this gradient **Orange Blend** (Figure 12.6).

The second blend will be used for the sky. Now Scroll through the list of blend names until you find the one named Black and White. Click on the name to highlight it; then click on the Duplicate button. Change the color on the right end of the gradient slider bar to 50 percent black, and

12.5

Duck à l'Orange,
Adobe Illustrator-
style.

the color on the left end to white. Move the midpoint diamond above
to 75 percent and make sure the Linear button is selected. Rename this
gradient **Gray Blend** and close the Gradient palette.

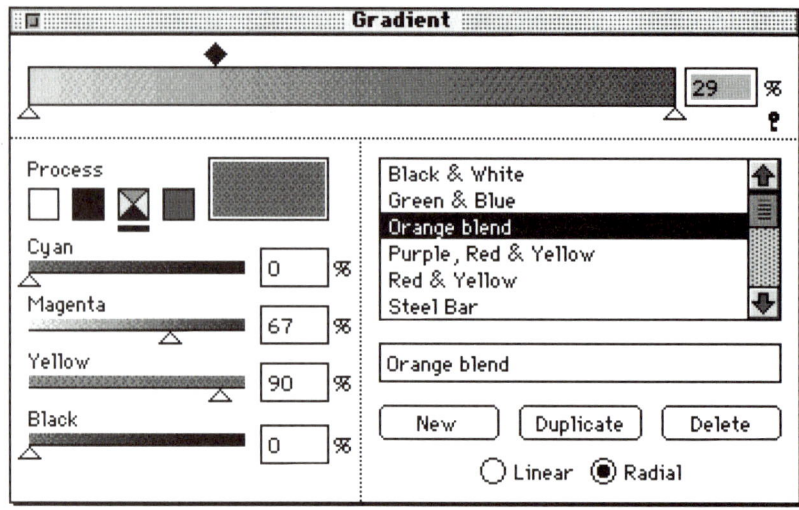

Drawing the Orange

This design is easiest to draw if we start with the most complex objects first, and add the background later. Open the rulers (⌘-R) in your document now, if they aren't already open.

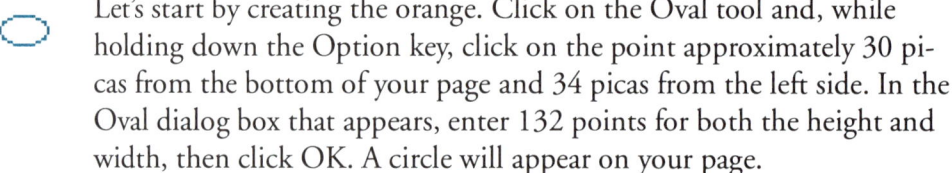

Let's start by creating the orange. Click on the Oval tool and, while holding down the Option key, click on the point approximately 30 picas from the bottom of your page and 34 picas from the left side. In the Oval dialog box that appears, enter 132 points for both the height and width, then click OK. A circle will appear on your page.

Use the Paint Style palette (⌘-I) and fill the circle with the orange blend you created earlier. With the Gradient tool, readjust the blend so that the lightest part is in the upper-left area of the circle.

Now let's create the stem of the orange. Click again on the Oval tool, and holding down the Option key, click on the artboard next to the orange circle. Enter a width of 10 points and a height of 7 points and click OK. Fill the oval with 20 percent magenta, 40 percent yellow, and 50 percent black. Stroke the oval with a 0.25-point rule of 90 percent cyan and 100 percent yellow. You can also enter the percentage values manually by clicking on the respective fields and typing. Use the Tab key to move to the next field.

Around this oval, use the Pen tool to create the green leaves as shown in Figure 12.7. To do this, click with the Pen tool anywhere on the circle, move away from the circle and click, then move back to the edge of the circle and click again to create a triangular shape. Continue around the circle until you have surrounded the circle with six green leaves. In the example, I have curved some of the lines to give the leaves a more rounded look.

12.7

The stem with leaves.

In the Paint Style palette, fill the leaves with 50 percent yellow and 50 percent cyan, and give them a 1-point stroke of 90 percent yellow and 60 percent magenta. If necessary, bring the oval to the front so that it is resting on top of the leaves.

 With the Selection tool, select and group (⌘-G) the leaves and stem, then move them over the top of the orange circle. Position them in the upper right area of the circle, as shown in Figure 12.8.

 With the grouped stem and leaves still selected, click on the Rotate tool and while holding down the Option key, click on the stem. Enter a rotation value of −15 degrees, and click OK.

Creating the Ducks

The "ducks" in the poster are easily created using the Pen tool to draw a "V" shape. Simply click once on your page, then click below and drag the mouse a little to create a curve. Click again above and to the right, again lower and to the left, and rejoin the final point to the first.

12.8

The finished orange.

 Use the Convert Direction Point tool if necessary on any of the points to create more of a curve. Fill the shape with the standard Black and White gradient from the Paint Style palette (⌘-I). Adjust the gradient with the Gradient tool so that the wing tips are darker than the body area, as shown in Figure 12.9.

12.9

Use the Pen tool to create bird-like shapes.

Make two or three birds with different wing positions; then use the Blend tool to create intermediate shapes between them. Click with the Blend tool on one bird, then on the other. Enter a Step value in the Blend dialog box for the number of birds you want to create, and click OK. The new birds that appear will be grouped; ungroup them now so that you can reposition the birds around the orange on your page—rotate a few of them to vary the look (Figure 12.10).

1 2 . 1 0

Place the birds around the orange and vary their positions by rotating a few.

Creating the Background

Now let's create the background. Double-click on the Oval tool in the Toolbox—a small plus sign will appear in the middle, meaning the shape will be drawn from the center out. You can also just hold down the Option key while using the regular Oval tool to achieve the same results. Click in the middle of your page and hold down the Shift key to draw a very large circle, one that extends to each margin line.

With the Scissors tool, cut the circle in half by clicking on each of the anchor points at the sides of the circle. Deselect all (⌘-Shift-A), and with the Selection tool, click on the bottom half of the circle and delete it. Reposition the remaining half circle now so that it is evenly centered between the left and right margins, with the top of the curve about 1 pica from the top margin of the page.

With the Pen tool, draw a line from the left margin to the right, approximately 15 picas from the bottom of the page.

Use the Direct Selection tool to select the right end of the line, hold down the Shift key, and click on the right anchor point of the large half circle above. Join them together with the Join command (⌘-J); then select and join the left sides together as well. Readjust the sides now, if necessary, to even the sides.

In the Paint Style palette (⌘-I), fill this shape with the Gray Blend gradient you created earlier. With the Gradient tool, click on the bottom of the arched shape, drag to the top, and release the mouse button. This repositions the blend so that the lightest color is at the bottom of the shape.

With the shape still selected, place it behind the other objects on the page using the Send to Back command (⌘-hyphen).

Use the Rectangle tool to draw a very large rectangle now, using the margin guides on all sides of the page as guides. Fill this rectangle with 100 percent black, and place it behind all the objects on the page (⌘-hyphen). The design should now look like Figure 12.11.

Adding the Type

The font I chose for the type in this poster is Avant Garde. It is a sans-serif typeface like Helvetica, but it has a more modern cut to the letters. If you do not have Avant Garde on your machine, use Helvetica Regular as a substitute.

In the black area below the picture, use the Type tool to enter the words **DUCK 'A L'ORANGE** and then open the Character palette (⌘-T). Change the font to Avant Garde (or Helvetica), and the size to 57 point type. Under the Type menu, change the alignment of the type to Center, and reposition it in the upper half of the black rectangle.

INSIDE INFO

To create the accent over the A, first hold down the Option key and press the key to the left of the number 1 in the top row on your keyboard. Now hold down the Shift key and type an A. The letter will appear with the accent in place.

Click with the Type tool below the larger type and change the point size in the Character palette to 14 point. Type the remaining text in all caps: **THE MEMPHIS CULINARY ACADEMY'S 21ST ANNUAL CHEF'S CHOICE COOK-OFF AND AWARDS JUNE 15–17, 1996.**

12.11

With the back-
ground added, the
design is nearly
complete.

MEMPHIS, TENNESSEE. Place a bullet between the year and the city name using the quick command Option-8. Use an en-dash (Option-hyphen) between the dates. Reposition the text so that it is centered in the area below the larger type (Figure 12.12).

12.12

The type should be centered within the black area at the bottom of the design.

DUCK À L'ORANGE

THE MEMPHIS CULINARY ACADEMY'S
21ST ANNUAL CHEF'S CHOICE COOK-OFF AND AWARDS
JUNE 15–17, 1996 • MEMPHIS, TENNESSEE

Adding the Finishing Touches

The design is almost finished, but let's add just a few more things. Use the Pen tool to add a horizon of sorts under the orange and the birds. You may wish to draw part of this using the Freehand tool to make curves for hills, then switch to the Pen tool to fit the sides and bottom into the frame of the design. Fill this shape with 50 percent black.

Use the Selection tool to select the orange, including the stem and leaves. With the Scale tool, hold down the Option key and click on any anchor point in the selected objects. In the Scale dialog box, enter 55 percent and click on the Copy key. Move this smaller orange into the upper-right corner of the design and center it in the black corner.

With the smaller orange still selected, Copy (⌘-C) it and Paste (⌘-V) the copy back into the document. Position this new orange in the upper-left black corner of the page. The finished design should look like Figure 12.5.

Creating a Magazine Layout

The opening spread of a magazine article can be fun and yet difficult to design. The concept or theme of the spread is dictated by the subject of the article, and sometimes that doesn't lend itself to much creativity. However, an interesting concept for even the driest of subjects can be developed with just little a brainstorming.

The important point is that the concept should lure the reader in. You want the reader to stop turning pages, look at the spread, and then begin reading.

For this project, we will design a two-page spread for an article about bees (Figure 12.13). The art used for this design comes from the Lesson 4 folder of the tutorials supplied with your Adobe Illustrator package. While this is not an overly complex design, it will give you good experience working with several aspects of the Illustrator program in a typical, real-world context.

Setting Up the Spread

To begin, open a new document (⌘-N) and go into the Document Setup dialog box (⌘-Shift-D). Since this is a spread, we will be placing items across the gutter area between two pages. In the lower left corner of the dialog box, click on Tile Imageable Areas (Figure 12.14). In the upper-right corner of the dialog box, change the Orientation to landscaped (the icon on the right) and enter these values in the Dimensions field: 1224 pt by 792 pt. This will enlarge the area of the artboard to accommodate two full-sized pages. Click on the OK button to exit the dialog box.

When the spread appears on your screen, open the rulers in this document (⌘-R). Reset the zero point of the rulers, if necessary, to coincide with the lower left corner of the artboard. Since the margin guides on the artboard are not centered correctly, you will need to adjust them. Click on the Page tool in the Toolbox, and then click and drag the pages on the artboard to position the bottom left corner at 5 picas in from the left edge of the artboard (the bottom should align with the bottom of the artboard).

One last thing we should do to set up is add a few more guidelines to the spread. Scroll over so that you can see the gutter line separating the two pages. Enlarge the view to 100 percent to make it easier to work with. From the vertical ruler, drag out two guidelines. Place one 4 picas to the left of the gutter line, and place the other 4 picas to the right of the gutter line.

12.13

The two-page spread for an article about bees.

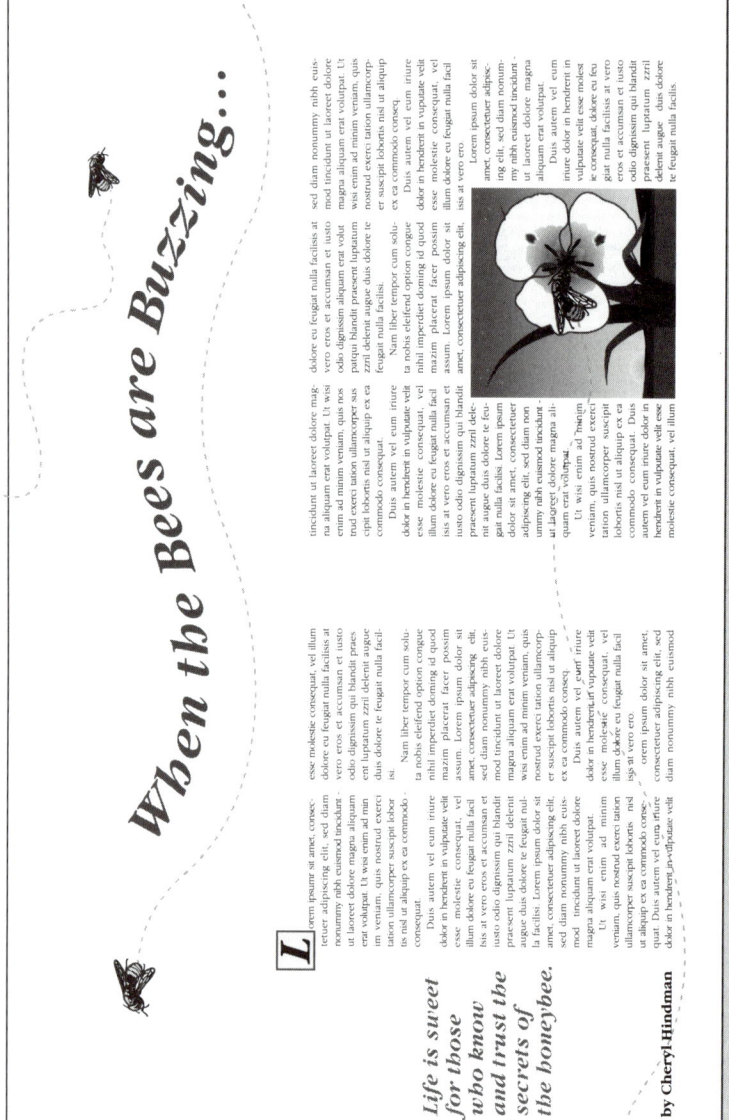

12.14

**The Document
Setup dialog box,
with the specifica-
tions for creating a
two-page spread.**

Document Setup

┌─ Artboard ──┐
│ Size: Tabloid ▼   Dimensions: 792 pt by 1224 pt │
│ ☐ Use Page Setup   Orientation: ☐ ☐ │
└──┘

┌─ View ─────────────────────┐ ┌─ Paths ──────────────────┐
│ ☒ Preview and print patterns│ │ Output resolution: 800 dpi│
│ ☐ Show placed images   │ │ ☐ Split long paths   │
│ ─────────────────────────── │ └───────────────────────────┘
│ ◉ Tile imageable areas   │ Ruler units: Points/Picas ▼
│ ○ Tile full pages   │ ☐ Use printer's default screen
│ ○ Single full page   │ ☐ Compatible gradient printing
└─────────────────────────────┘
                                        [Cancel] [OK]

The final guideline to add is a horizontal one. Click and drag one from
the horizontal ruler and place it 5 picas from the bottom of the page.
Your document should now look like Figure 12.15. Save your document now (⌘-S), and give it a name.

12.15

**The template for
the two page
spread.**

Adding Text Blocks to the Spread

Let's add the main text of the article to the spread now. This will allow us to design around the text. With the Rectangle tool selected, hold down the Option key and click anywhere on the spread (we'll position the box in a minute). In the Rectangle dialog box enter a width of 156 points and a height of 400 points, then click OK.

With the Selection tool, click on the rectangle and drag it to align with the horizontal guideline you placed 5 picas from the bottom of the pages. Move the box horizontally so it aligns 20 picas from the left side of the artboard.

Importing the Text

Select the Area Type tool now from the Toolbox, and click in the upper-left corner of the rectangle. A flashing insertion cursor will appear. In the File menu, select Import Text. The text we will use is *dummy text*, a file of imaginary words that will fill the space appropriately for our needs. In the Illustrator folder, open the Tutorials folder and then the Lesson 5 folder. Select the text file called On Health Text and click on the Import button.

The text that flows into the box will need to be styled. Click on the text with the Type tool and Select All (⌘-A). Open the Character palette (⌘-T) and change the text to 11 point Garamond Light on 14 point leading. If you do not have this font, select any serif font of your own.

Open the Paragraph palette now (⌘-Shift-P), and give the text a first line indent of 18 points. Select the Justified alignment (the second icon from the right in the palette).

Adding More Text Blocks

Since the article runs across two pages, we need to add a few more rectangles for the text to flow through. Deselect everything (⌘-Shift-A), and then use the Group Selection tool to click and drag on the text rectangle (only the rectangle should be selected when you do this, *not* the text).

Hold down the Option and Shift keys as you drag, to copy the rectangle and constrain the move.

Place this new rectangle to the right of the first, against the vertical guideline that you placed 4 picas from the gutter. Release the mouse button first, *then* the Option and Shift keys. The text will flow into the new text block.

WATCH OUT!

Make sure you select only the text rectangle and not the text each time you use the Group Selection tool to move and copy the blocks.

Use this new text block to create another text block, placing the new rectangle on the right hand page, against the guideline that is 4 picas to the right of the gutter. Create another block from this one and move it approximately 1 pica to the right of the last. Create another block from this rectangle, and move this last copy 1 pica to the right of the middle rectangle. Make sure you are always copying the last rectangle created. This links the blocks in the correct order so that the text will flow properly.

With the blocks in place, you may need to copy and paste more text to the end to make this layout look correct (of course, in real life you'll have more than enough text to fill all the blocks). The spread should now look like Figure 12.16.

Creating the Text Wrap

For good measure, save your file now (⌘-S). From the Tutorials folder, open the Lesson 4 folder and then open the Illustrator file titled Flower.Finish. Select all (⌘-A), and use the Scale tool with the Option key to reduce the size of the artwork to 60 percent. Copy (⌘-C) this smaller version to the Clipboard, and then close the Flower.Finish file without saving it.

12.16

The spread with
text and text
blocks added.

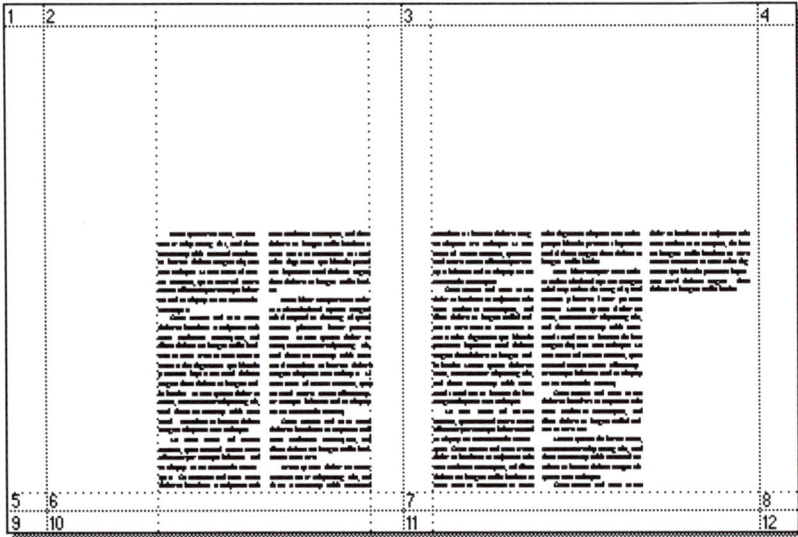

On the magazine spread, Paste (⌘-V) the artwork into the document. Position the artwork over the middle column on the right page, so that it aligns with the bottom of the text. Deselect everything (⌘-Shift-A), and use the Selection tool to click on the large square that makes up the background of the artwork. Under the Filter menu, choose Objects ➤ Offset Path. Enter an offset value of 6 points and click OK. This creates a buffer around the outside of the artwork that we will use to create the text wrap.

Use the Selection tool to click on the text blocks (all will become selected when you click on one), and the buffer rectangle you just created (*not* the artwork). Under the Type menu, select Make Wrap. The text will re-flow itself so that it wraps around the buffer rectangle, leaving a margin of space between the text and the artwork as shown in Figure 12.17.

Adding the Headline, Deck, and Byline

Reduce the size of your page view so you can see the better part of both pages. Click on the Freehand tool and use it to draw a wavy line that extends across both pages. It shouldn't extend to the edges of the page, but should be centered over all the text blocks in the white space above

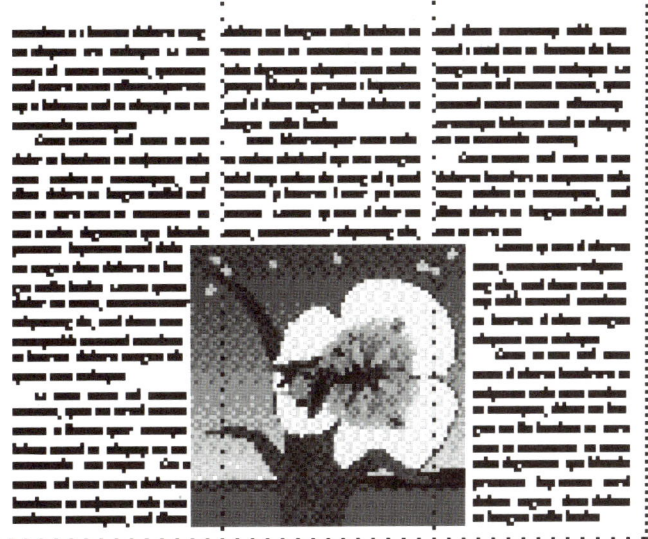

them. Copy the line (⌘-C), and Paste (⌘-V) the copy back on the page,
a little lower than the first line.

Use the Type or Path Type tool now to click on the left end of the first
wavy line. Type in the headline **When the Bees are Buzzing**… and then
open the Character palette. Style the type as 58 point Garamond Bold
Italic. Use the Selection tool to click and drag on the large vertical bar at
the front of the type to reposition it on the line.

Enlarge your page view so you can see the white space to the left of the
text blocks on the left page. With the regular Type tool selected, click
on the margin guide and type in the deck **Life is sweet for those who
know and trust the secrets of the honeybee**. In the Character palette,
style the type as 24 point Garamond Bold Italic. Use the Selection tool
to vertically center the type next to the text block.

Click with the Type tool in the lower-right corner of the page now,
where the left margin meets the guideline positioned at the 5 pica mark.
Type in the byline **by Cheryl Hindman** and then style the byline as 16
point Garamond Bold.

Open the Paint Style palette now, and click on the deck with the Selection tool. Fill the type with 100 percent cyan and 50 percent magenta.

Click on the headline now and color it 30 percent cyan and 100 percent magenta. The layout should now look like Figure 12.18.

Adding the Flying Bees

 The flying bees in the layout are smaller duplicates of the bee in the artwork on the right page. With the Zoom tool, enlarge the area around the bee in the artwork. Use the Selection tool to carefully select the bee—it isn't grouped, so you may need to select all of the artwork and then hold down the Shift key to deselect the portions you don't need. When you have isolated the bee, group it (⌘-G) and then copy it to the Clipboard (⌘-C).

Return your page view to 100 percent and then Paste (⌘-V) a copy of the bee back on the page. With the new bee still selected, use the Scale tool with the Option key to reduce its size to 80 percent. Place this bee in the upper-left corner of the right page, above the headline.

12.18

The two-page spread with type added.

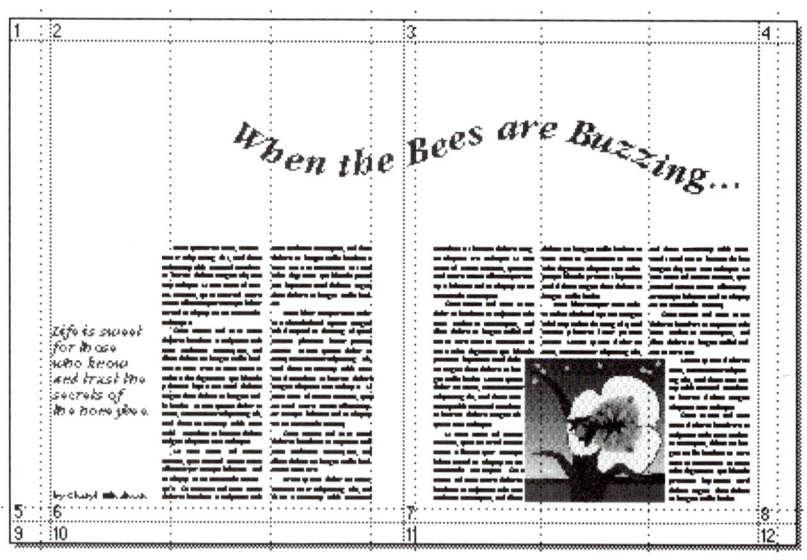

With the bee still selected, click on the Reflect tool and then hold down the Option key while clicking on the bee. In the Reflect dialog box, click on Vertical and then click on the Copy button. A mirror image of the first bee will appear on your page. Move this copy to the left page and position it to the left and below the headline type.

With the extra wavy line you created earlier, create the "bee trail" by positioning the left end of the line behind the bee. In the Paint Style palette, change the line stroke to 20 percent magenta, 40 percent yellow, and 20 percent black. Make the line 2 points in width and make the line caps round. Click on the Dashed button, and enter a dash of 4 points and a gap of 8 points. Position the line (with the bee) so that it matches the curves of the headline above it.

Use the Freehand tool to create other bee trails—one for the bee in the upper-left corner of the right page, and one for the bee in the artwork below. If you create one that runs across type, be sure to place it behind the text boxes (⌘-hyphen) so that the type is placed over it.

Adding the Pop Cap

The final element to add to this layout is the pop cap at the beginning of the text. This is a single letter set over a box stroked and filled with colors sampled from the artwork to the right.

Begin by creating the letter "L", and styling it to 48 point Garamond Bold Italic. With the Rectangle tool, create a box around the letter, slightly larger on all sides than the letter itself. Bring the letter to the front (⌘-=) and then click on the box. Fill the box with a custom color: 30 percent gold. Give the box a 2 point stroke of 40 percent cyan and 100 percent magenta.

Group the letter and the box together (⌘-G) and position them at the beginning of the first line of type. The bottom of the box should be even with the baseline of the first line.

You're done! Glance back at Figure 12.13 to see how closely you've matched the original design.

Summary

Congratulations! Now that you have the principles of Illustrator down, all you need to do is set your mind free and see where your designs take you. With the powerful tools that Adobe Illustrator provides, you are limited only by your imagination.

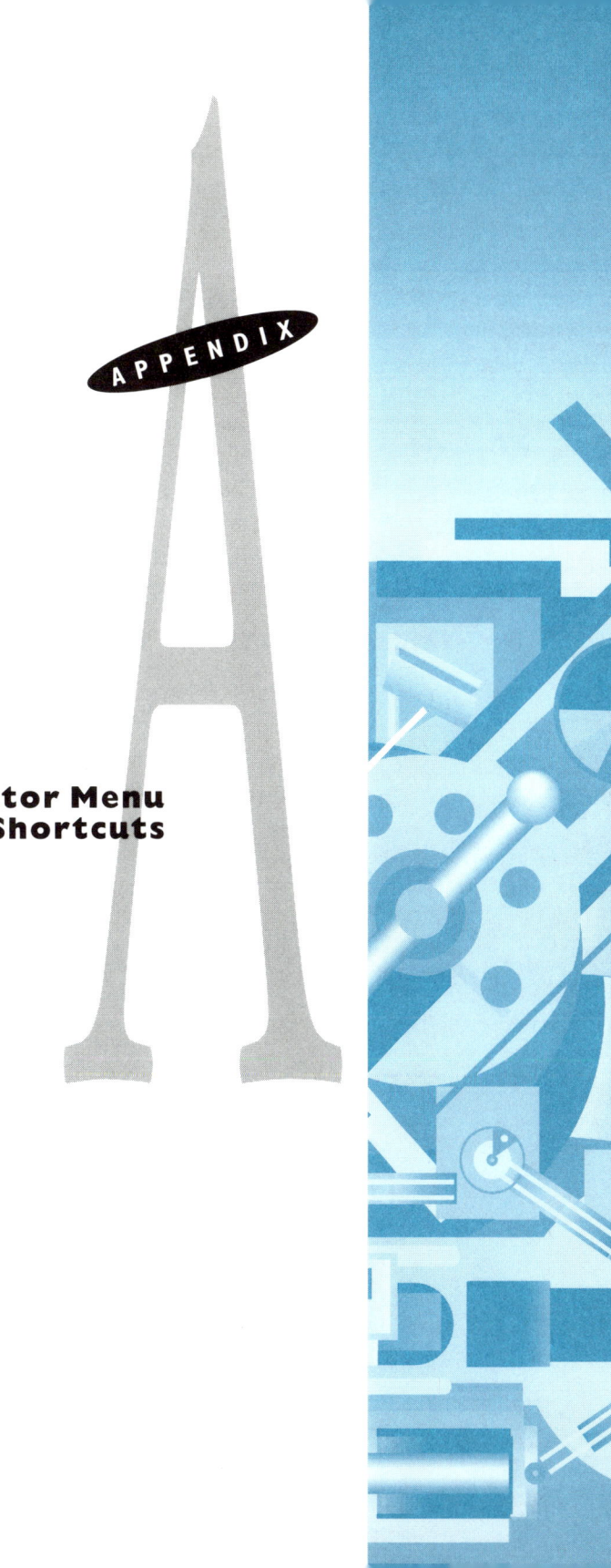

Adobe Illustrator Menu and Keyboard Shortcuts

Illustrator's menu commands and keyboard shortcuts are often the quickest and easiest ways to get the effect you want. You'll probably soon memorize those you use most often; but until you do (or when you want to try something different), you can consult the following reference guide.

The Illustrator Menus

Across the top of your screen you will see the Adobe Illustrator menu bar, with nine menu options (in addition to the standard Apple menu). Each of these menus contains commands that operate different aspects of the Illustrator program. If you click on any of the menu headings and hold down your mouse key, you will see a listing of the commands in that menu.

The File Menu

The File menu (see Figure A.1) contains commands for document management, such as saving, opening, and closing files.

New (⌘-N) opens a new Adobe Illustrator document window with a blank artboard.

Open (⌘-O) opens an existing Adobe Illustrator document.

Close (⌘-W) closes an open Adobe Illustrator document.

Save (⌘-S) saves changes made to an open Adobe Illustrator document.

Save As saves an open Adobe Illustrator file under a different name or in a different format.

Revert to Saved reverts back to the last saved version of an open document, eliminating the current on-screen version.

A.1

File menu commands control the look and behavior of a document.

```
┌─────────────────────────────┐
│ File                        │
├─────────────────────────────┤
│ New                    ⌘N   │
│ Open...                ⌘O   │
│                             │
│ Close                  ⌘W   │
│ Save                   ⌘S   │
│ Save As...                  │
│ Revert to Saved             │
│                             │
│ Place Art...                │
│ Import Styles...            │
│                             │
│ Document Setup...      ⌘⇧D  │
│ Page Setup...               │
│ Print...               ⌘P   │
│                             │
│ Preferences             ▶   │
│                             │
│ Quit                   ⌘Q   │
└─────────────────────────────┘
```

Place Art imports another EPS file for placement within an open Illustrator document.

Import Styles imports custom colors, gradient color blends, patterns and graphs from another Illustrator file into the current Illustrator document. If any style in the current Illustrator document has the same name as one you're importing, it will be overwritten with the newly imported version.

Document Setup (⌘-Shift-D) brings up the Document Setup dialog box, which contains various settings that control the way the artboard looks and responds.

Page Setup brings up the Page Setup dialog box, which controls the way your document is printed.

Print (⌘-P) prints your document to the output device selected in the Chooser.

Preferences brings up a submenu containing four choices: General, Color-Matching, Hyphenation Options and Plug-Ins. The General Preferences dialog box commands control tool and keyboard behavior. The Color-Matching dialog box is used when calibrating a color monitor. The Hyphenation Options dialog box lets you create a customized hyphenation dictionary, as well as select hyphenation rules from one of twelve different languages. The Plug-Ins preference option lets you choose the folder from which Illustrator will load plug-in filters for use with the program. We'll discuss each of these preference areas in greater detail later in the book.

Quit (⌘-Q) closes the Adobe Illustrator application. If a document is open when you invoke the Quit command, you will be prompted to save your document before quitting the application.

The Edit Menu

The Edit menu (Figure A.2) contains commands that relate to the editing of objects and text in a document.

A.2

The Edit menu contains commands for editing objects and text.

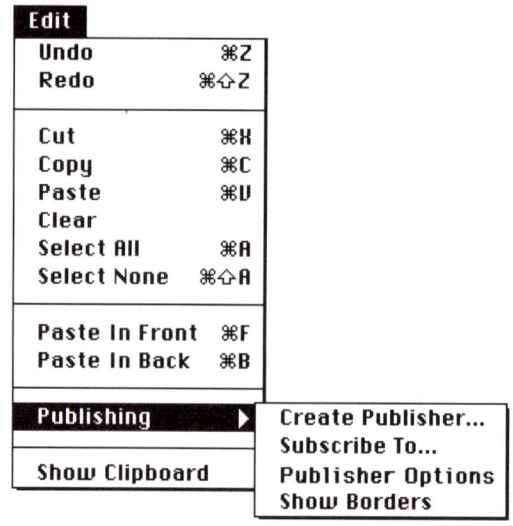

Undo (⌘-Z) cancels the last operation performed. Depending on the number of levels selected in the General Preferences dialog box, Illustrator can undo up to 200 operations. This means that by repeatedly invoking the Undo command, you can methodically erase what you have just done. This lets you literally undo "mistakes" that you may have made without deleting the entire drawing.

Redo (⌘-Shift-Z) reinstates what was undone by the Undo command. Depending on the number of levels selected in the General Preferences dialog box, Illustrator can redo up to 200 undo operations.

Cut (⌘-X) removes a selected path, grouped object, or text from the screen. The cut object or text will temporarily reside on the Clipboard until you replace it by performing another Cut or Copy operation. This allows you to move the cut object and paste it elsewhere.

Copy (⌘-C) creates a duplicate copy of a selected object or text in the Clipboard. By using the Paste command, you can place the copy into the same or another document.

Paste (⌘-V) retrieves a cut or copied object from the Clipboard and inserts it back into the current document.

Clear (Delete key) deletes a selected object or text from the current document. This is a final and irreversible command.

Select All (⌘-A) selects all objects in a document (including text).

Select None (⌘-Shift-A) deselects all selected objects in a document.

Paste In Front (⌘-F) pastes the contents of the Clipboard in front of all other objects in a document.

Paste In Back (⌘-B) pastes the contents of the Clipboard behind all other objects in a document.

Publishing brings up a submenu containing four options: Create Publisher, Subscribe To, Publisher Options, and Show Borders. These options allow you to create and share files with other documents and applications. Whenever a "published" file is edited and changed, it will automatically be updated in any other documents where it is imported.

Show Clipboard opens the Clipboard window to display its current contents.

The Arrange Menu

The Arrange menu contains commands that control the way objects are moved and arranged in a document (Figure A.3).

A.3

The Arrange menu commands help you move and arrange objects in a document.

```
┌─────────────────────────────┐
│ Arrange                     │
├─────────────────────────────┤
│ Repeat Transform...    ⌘D   │
├─────────────────────────────┤
│ Move...               ⌘⇧M   │
│ Bring To Front         ⌘=   │
│ Send To Back           ⌘-   │
├─────────────────────────────┤
│ Group                  ⌘G   │
│ Ungroup                ⌘U   │
├─────────────────────────────┤
│ Lock                   ⌘1   │
│ Unlock All             ⌘2   │
│ Hide                   ⌘3   │
│ Show All               ⌘4   │
└─────────────────────────────┘
```

Repeat Transformation (⌘-D) duplicates your most recent transformation command as many times as needed. For instance, if you have several boxes that need to be rotated to a 90° angle, you could rotate one of them, then simply click on the next box and select the Repeat Transformation command. This command works when used immediately after the Move, Scale, Rotate, Reflect, and Shear commands.

Move (⌘-Shift-M) opens the Move dialog box (Figure A.4). If you already know the precise distance and direction that you want an object to move, the Move dialog box is the easiest method to use. You can move an object a specified horizontal or vertical distance, as well as to a new angle, by entering the amount in the dialog box. If you click on the Copy button in this dialog box, a copy will be made at the specified distance and angle, leaving the original untouched.

Bring To Front (⌘-=) moves the selected object to the top layer, in front of all the other objects in a document.

A.4

Numbers entered into the Move dialog box will move and rotate an object in precise amounts.

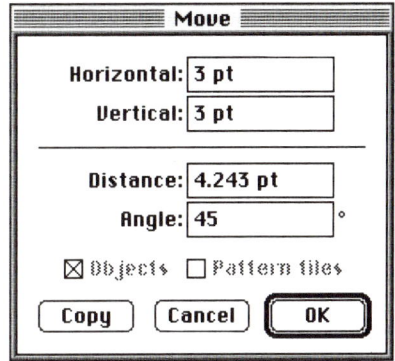

Send To Back (⌘-hyphen) moves the selected object to the bottom layer, behind all of the other objects in a document.

Group (⌘-G) creates a group out of the currently selected objects in a document. When a group is created, all items in the group will move and act as one object when clicked on with the Selection tool. Any styles applied to the group will be applied to all items in the group.

Ungroup (⌘-U) releases the grouping mode and returns all objects to their solitary status.

Lock (⌘-1) essentially renders an object unselectable. This is a helpful command to use when dealing with multiple overlapping objects. Once an object is locked, it cannot be selected, moved, or styled until it is unlocked.

Unlock All (⌘-2) releases all locked objects in a document and returns them to active duty.

Hide (⌘-3) makes a selected object invisible in all viewing modes. However, a hidden object will still print.

Show All (⌘-4) returns hidden objects to view in a document.

The View Menu

The View menu commands control the way a document as a whole is displayed on your screen (Figure A.5).

A.5

The View menu contains options for changing the way you view a document.

View	
✓Preview	⌘Y
Artwork	⌘E
Preview Selection	⌘⌥Y
Show Template	⌘⇧W
Show Rulers	⌘R
Hide Page Tiling	
Hide Edges	⌘⇧H
Hide Guides	
Zoom In	⌘]
Zoom Out	⌘[
Actual Size	⌘H
Fit In Window	⌘M
New View...	⌘⌃V
Edit Views...	

Preview (⌘-Y) is one of three viewing modes in Illustrator. Preview shows your design on screen the way it will actually look when printed, with all styles and color in place. Unlike earlier versions of Illustrator, version 5.5 lets you edit a file directly in Preview mode. However, depending on the complexity of your file and the amount of RAM in your Mac, the program is almost sure to run slower in Preview mode.

The **Artwork** (⌘-E) mode shows only the outlines of objects as they are drawn and styled. This is the fastest mode to work in, especially with a complex design.

Preview Selection (⌘-option-Y) is essentially a blend of the first two viewing modes. In Preview Selection mode, all objects are shown in Artwork mode except for the currently selected object or objects, which will appear in Preview mode.

Show Template (⌘-Shift-W) shows the outline of an opened template. Any PICT or MacPaint file can be opened and used as a drawing template in Illustrator. Although the template will appear on the screen, it will not print. When a template is showing, this menu option changes to read Hide Template.

Show Rulers (⌘-R) adds a horizontal and vertical ruler to the sides of an open document window. The units of measure used in the rulers are set in the General Preferences dialog box. When the rulers are showing, this menu option changes to read Hide Rulers.

Hide Page Tiling hides the page tiling currently showing in a document window, as specified in the Document Setup dialog box. When page tiling has been hidden, this menu option changes to read Show Page Tiling.

Hide Edges (⌘-Shift-H) hides the defining edges and points of the currently selected object. When the edges are hidden, this menu option changes to read Show Edges.

Hide Guides hides all guides that have been created on a page. When the guides have been hidden, this menu option changes to read Show Guides.

Zoom In (⌘-]) enlarges the view of the entire page in set increments. From 100 percent, you can zoom in to a 150, 200, 300, 400, 600, 800, 1200, or 1600 percent magnified view.

Zoom Out (⌘-[ ) reduces the view of the entire page in set increments. From 100 percent, you can zoom out to a 66.67, 50, 33.33, 25, 16.67, 12.5, 8.33, or 6.25 percent view of the original size.

Actual Size (⌘-H) brings the page view back to 100 percent.

Fit In Window (⌘-M) fits the image and page view into the current document window. The actual size you get with this option depends on the size of the current document window as well as your monitor size.

New View (⌘-control-V) allows you to create up to 25 custom-sized views of a single document. All sizing, layering and viewing options are kept intact in each view.

Edit Views lets you edit or delete any custom-sized views that you have created in a document.

The Object Menu

The Object menu commands control the way objects in a document are styled (Figure A.6). Here you can find commands for creating custom paint and pattern fill preferences, as well as other object-styling commands. The menu also contains five submenus to assist you in creating guides, masks, compound paths, crop marks, and graphs.

A.6

The Object menu commands help you style the objects in your document.

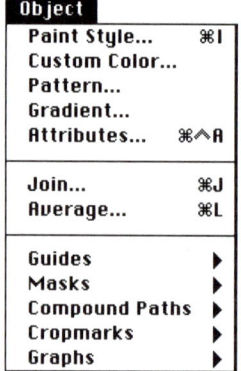

Paint Style (⌘-I) brings up the Paint Style dialog box (Figure A.7), where you can set the color and tint for objects and text in a document. This dialog box is also a palette than can be left open on the desktop as you work. In the upper-right corner of the box is a submenu that lets you control which portions of the palette are displayed, making it adjustable in size.

Custom Color brings up the Custom Color dialog box (Figure A.8). Here, you can create your own custom color combinations using the four standard printing colors: Cyan, Magenta, Yellow and Black. Custom colors can be named, saved and appended to other documents as needed.

Pattern brings up the Pattern dialog box (Figure A.9). Here you can create customized patterns to be used as "fill colors" for objects in your design. Once you have created a pattern in a document, it can be selected and saved as a customized fill pattern using this dialog box. Chapter 7 shows how to work with Patterns.

A.7

The Paint Style dialog box is also an adjustable palette that can be left on the desktop for easy access as you work.

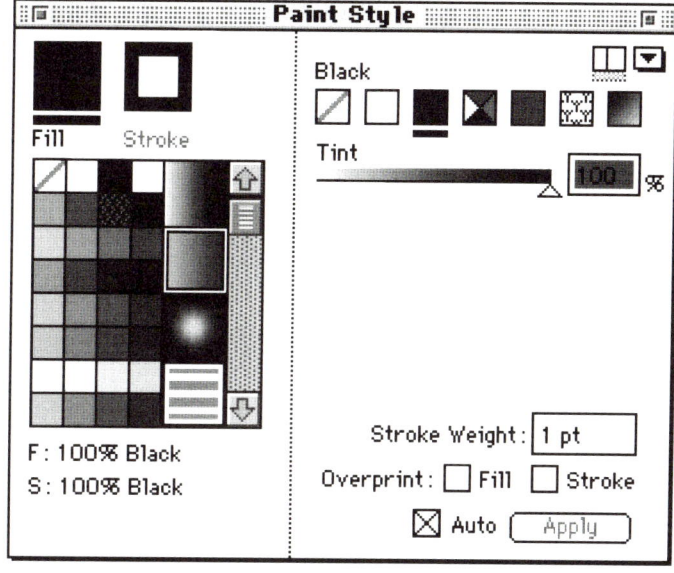

A.8

The Custom Color dialog box allows you to create and name your own color combinations.

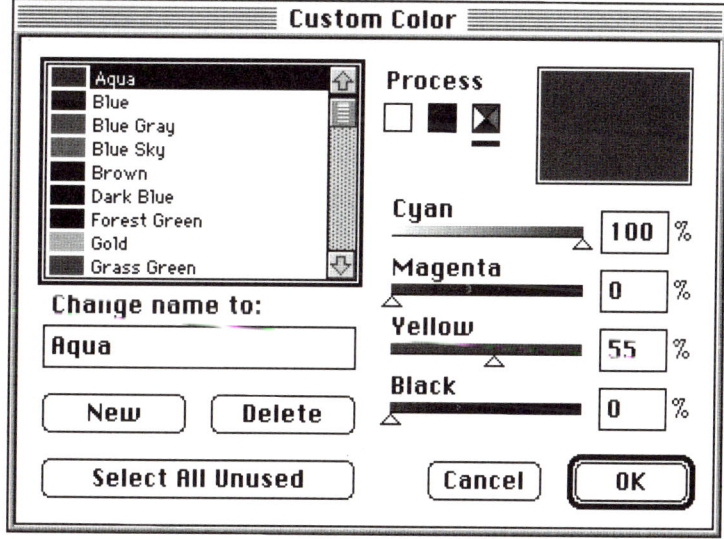

A.9

The Pattern dialog box shows a list of patterns that can be used to fill objects.

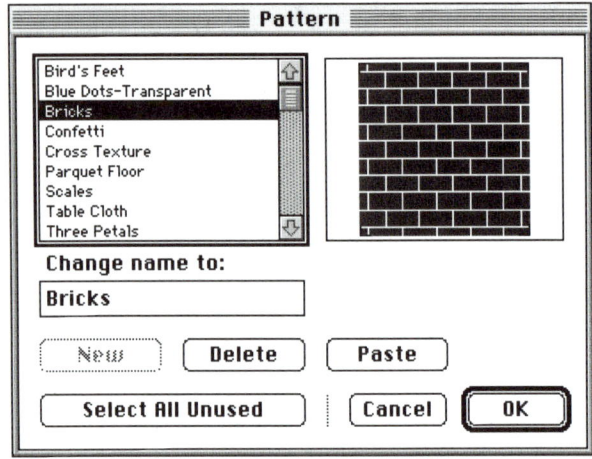

Gradient brings up the Gradient dialog box (Figure A.10). Here, you can create custom blends of color in linear and radial patterns. These color blends can then be named and applied to objects in your document. Like Paint Style, this is also a palette that can be left on the desktop and adjusted to show only the top portion of the box.

A.10

The Gradient dialog box is used to create blends of color.

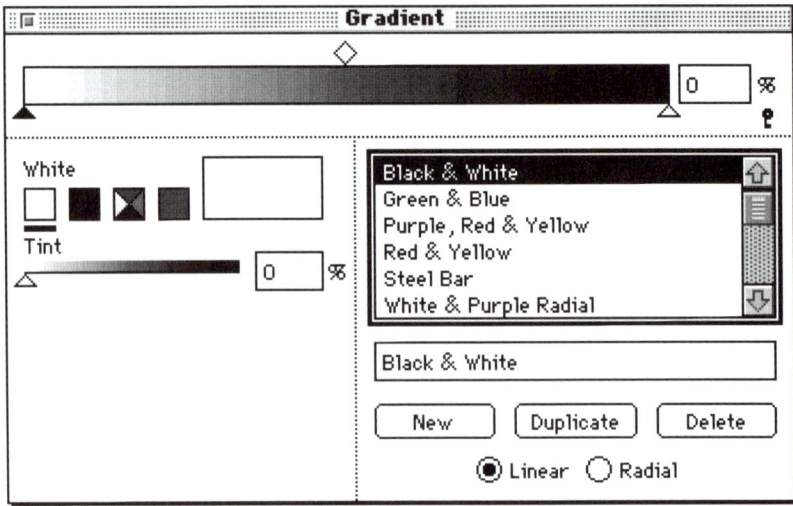

Attributes (⌘-control-A) brings up the Attributes dialog box (Figure A.11). This is a multipurpose dialog box that gives limited information about currently selected items in a document. This box contains information about masking and output resolution, as well as controls for reversing the direction of a path. The Attributes dialog box also contains a Note area, where you can annotate information about objects for future use. For more detailed information about a document, use the Document Info dialog box, discussed later in this chapter.

```
┌─────────────────────────────────────────┐
│═══════════════ Attributes ══════════════│
│ ┌─────────────────────────────────────┐ │
│ │ Note:                               │ │
│ │ ┌─────────────────────────────────┐ │ │
│ │ │ the word "text" is masked by a box│ │
│ │ │ containing a scale pattern│       │ │
│ │ │                                 │ │ │
│ │ │                                 │ │ │
│ │ └─────────────────────────────────┘ │ │
│ │                                     │ │
│ │ ⊠ Show center point  ☐ Reverse path direction│
│ │                                     │ │
│ │ Output resolution: │800│ dpi        │ │
│ │                                     │ │
│ │ The current selection contains a mask and │
│ │ something affected by a mask.       │ │
│ │                                     │ │
│ │          ┌ Cancel ┐  ┌══ OK ══┐     │ │
│ └─────────────────────────────────────┘ │
└─────────────────────────────────────────┘
```

Join (⌘-J) is a command that will join two selected open points of a path together, closing the path.

Average (⌘-L) aligns a group of selected objects along a central axis. For example, if you want to align three circles on the same horizontal axis, selecting first the circles and then the Average command will cause the circles to be perfectly aligned. Average will align objects to either the vertical or horizontal axis or average them along both. You can choose how objects are aligned in the Average dialog box (Figure A.12).

A . 1 2

The Average dialog
box aligns objects
along a selected
axis.

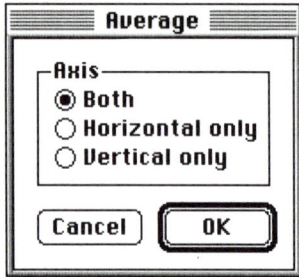

A . 1 3

Submenus under
the Object menu
contain commands
for Guides (A),
Masks (B), Com-
pound Paths (C),
Cropmarks (D),
and Graphs (E).

The next few menu commands all have small submenus that are shown in Figure A.13.

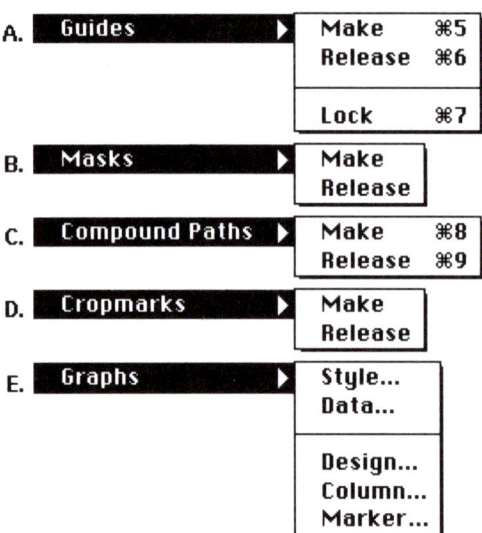

Guides contains a submenu for making, releasing, and locking guides in a document (Figure A.13a). Guides are nonprinting lines that you draw for the purpose of aligning objects and text in a document.

Masks contains a submenu for making and releasing masks (Figure A.13b). A mask is a combination of two different items, such as text and a background pattern, that allows the pattern in the background to show only through the outlines of the text.

Compound Paths contains a submenu for making and releasing compound paths (Figure A.13c). A compound path is a group of overlapping paths that appear transparent.

Cropmarks contains a submenu for making and releasing crop marks (Figure A.13d). In order to use this option, you need to draw a separate rectangle around your design. Adobe Illustrator will use (and then delete) this rectangle to create the crop marks.

Graphs contains a submenu for creating customized graphs in Adobe Illustrator (Figure A.13e). The Style option in this submenu brings up a detailed Graph Style dialog box that allows you to select from numerous graph styles (Figure A.14).

A.14

The **Graph Styles** dialog box contains numerous graph style options.

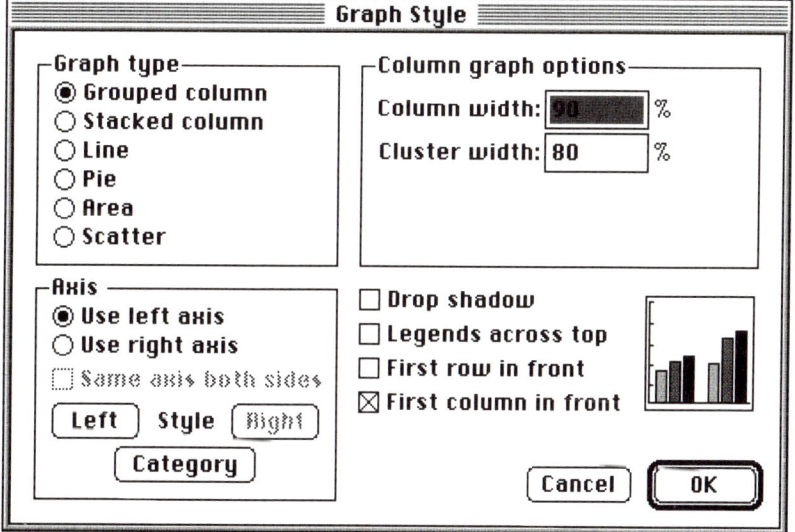

The Font Menu

The Font menu (Figure A.15) contains a list of the fonts currently available on your system. If you have a lot of fonts loaded, then this list can become quite long. Type Reunion, a utility included with Adobe Illustrator, reduces font menus by up to 80 percent by listing fonts by family. Other font utilities, such as Suitcase II and Master Juggler, allow you to organize your fonts into specialized "suitcases," displaying only those

A.15

The Font menu displays the fonts available for use on your system.

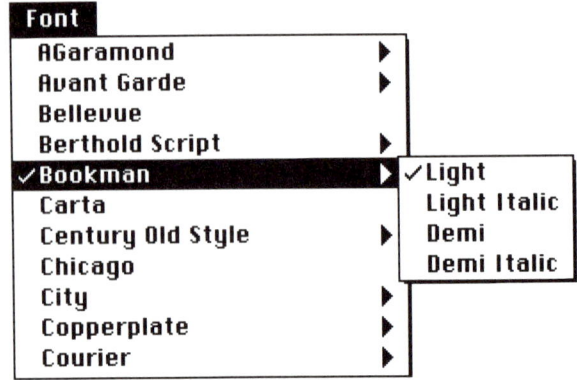

fonts you need at any given time. This not only saves space in the Font menu, it saves memory, too.

The Type Menu

The Type menu contains commands that control and style the text in your document (Figure A.16). There are commands for changing the point size, leading, and alignment of type, along with special controls for wrapping text around objects and turning text into an object itself.

A.16

The Type menu gives you access to commands for styling text.

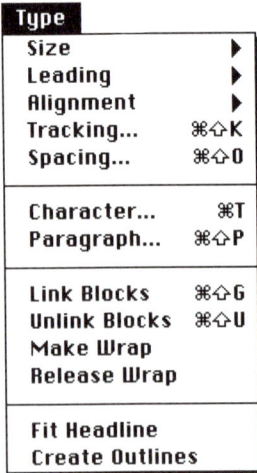

Chapter 6 offers a complete guide to working with type in Illustrator, including several exercises. But for a quick preview, type in a little text and try out some of the following options.

Size contains a submenu listing the different point size options for type (Figure A.17). There are 15 preset point size options as well as an Other option for entering your own specific point size.

A.17

The Size submenu lists point size options for sizing type.

Size ▶		✓Other... ⌘⇧S
		6 pt
		7 pt
		8 pt
		9 pt
		10 pt
		11 pt
		12 pt
		14 pt
		18 pt
		21 pt
		24 pt
		36 pt
		48 pt
		60 pt
		72 pt

Leading contains a submenu for choosing the leading for a selected area of type (Figure A.18). Leading is the amount of vertical space measured in points between the baselines of two lines of text. The Leading submenu contains 16 preset leading options as well as an Other option for entering your own preferred leading measurement. Auto-leading is the default measurement, which sets the leading at 120 percent of the type size for the selected portion of text (for example, 10-point type will have 12-point leading).

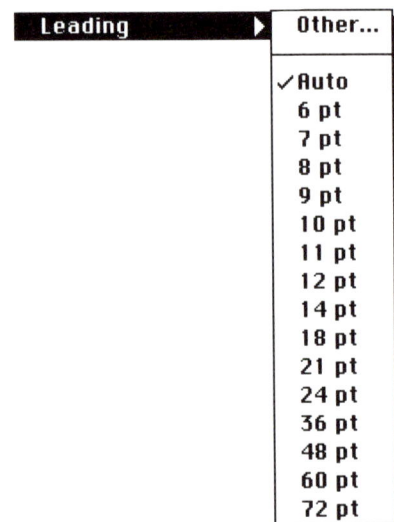

A.18

The Leading sub-menu lists leading size options available for use.

Alignment contains a submenu for setting the alignment of text (Figure A.19). There are five alignment options: Left, Center, Right, Justify, and Justify Last Line. Text is aligned based on its original insertion point.

Tracking/Kern (⌘-Shift-K) automatically opens the Character dialog box/palette with the cursor in position to change the Tracking/Kerning option (Figure A.20). Depending on what you have selected on your screen, this option will read either Tracking or Kern (not both). Tracking controls the amount of space between groups of more than two characters. Kerning controls the amount of space between just two characters.

A.19

The Alignment submenu allows you to align a block of text in five different ways.

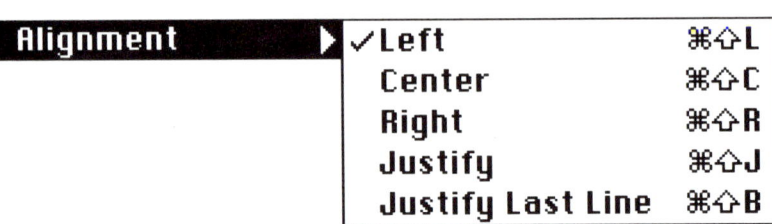

A.20

The Tracking/Kern command automatically opens the Character dialog box and places the cursor in the Tracking/Kerning option box.

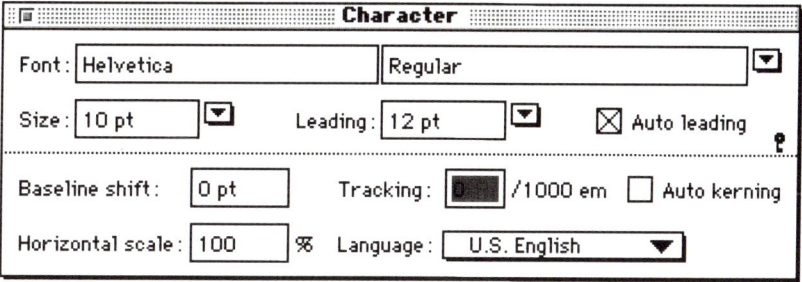

Spacing (⌘-Shift-O) automatically opens the Paragraph dialog box/palette with the cursor in position to change the Word Spacing option (Figure A.21). To the right of this is the Letter Spacing option. Both spacing options control the way words and letters are spaced in justified paragraphs of text. Illustrator will use the Minimum, Desired, and Maximum values when it must adjust the amount of space between letters and words to obtain a justified block of text.

A.21

The Spacing command automatically opens the Paragraph dialog box, where the Word and Letter Spacing options can be changed.

Character (⌘-T) opens the Character dialog box (see Figure A.20). This dialog box contains various controls for altering the font, size, leading, baseline shift, horizontal scale, and kerning or tracking of a selected area of text. It is also a palette that can be left open on the desktop for easy access while you are working.

Paragraph (⌘-Shift-P) opens the Paragraph dialog box (see Figure A.21). This is another desktop palette that can be left open as you work. Its various commands control the way text is spaced and aligned. The Paragraph dialog box contains commands for alignment, indentation, hyphenation, word and letter spacing, and an extra leading amount to be added before paragraphs.

Link Blocks (⌘-Shift-G) links a selected block of text to another blank object, allowing the text to continue into the second object. Most commonly, this would be used to link two rectangles to create standard columns of text.

Unlink Blocks (⌘-Shift-U) unlinks two linked text blocks. Text is removed from the second object in the broken link, and is in limbo until you link the original text block to a new object.

Make Wrap causes text to wrap around an object placed over a block of text.

Release Wrap releases the wrapping command, causing text to ignore an object placed over it and flow behind the object in a normal block.

Fit Headline causes type entered into a rectangle with the Area Type tool to be enlarged to fit across the width of the available area. With an Adobe multiple master font, it will increase the point size and width of the font to fill the space. With other fonts, it will increase the tracking value of the type to fit the space.

Create Outlines turns type into outlined objects that can be edited and manipulated. Once type is converted into outlines it is no longer considered type, and therefore its attributes can no longer be altered using type commands. It can, however, be painted and edited like any other object.

The Filter Menu

The Filter menu gives you access to over 40 plug-in filters that are now a part of Illustrator 5.5 (Figure A.22). *Filters* are special modules that simplify designing by doing a lot of the tedious manipulations for you. The filters vary widely in purpose; and what follows is a brief survey of them. You'll find detailed explanations of the Text filters in Chapter 6; the other filters are discussed in Chapter 9.

Last Filter (⌘-Shift-E) invokes the last filter used and applies it to the object currently selected on your screen. Once you've used a filter in the current session, its name will appear in this space and it will be invoked when this command is selected.

Colors brings up a submenu containing filters that adjust the color within an object (Figure A.23). This is a more complex way of adjusting color than is found in the Paint palette, and includes a command for inverting colors to their exact opposites in the color wheel.

A.22

The Filter menu contains plug-in filters for creating special effects in Adobe Illustrator.

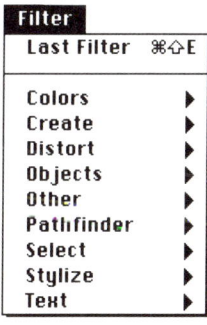

A.23

The Colors sub-menu contains sophisticated controls for adjusting color.

The **Create** submenu offers filters for creating different types of objects (Figure A.24). These filters make drawing their objects a piece of cake. The Star filter, for example, brings up the Create Star dialog box (Figure A.25). Here you can specify the number of points, the inside radius and outside radius to automatically generate a perfect star in your design.

A.24

The Create submenu contains several creation filters that make automate drawing certain certain objects.

A.25

The Create Star dialog box automatically renders perfect stars.

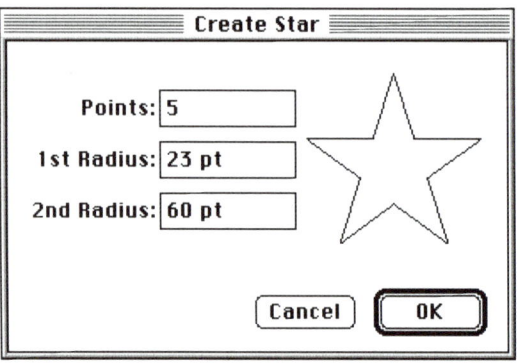

Distort brings up a submenu containing filters for automatically distorting objects (Figure A.26). Included are filters that roughen the outline of the object and twirl the outside points of an object around its center.

Objects gives you a submenu with filters that control object transformation and movement (Figure A.27). Here you'll find filters for object alignment and duplicating paths at an offset.

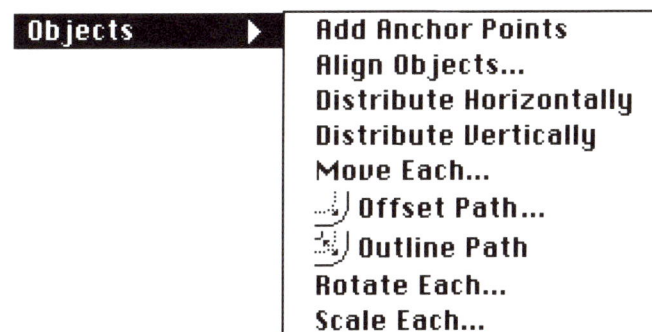

A.26

The Distort sub-
menu contains
filters that auto-
mate figure
distortion.

A.27

The Objects filters
align objects and
duplicate paths.

Other brings up the Document Info dialog box, which provides detailed information about various elements of the current document (Figure A.28). The information is distributed into seven categories, making it easy to tune into the area you are most interested in.

Pathfinder gives you a submenu with several filters for combining, isolating, subdividing, and building paths (Figure A.29). These filters allow you to create transparent effects by combining and overlapping paths to create a new compound path.

Select contains submenu choices that make it easy to select several objects in a document at once, based on similar features (Figure A.30). You can select objects based on fill color and style, stroke color and weight, masks, and stray points.

A.28

The Document Info dialog box displays information about different aspects of the current document.

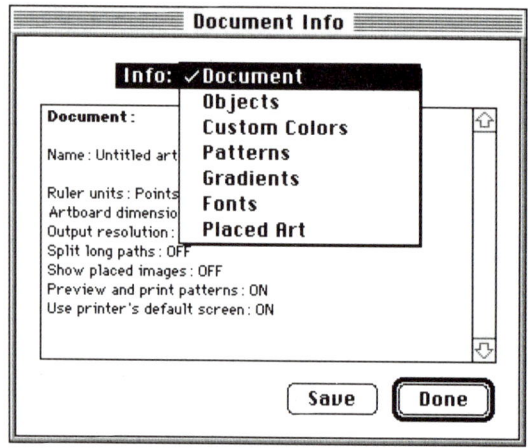

A.29

The Pathfinder filters allow you to create transparent effects by combining multiple object paths into a compound path.

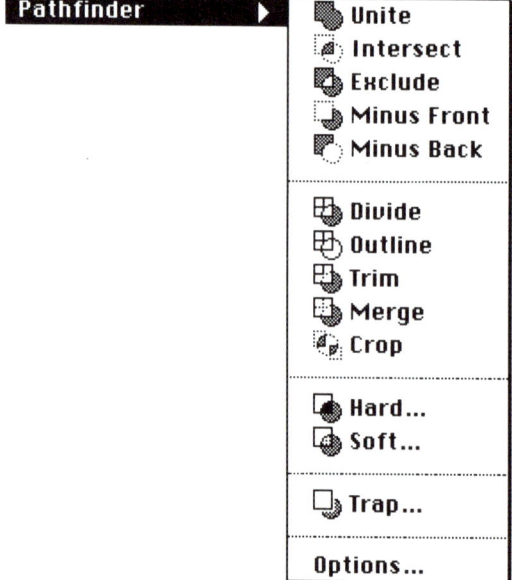

The **Stylize** submenu offers several special-effect filters for you to choose from (Figure A.31). The Bloat, Calligraphy, and Punk filters stylize objects when applied, and the Arrowhead and Drop Shadow filters automate the creation of their respective elements (Figure A.32).

A.30

The Select sub-menu options let you select objects in a document based on similar features.

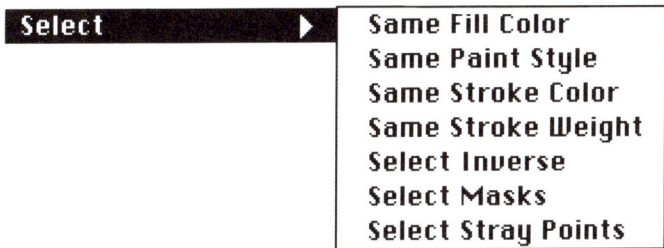

A.31

The Stylize filters create special effects when applied to objects.

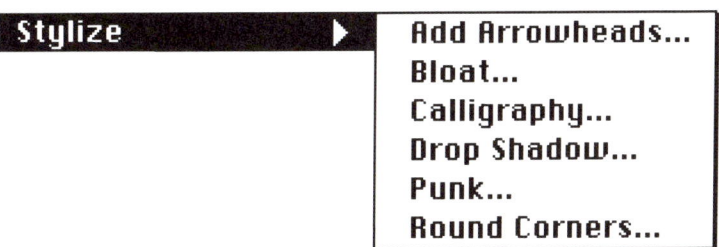

A.32

The Arrowhead filter offers 27 different arrow heads and tails to choose from.

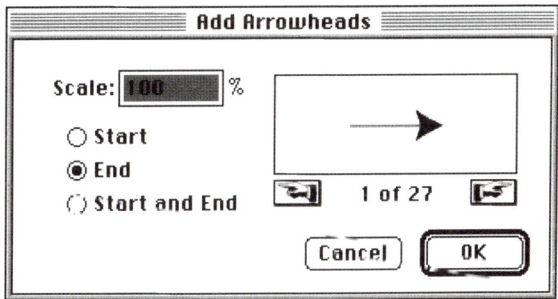

Text brings up a listing of the amazing new text filters that give you word processing and page layout control in Illustrator (Figure A.33). Included in this submenu are filters for changing the case of letters and checking spelling, as well as a filter that creates rows and columns of text and one that lets you search for and replace fonts in a document (Figure A.34).

A.33

The Text submenu offers filters that aid in editing text.

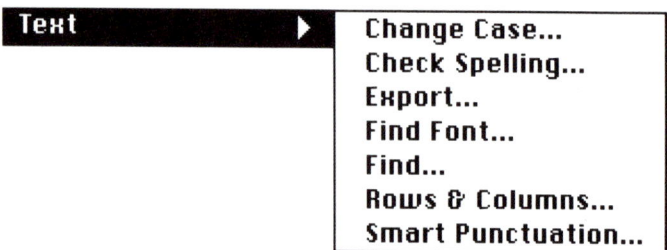

A.34

The Find Font filter lets you search your document for a particular font and automatically replace it with another.

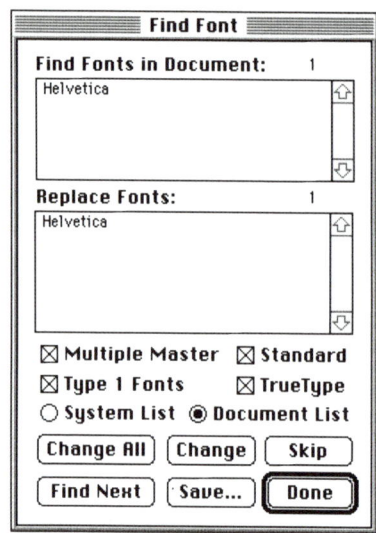

The Window Menu

The Window menu is the final menu listed in the menu bar (Figure A.35). It contains commands that show (open) and hide (close) palettes and windows on your screen. Some of these commands simply duplicate options available in other menus, such as the Show Paint Style command. However, a few important commands in this menu are not found anywhere else, and are in fact excellent contributions to this latest version of Adobe Illustrator.

New Window opens a new document window containing the same elements as displayed in the original document window.

A.35

The Window menu opens and closes palettes and windows on your desktop.

This is an easy way to create different views of the same file. The second window is given the same name as the first, with a 2 added after the name.

Show/Hide Toolbox (⌘-control-T) opens and closes the Toolbox palette on your desktop.

Show/Hide Layers (⌘-control-L) opens and closes the Layers palette on your desktop (Figure A.36). This palette controls the creation of layers in a document and how they are used and displayed.

A.36

The Layers palette and its submenu help you create and display layers of objects in your document.

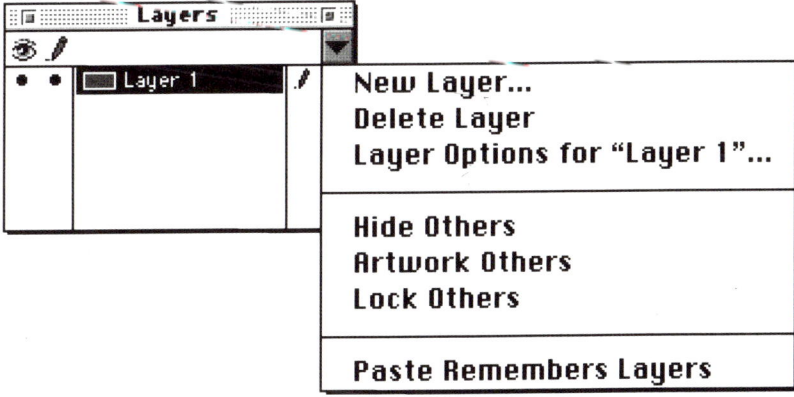

Show/Hide Info (⌘-control-I) opens and closes the Info palette (Figure A.37). This handy palette gives information about the currently selected tool. Elements such as cursor position, object size, and rotation angle are displayed and changed as you click on different tools and objects.

| X: 116.333 pt | W: 0 pt | D: 0 pt |
| Y: 612 pt | H: 0 pt | ∠ 0° |

Show/Hide Paint Style opens and closes the Paint Style palette (shown earlier in Figure A.7) on your desktop.

Show/Hide Gradient opens and closes the Gradient palette (shown earlier in Figure A.10) on your desktop.

Show/Hide Character opens and closes the Character palette (shown earlier in Figure A.20) on your desktop.

Show/Hide Paragraph opens and closes the Paragraph palette (shown earlier in Figure A.21) on your desktop.

Show/Hide Tab Ruler (⌘-Shift-T) opens and closes the Tab Ruler palette (Figure A.38). Using this palette, you can set tabs in text at positions you specify. The Tab Ruler comes with tabs preset at three-pica intervals.

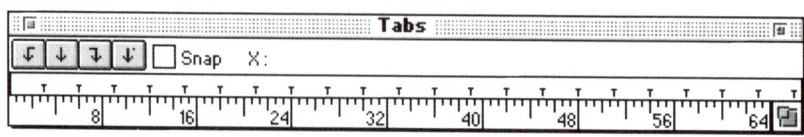

The bottom of the Window menu also displays the names of all the open Adobe Illustrator documents currently on your screen. You can easily flip between them by selecting a document name from the list in this menu. The name with a check mark to its left is the currently selected document window.

Keyboard Shortcuts

Illustrator's keyboard shortcuts offer a quick way of accomplishing the most important tasks in working with the program.

File Shortcuts

New	⌘-N
Open	⌘-O
Close	⌘-W
Save	⌘-S
Document Setup	⌘-Shift-D
Print	⌘-P
Quit	⌘-Q
General Preferences	⌘-K

Object Editing Shortcuts

Undo	⌘-Z
Redo	⌘-Shift-Z
Cut	⌘-X
Copy	⌘-C
Paste	⌘-V
Select All	⌘-A
Select None	⌘-Shift-A
Paste In Front	⌘-F

Paste In Back	⌘-B
Repeat Transform	⌘-D
Move	⌘-Shift-M
Bring to Front	⌘-=
Send to Back	⌘-hyphen
Group	⌘-G
Ungroup	⌘-U
Lock	⌘-1
Unlock All	⌘-2
Attributes	⌘-Control-A
Join	⌘-J
Average	⌘-L
Make Guides	⌘-5
Release Guides	⌘-6
Lock/Unlock Guides	⌘-7
Make Compound Paths	⌘-8
Release Compound Paths	⌘-9

Viewing Shortcuts

Hide	⌘-3
Hide All But Selected Objects	⌘-Option-3-any tool
Show All	⌘-4
Preview Mode	⌘-Y
Artwork Mode	⌘-E
Preview Selection Mode	⌘-Option-Y
Show/Hide Template	⌘-Shift-W
Show/Hide Rulers	⌘-R
Hide Edges	⌘-Shift-H
Zoom In	⌘-]

Zoom In (alternate)	⌘-spacebar-any tool
Zoom Out	⌘-[
Zoom Out (alternate)	Option-Zoom tool
Actual Size	⌘-H
Actual Size (alternate)	Double click on Zoom tool
Fit in Window	⌘-M
Fit in Window (alternate)	Double click on Hand tool
New View	⌘-Control-V

Type Editing Shortcuts

Adjust Size	⌘-Shift-S
Adjust Tracking	⌘-Shift-K
Adjust Spacing	⌘-Shift-O
Left Alignment	⌘-Shift-L
Center Alignment	⌘-Shift-C
Right Alignment	⌘-Shift-R
Justify Alignment	⌘-Shift-J
Justify Last Line	⌘-Shift-B
Link Blocks	⌘-Shift-G
Unlink Blocks	⌘-Shift-U
Increase Point Size	⌘-Shift->
Decrease Point Size	⌘-Shift-<
Increase Leading	Option-Up Arrow
Decrease Leading	Option-Down Arrow
Increase Kerning/Tracking	Option-Right Arrow
Decrease Kerning/Tracking	Option-Left Arrow
Increase Baseline Shift	Option-Shift-Up Arrow
Decrease Baseline Shift	Option-Shift-Down Arrow
Select Word to Right	⌘-Shift-Right Arrow

Select Word to Left	⌘-Shift-Left Arrow
Select Paragraph Above	⌘-Shift-Up Arrow
Select Paragraph Below	⌘-Shift-Down Arrow

Palette/Dialog Box Shortcuts

Show Toolbox	⌘-Control-T
Show Paint Style Palette	⌘-I
Show Character Palette	⌘-T
Show Paragraph Palette	⌘-Shift-P
Show Layers Dialog Box	⌘-Control-L
Show Info Dialog Box	⌘-Control-I
Show Tab Ruler	⌘-Shift-T
Use Last Filter	⌘-Shift-E
Display Last Filter Dialog Box	⌘-Option-Shift-E

Page numbers in *italics* refer to figures; page numbers in **bold** refer to primary discussions of the topic.

Symbols & Numbers

⌘ Command key, 19, 20
   and Freehand tool to erase, 38
   and paint swatches, 158
   for Selection tool, 48
… (ellipsis), menu commands with, 20
24-bit video card, 6–7
45-degree angle, constraining line to, 34, 44

A

accents, adding to text, 288
Actual Size (View menu), 309
Add Anchor Point tool, 22, 78, 195
Add Anchor Points filter, **219**, *220*
Add Arrowheads filter, **240**
Add Guides command, 126
Adjust Colors filter, **204–205**, *205*
Adobe Acrobat, 11, **270–271**
Adobe Illustrator
   compatibility, 9–11
   double-clicking file icons to start, 16
   hardware requirements, **6–8**
   origins, **3**
   software requirements, 8
   starting, **15**
   users of, **5**
   version 5.5 new features, **3–5**
   what it is, **2–5**
Adobe Photoshop, 9, 101
   importing files from, 107
Adobe Premier, 11
Adobe Separator, 227, **271–276**
   adding printer marks with, **274**
   making separations, **274–275**
Adobe Type Manager (ATM), 8, **268–269**
Aldus Freehand, 9
Align Objects filter, **220**, *220*
alignment
   with Average dialog box, 313, *314*
   guides for text and objects, 105
   of type, **152**
Alignment (Type menu), *318*, 318
Ami Professional, importing text file from, 122
anchor points, 31, *32*, 74, *75*
   adding to path, **77–78**, 195
   as central point of focus for transformation, 84

converting to directional anchor point, **78–79**, *79*
   deleting, **80–81**
   filter to add multiple, **219**, *220*
   tools for, 22
   for type, 54
angled objects, Shear tool to create, 93
angles, setting precise for sheared object, 94, *95*
angular corners, for stroked path, 163
annotation, for printed file, 227, 228
Apple menu, Control Panels, 268
AppleWorks, importing text file from, 122
Area graph, 247, *248*
Area Select (General Preferences dialog box), 27
Area Type tool, 23, **119**, 124
Arrange menu, **306–307**, *306*
   Group, 50, 307
   Send to Back, 44, 192, 307
   Ungroup, 50, 307
arrow, menu commands with, 20
arrow keys, to move selected objects, 83
arrowheads, filter for, **240**
art paths, converting text paths to, **121–122**
Artboard, **16–18**, *17*
   dividing into printable sections, 113
artwork. *See also* imported images
   adding to type, **196–197**
   importing, **105–107**, **130–131**
   text wrap around, **127–129**
Artwork mode, 30–31, 42, 69
   bounding box in, 107, 119
   for type special effects, 194
Artwork (View menu), 308
ASCII text
   for imported data for graph, 256
   importing, 123
Attributes (View menu), 313
Auto Hyphenation, **135–136**
Auto-Leading feature, 146, 317, *318*
Auto Trace Gap (General Preferences dialog box), 27, 104
Auto-Trace tool, 23, **102–103**
Avant Garde font, 288
Average (View menu), 313, *314*
Axis settings (Graph Style dialog box), **248**

B

backward compatibility, 10, 172

bar graphs, applying design to, **262–263**
Baseline Shift, 27, 151
beveled corners, for stroked path, 163
beveled shadows, 193
bitmapped images, as templates, 100, 101
black fill, overprinting other colors with, 226
black flag, to open extended Character palette, 149
Black and White button, in Paint Style palette, 159
Bleed (PPD file setting), 273
Blend dialog box, *199*
Blend Front to Back filter, **205**, *206*
Blend Horizontally filter, **206–207**
Blend tool, 24, **197–201**
   morphing with, **200–201**
   to simulate motion, **199**, *200*
Blend Vertically filter, **207**, *207*
Bloat filter, **240**, *241*
borders, stroking, 61
bounding box, for text, 119
Bounding Box (PPD file setting), 273
box, three-dimensional effect, **183–185**
Bring to Front command, 196, 306
Brush dialog box, *39*
Brush tool, 22
   changing to cross hair cursor, 27
   to create curves, **38**
business cards, **278–281**

C

calligraphic mode, 38, *39*
Calligraphy filter, **241**, *241*, 242
Canvas images, importing, 106
Caps (Paint Style palette), *158*, *162*, 162
case of type, changing, **139**, *139*
category labels, in graph worksheets, 254
center alignment, 152, *153*
center point, drawing shapes around, 40, *41*
center tab stops, 153
centering words, keyboard shortcuts for, 67
Change All (Find Font dialog box), *144*, 144
Change Case filter, 4, 139
Change Case filter dialog box, *139*
Change (Find Font dialog box), *144*, 144
Change Placed Art (File menu), 107
Character (Type menu), 320
Character palette, **63**, *63*, 143, *320*, 320
   Baseline Shift, **151**

font changes with, 67, 280, 294
Kerning, 148, 318
opening extended version, 149
to set leading, 146
Size field, 145
Tracking field, 149, 318
character shapes, by Adobe Type
  Manager, 269
Check Spelling filter, 4, **133**, *134*, **135**
chiseled type, **193–194**, *194*
choke, 175
circles, 23, **41–42**, 51
Clear (Edit menu), 305
Clipboard, 49, 298
  to copy type, 54
  for data entry to graph worksheet, **257**
  sending PICT image to, 109
clockwise rotation, 86
clockwise spiral, 213
Close (File menu), 302
closed paths, 73, *74*
  from Brush tool, 38
  center points of, 77
  creating open path from, 22
  as text box, *120*, 120
cluster width, in graphs, 249
CMYK color, *See* process colors
color, **156–177**
  for closed paths, 73
  custom, **163–167**
  default settings for, 68
  fill patterns, **172–174**
  filters for, **204–210**
  gradient fills, **168–172**
  of graph components, 260
  guidelines for using, 156
  of imported images, 107
  for layers, 110
  for objects, **58–61**
  storing combinations, 157–158
  trapping, **174–177**
color bars, 274
color blends, 205
Color/Grayscale, for mosaic filter, 211
color matching systems, **165–167**
  Focoltone Colour System, **167**
  Pantone, **166**
  Toyo Ink Electronic Color Finder
    1050, 166
  Trumatch Color Swatching System,
    167
Color Selector buttons (Paint Style
    palette), *158*, **159–160**

color separations, 3, 271. *See also* Adobe
    Separator
  printing, **275–276**
  saving, **275**
Color tools, 24
Column Graph options (Graph Options
    dialog box), 249, *250*
Columns field, in Rows & Columns
    filter, 126
columns of text, 4, 125–126, *127*
commands, gray on menus, 19–20
Compatibility box, for Illustrator version
    for saved file, 108
Compatible Gradient Printing option
    (Document Setup dialog box),
    171
compound path, 181
Compound Paths (View menu), *314*, 315
Connect Data Point, as line graph
    option, 250
Constrain Angle option (General
    Preferences dialog box), 26
constrained shapes, **41–42**
constraining line, to 45-degree angle, 34
Control key, 20
control panel, for Adobe Type Manager,
    268, *269*
Convert custom colors to process option
    (Trap dialog box), 176
Convert Direction Point tool, 22, 286
Copy (Edit menu), 49, 51, 305
corner points, 77, *77*
Corner Radius option (General
    Preferences dialog box), 26
corners, for offset path, 222
counterclockwise rotation, 86
counterclockwise spiral, 213
Courier font, *141*
Create Outlines (Type menu), 320
Crop filter, **234–235**, *234*
crop marks, 214, 274
Cropmarks (View menu), *314*, 315
Current Tool option, on status bar, 18
Cursor Key (General Preferences
    dialog box), 27, 74
curved lines
  Brush tool to create, 38
  changing straight lines to, **78–79**
  corner points for, 77, *77*
  direction points for, 31, 75, *76*
  Freehand tool to create, **36–38**
  moving, 47
  Pen tool to create, **34–36**
  smooth points for, 76, *76*
Custom button, and Paint Style palette
    slider bars, *159*, 159

Custom Color (Object menu), 310
Custom Color button (Paint Style
    palette), 164
Custom Color dialog box, *164*, 164, *311*
  Select All Unused, 165
custom colors, **163–167**
  and color separations, 274
  creating, **164**
  deleting, **165**
  filter to convert to process color, **208**,
    208
Custom Colors (Document Information
    dialog box), 115, 224
Custom Patterns (Document Information
    dialog box), 115, 225
Custom to Process filter, **208**, *208*
customizing graphs, **259–266**
Cut (Edit menu), 305
cylinders, **185–187**, *187*

D

Dashed Lines (Paint Style palette), *158*,
    161, *162*
data entry for graphs, **254–257**
  importing data for, **256–257**
  manual, **255–256**
  Paste command for, 257
Date and Time option, on status bar, 18
dBASE, importing text file from, 122
decimal tab stops, 153
default settings. *See also* General
    Preferences dialog box
  for color, 68
  for PPD (PostScript Printer
    Definition) file, **272–273**
degrees, rotating object by precise
    amount, 85
Delete Anchor Point tool, 22, 80, 81
Delete Riders filter, **228**
deleting
  anchor points, **80–81**
  custom colors, **165**
  fill patterns, **174**
  gradient fills, **171**
  paint swatches, 158
  tabs, 154
  templates from view, 104
  text objects, 125
Desaturate filter, **209**
Desaturate More filter, **209**
deselecting objects, 50, 186
Design dialog box, 261, *262*
designs, positioning on page, 25, **114**
desktop interface, **16–25**
  dialog boxes, **18–19**

drawing surface, **16–18**, *17*
menu bar, **19–20**
palettes, 19
dialog boxes, **18–19**
    commands for, 20
    to create shapes, **40–41**
    keyboard shortcuts, end paper, 332
dictionary for spell check
    adding word to, 133
    changing, 135
    user-customizable for spell check, 4
digital drawing tablet, 7
Direct Selection tool, 21, 47, 50, 80, 81,
        82–83, 186, 287
    for compound paths, 181
    to select anchor point, 74
    for straight line size adjustment, 33
direction lines, 34
direction points, 75, *76*
    adjusting, 79, 81
    on curved lines, 31, *34*, 34
discretionary hyphens, inserting, 136
Distill program (Adobe Acrobat), 270
Distort filters, **215–219**
Distribute Horizontally filter, **221**
Distribute Vertically filter, **221**
Divide filter, **231–232**, *232*
Document Information dialog box,
        114–115, *115*, **224–225**, 323, *324*
Document Setup (File menu), 16, 166, 303
Document Setup dialog box, 17,
        111–113, 291, *293*
    Compatible Gradient Printing
        option, 171
    Show Placed Images, 107
    Single Full Page option, 111, *112*
    Tile Full Pages option, *112*, 112–113
    Tile Imageable Areas, *113*, 113
document windows, 16, 42
Done (Find Font dialog box), *144*, 145
DOS system, Encapsulated PostScript
        format (EPS), 11
double-clicking, file icons to open
        Illustrator, 16
drawing
    graphs, **252–253**
    lines, **31–38**
    shapes, **39–42**
drawing surface, **16–18**, *17*. See also
        Artboard
Drawing tools, 22–23
drop caps, 127
Drop Shadow (Graph Style dialog box),
        252
drop shadow effect, 93

Drop Shadow filter, **242**, *242*
drop shadows, **192–193**, *193*
duplicates, shearing, 94
duplicating
    gradient fills, 170
    objects with Move dialog box, **48–49**

E

Edge-to-Edge Lines, as line graph option,
        250
Edit Behavior (General Preferences
        dialog box), 28
Edit menu, **304–305**, *304*
    Copy, 49, 51, 305
    Paste, 49, 51, 296, 305
    Select All, 50, 305
Edit Views (View menu), 309
editing, 72
    graph data, **257**
    layer available for, 110
    type, 56
electronic drawing tablet, 38
ellipses, smart punctuation vs. regular, 138
ellipsis (...), menu commands with, 20
em dash, 137, 138
em space, 147
embossed type, **193–194**
Emulsion (PPD file setting), 272
en dash, 138
Encapsulated PostScript format (EPS), 7, 9
    IBM PC-compatible, 11
    importing, 106
    saving, 107, **108**
endpoints, 75
    style for, 162
entering type, 54. *See also* data entry
        for graphs
entry line, in Graph Data worksheet, 255
EPS format dialog box, Include Placed
        Images, *108*
Eras font, *141*
Error Handler, in rider, 228
Exclude filter, **230**, *230*
exercises
    business cards, **278–281**
    columns and text wrap, 130
    five-ring logo, **51–53**
    flower drawing, **42–46**
    food label, **65–69**
    half-circle creation, **81–82**
    magazine layout, **290–299**, *292*
    poster advertisement, **282–290**
    rotating and scaling, **89–91**
    sale ad, **56–58**
exporting, **108–109**

gradient fills, **171–172**
eye icon, in Layers palette, 110
Eyedropper tool, 24
    changing to cross hair cursor, 27

F

families of fonts, 141
feelings, color and, 156
File box (Paint Style palette), 59
file icons, double-clicking to open
        Illustrator, 16
File menu, **302–304**, *303*
    Change Placed Art, 107
    Document Setup, 16, 166, 303
    Import Styles, 166, 261, 303
    Import Text, 130
    keyboard shortcuts, endpaper, 329
    New, 42, 51, 102, 302
    Open, 102, 302
    Place Art, 106, 130
    Preferences, 25
    Preferences, Hyphenation Options,
        135
    Print Composite, 278
    Save, 46, 302
    Save As, 108, 302
file sharing, Adobe Acrobat for, 11,
        270–271
Fill & Stroke for Mask filter, **210**
Fill button (Color palette), 68
Fill Lines, as line graph option, 250
fill patterns, **172–174**, *173*
    changing, 173
    creating, **173**
    deleting, **174**
    transforming, 27
Filter menu, **321–325**
    Colors, **204–210**, *321*, 321
    Colors, Adjust Colors filter,
        204–205, *205*
    Colors, Blend Front to Back filter,
        205, *206*
    Colors, Blend Horizontally filter,
        206–207
    Colors, Blend Vertically filter, **207**,
        207
    Colors, Change Custom to Process,
        167
    Colors, Custom to Process filter, **208**,
        208
    Colors, Desaturate filter, **209**
    Colors, Desaturate More filter, **209**
    Colors, Invert Colors filter, **209**

Colors, Saturate filter, **209–210**
Colors, Saturate More filter, **210**
Create, **210–214**, *322*, 322
Create, Fill & Stroke for Mask filter, **210**
Create, Mosaic filter, **210–212**
Create, Polygon filter, **212**, *212*
Create, Spiral filter, **213**
Create, Star filter, **213**, *213*
Create, Trim Marks filter, **214**, *214*
Distort, **215–219**, *322*, *323*
Distort, Free Distort filter, **215**, *215*
Distort, Roughen filter, **216**, *216*
Distort, Scribble filter, **217**, *218*
Distort, Tweak filter, **218**, *218*
Distort, Twirl filter, **218–219**, *219*
Last Filter, 321
Objects, **219–224**, *322*, *323*
Objects, Add Anchor Points filter, **219**, *220*
Objects, Align Objects filter, **220**, *220*
Objects, Distribute Horizontally filter, **221**
Objects, Distribute Vertically filter, **221**
Objects, Move Each filter, **221**, *222*
Objects, Offset Path filter, 193, 194, **221–222**, *222*, 296
Objects, Outline Path filter, **222–223**
Objects, Rotate Each filter, **223**, *223*
Objects, Scale Each filter, **223–224**, *223*
Other, 114, **224–228**, 328
Other, Delete Riders filter, **228**
Other, Document Information filter, **114–115**, *115*, **224–225**, *323*, *324*
Other, Make Riders filter, **227–228**, *228*
Other, Overprint Black filter, **226**, *226*
Pathfinder, **229–237**, *323*, *324*
Pathfinder, Crop filter, **234–235**, *234*
Pathfinder, Divide filter, 181, **231–232**, *232*
Pathfinder, Exclude filter, **230**, *230*
Pathfinder, Hard filter, **235**, *235*
Pathfinder, Intersect filter, **229**, *230*
Pathfinder, Merge filter, **233–234**, *234*
Pathfinder, Minus Back filter, **231**, *232*
Pathfinder, Minus Front filter, **231**, *231*

Pathfinder, Options filter, **237**
Pathfinder, Outline filter, **232**, *233*
Pathfinder, Soft filter, **235–236**, *236*
Pathfinder, Trap filter, 5, 175, **236**, *237*
Pathfinder, Trim filter, **233**, *233*
Pathfinder, Unite filter, **229**, *229*
Select, **237–239**, 323, *325*
Select, Same Fill Color filter, **238**
Select, Same Paint Style filter, **238**
Select, Same Stroke Color filter, **238**
Select, Same Stroke Weight filter, **238**
Select, Select Inverse filter, **238–239**
Select, Select Masks filter, **239**
Select, Select Stray Points filter, **239**
Stylize, **239–243**, 324, *325*
Stylize, Add Arrowheads filter, **240**, *325*
Stylize, Bloat filter, **240**, *241*
Stylize, Calligraphy filter, **241**, *241*, *242*
Stylize, Drop Shadow filter, **242**, *242*
Stylize, Round Corners filter, **243**
Text, 243, *325*, *326*
Text, Check Spelling, 133
Text, Find Font, 144, *326*
Text, Revert Text, 122
Text, Rows & Columns, 125
Text, Smart Punctuation filter, 137
Find Font filter, 143, *326*
Find Fonts dialog box, *144*
Find Next (Find Font dialog box), *144*, 145
First Column in Front (Graph Style dialog box), 252
First Line field (Paragraph palette), 152
First Row in Front (Graph Style dialog box), 252
Fit Headline (Type menu), 320
Fit In Window (View menu), 22, 309
flashing insertion point, 56, *57*
flatness, in rider, 227–228
Focoltone Colour System, **167**
folder, for Adobe Illustrator, 15
font cache, 269
Font menu, **315–316**, *316*
font utility, 8
fonts, 8, 63, *64*, **141–145**, *141*
    categories of, **142–143**
    changing, 143
    for graph text, **260–261**
    and memory needs, 6
    searching and replacing, 4, **143–145**

Fonts (Document Information dialog box), 115, 225
forward compatibility, 10
four-color printing, 165
fractions, smart punctuation vs. regular, 138
FrameMaker, importing text file from, 122
Free Distort filter, **215**, *215*
Free memory option, on status bar, 18
Freehand Tolerance option (General Preferences dialog box), 26, 36–37, *37*, 43, 103
Freehand tool, 23, 43, 44, 290, 296
    changing to cross hair cursor, 27
    to create curves, **36–38**
Futura typeface, 142

G

Gap value, for dashed lines, 161
General Information, for document, 114, 224
General Preferences dialog box, 25–26, *26*
    Auto Trace Gap, 27, 104
    Cursor Key increments, 27, 74
    Edit Behavior, 28
    Freehand Tolerance, 26, 36–37, *37*, 43, 103
    Keyboard Increments, 27
    Tool Behavior controls, **26–27**
Gradient (View menu), 312
Gradient button, and Paint Style palette slider bars, 159, *161*
Gradient dialog box, *312*
Gradient Fill tool, 24, 171, 195
gradient fills, **168–172**, 286
    creating, **168–170**, 282–283
    creating with multiple colors, 171
    deleting, **171**
    duplicating, 170
    for metallic type, 195
    positioning within objects, **171**, 288
    printing and exporting, **171–172**
    for three-dimensional effect, 187, 188
    with woven look, *182*
Gradient palette, 168, *169*, 282, *284*
gradient tint bars, 274
Gradients (Document Information dialog box), 115, 225
Graph Axis Style dialog box, 248, *249*
Graph Column Design dialog box, 262–263, *263*
Graph Data dialog box, 253, **254–257**, *254*
    Cell Style button, 259

manipulating data with, **258–259**
Transpose command, 258
Graph dialog box, dimensions of graph
in, 253
Graph Marker Design dialog box, 264,
265
Graph Style dialog box, **246–252**, *247,
315*
Axis settings, **248**
Graph Options, **249–251**
graph styles, integrity of gradients, 172
Graph tool, 25, 246
graph worksheet
customizing cells, **259**
transposing rows and columns in, **258**
graphic area, converting to text area,
119–120
graphics, *See* artwork
graphs, **246–266**
creating specialized designs, **261–264**
customizing, **259–266**
data entry for, **254–257**
drawing, **252–253**
drawing outline to predetermined
dimensions, **253**
editing data, **257**
fonts for text in, **260–261**
manipulating data elements, **258–259**
manually drawing outline, **253**
types of, **247**, *248*
Graphs (View menu), *314*, 315
gray commands, 19–20
Greek Type limit, setting preferences, 28
Group (Arrange menu), 50, 307
Group Selection tool, 21, 124, 130, 295
for graph customizing, 260
Grouped column graph, 247, *248*
options for, 249, *250*
grouping objects, **49–50**, 52
graph elements, 259–260
transformation tools for, 84
guides
creating, **104–105**, 291
for perspective, 188
ruler, **105**
Guides (View menu), *314*, 314
Guides Lock command, 105
gutters, 291
artwork in, 113

H

half-circle, creating, **81–82**
halftone dot shape, in rider, 227
Halftone (PPD file setting), 273
Hand tool, 22

Hard filter, **235**, *235*
hardware requirements, **6–8**
headlines
adding, 296
forcing fit, 320
point size for, 64, 145
Height/Width option (Trap dialog box),
176
Helvetica font, *141*
hidden layers, 110
Hide (Arrange menu), 307
Hide Edges (View menu), 309
Hide Guides (View menu), 309
Hide Page Tiling (View menu), 309
Hide/Show Template command, 102, 104
horizontal axis
aligning objects along, 220
for Reflect tool, 96
horizontal distribution, of objects, 221
horizontal guides, 105, *106*
for column and row edges, 126
horizontal mirror image, 93
horizontal percentages, for scaling
object, 88
horizontal scale of letters, *64*, 64–65,
151–152
hyphenation, automatic, **135–136**
Hyphenation Options dialog box, *136*

I

I-beam cursor, 54, 119
IBM PC-compatibility, Encapsulated
PostScript format (EPS), 11
Image (PPD file setting), 273
images, *See* artwork
Import Styles (File menu), 166, 261, 303
Import Text (File menu), 130
imported images, **105–107**
color of, 107
PICT, 9
saving with file, 107
sizing, 130
styles for, **107**
importing
data to graph worksheet, 256–257
text, **122–124**
text to magazine layout, **294**
inches, as ruler measurement unit, 28
Include Placed Images (EPS format
dialog box), *108*
indentation, **152**
Info palette, 23, 42, *43*, 66
inserting
discretionary hyphens, 136
type, **118–122**
insertion point

entering type at, 23
flashing, 56, *57*
selecting type by, 55–56
for text, 119
Intersect filter, **229**, *230*
Invert Colors filter, **209**

J

jagged edge, filter to create, 216
Japan, Toyo Ink Electronic Color Finder
1050, 166
Join command, 75, 195, 197, 313
Joins (Paint Style palette), *158*, 163
justify alignment, 152, *153*
Justify Last Line alignment, 152, *153*

K

kerning, **147–148**
setting preferences, 27
keyboard, 7
Keyboard Increments (General
Preferences dialog box), 27
keyboard shortcuts, endpaper, **19**,
329–332
for centering words, 67
on menus, 20

L

labels, for printers, 274
landscape orientation, 272
landscapes, perspective in, 188
Last Filter (Filter menu), 321
layers, **109–111**
creating, 110
hiding and locking, **110–111**
Layers palette, 110, *327*
leading
for lines of type, 146, *147*
setting preferences, 27
Leading (Type menu), 317
Learned Words dialog box, 133, *134*
Left alignment, 152, *153*
left tab stops, 153
legend labels, in graph worksheets, 254
legends, options for pie graphs, 250–251
Legends Across Top (Graph Style
dialog box), 252
Legends in Wedges, as pie graph option,
251
letters
adding accents to, 288
horizontal spacing between, 147
spacing of, **149–151**
ligatures, smart punctuation vs.
regular, 138

Line graph, 247, *248*
 options for, 250
 placing markers on, **264**, *265*
line screen, for Adobe Separator, 273
line segments, 31, 72. *See also* paths
 moving, **82–83**
line spacing, by Adobe Type Manager, 269
line weights, scaling during transforms,
  27, 86, 87
linear blend, *170*, 170
lines. *See also* curved lines
 adjusting size of straight, 33
 changing straight to curved, **78–79**
 creating wavy, 35–36
 drawing, **31–38**
 moving, 47
 Pen tool for straight, **32–34**
 stroking, 61, 69
 stroking vs. filling, 73
 variable width with Brush tool, 38
Link Blocks (Type menu), 320
linking text blocks, **124–125**
list, of hyphenation exceptions, 135
Lock (Arrange menu), 307
Lock Width/Height, for mosaic filter, 211
locked layers, 110
locking guides, 105
Lotus 1-2-3, importing text file from, 122

M

MacDraw, 270
 importing images from, 106
Macintosh System software, 8
MacLink (DataViz), 101
MacPaint
 file as template, 101
 importing files from, 107
MacWrite, importing text file from, 122
magazine layout, **290–299**, *292*
 adding text blocks, **294–295**
magnifying glass icon, 22
Make Guides command, 104, 279
Make Riders filter, **227–228**, *228*
Make Wrap (Type menu), 129, 131,
  296, 320
margins, 152
 centering guides, 291
 preventing loss of work in, when
   printing, 113
Mark Data Points, as line graph
   option, 250
marquee, 53
 Direct Selection tool to draw, 83
 Selection tool for, 50
masking, **191–192**, *191*
 fill and stroke objects for, 210

 selecting, 239
Masks (View menu), *314*, 314
math coprocessor
 for Offset Path filter, 221
 for Outline Path filter, 222
mathematical formulas, 9
Measure tool, 23
measurements, Info palette to list, 42
memory, 6
 currently available, 18
 font cache, **269**
 for Mosaic filter, 212
menu bar, **19–20**, 302
Merge filter, **233–234**, *234*
metallic type, **194–196**, *194*
Microsoft Word, importing text file
   from, 122
millimeters, as ruler measurement
   unit, 28
Minus Back filter, **231**, *232*
Minus Front filter, **231**, *231*
mirror images, Reflect tool to create, 24,
  91–93
misregistration, trapping to allow for, 174
Miter Limit field (Paint Style palette),
  163, 163
Mix Hard filter, 235
mixing rate, for Soft filter, 235
moire, 227
monitors, 6
morphing, with Blend tool, **200–201**
Mosaic filter, **210–212**
motion, Blend tool to simulate, **199**, *200*
mouse, 7
Move command, 186, 306
Move dialog box, *48*, 48, 186
Move Each filter, **221**, *222*
moving
 line segments, **82–83**
 objects, **47–49**
 page to position design, 25, **114**
 tabs, 154
 type, **57–58**
MultiMate, importing text file from, 122
Multiple Master typefaces, 143
multiple objects, selecting, 49

N

negative image, from Adobe Separator, 273
new document window, 42
New (File menu), 42, 51, 102, 302
New Size, for mosaic filter, 211
New View (View menu), 309
New Window (Window menu), **326–327**
newsletters, linked blocks on separate
   pages, 125

newspaper text, point size for, 145
"no color" button, 68
No Legends option, for pie graph, 251
Non-Uniform button (Scale dialog box),
  88, 184, 186
Number of tiles, for mosaic filter, 211
Number of Undos option, on status
   bar, 18
numbers, in graph labels, 255

O

object editing, keyboard shortcuts,
   endpaper, **329–330**
Object Information (Document
   Information dialog box), 115, 224
Object menu, **310–315**, *310*
 Compound Paths, Make, 191
 Custom Color, 164
 Gradient, 168, 282
 Graphs, Column, 262
 Graphs, Data, 257
 Graphs, Design, 261
 Graphs, Marker, 264
 Graphs, Style, 246
 Paint Style, 59
 Pattern, 173
objects. *See also* transforming objects
 anchor point deletion and shape
   of, 80
 color for, **58–61**
 creating object from intersection of,
   229, *230*
 deselecting, 50
 filter to distort, 215
 filters for, **219–224**
 grouping, **49–50**, 52
 guides to align, 105
 manipulating, **46–50**
 moving, **47–49**
 paths for, *73*
 positioning gradient within, **171**
 uniting overlapping, 229
OfficeWriter, importing text file from, 123
Offset Path filter, 193, 194, **221–222**,
  222, 296
Open (File menu), 302
open paths, 73, *74*
 creating from closed path, 22
 endpoints for, 75, 162
 from stack of grouped objects, **232**,
  233
opening
 files in Adobe Separator, 271

new document, 278
PDF file in Illustrator, **270–271**
Option key, 20
   and Copy command for PICT image,
      109
   and paint swatches, 158
   with Scale tool, 184
   and transformation, 84
Options filter, **237**
Orientation (PPD file settings), 272
Other Filters folder, 204
   Revert Text Path filter, 122
Outline filter, **232**, *233*
Outline Path filter, **222–223**
outlines, converting text to, 176–177,
   190–191, 320
Oval dialog box, 284
Oval tool, 23, 39, 43, 66–67, 287
   and center points, 77
   for circles, 41, 81, 284
Overprint Black filter, **226**, *226*

P

page layout applications, 4
Page Setup (File menu), 303
Page Setup dialog box, Printer Effects, 10
Page Size (PPD file settings), 272
Page tool, 25, **114**, 291
PageMaker, 9
pages
   size of, 111
   tiling, **111–113**
Paint Style (Object menu), 310
Paint Style palette, **58–61**, *59*, **157–163**,
   158, 284, *311*
   Caps, *158*, **162**, 162
   Color Selector buttons, *158*, **159–160**
   Custom Color button, 164
   Custom to Process filter and, 208
   for customizing graphs, 260
   Dashed Lines, *158*, **161**, *162*
   double-clicking gradient name, 169
   Joins, *158*, **161–163**
   Miter Limit field, *163*, 163
   Paint Swatches, **157–159**, *158*
   Stroke box, 61, *62*
Paint Swatches (Paint Style palette),
   157–159, *158*
Paint tool, 24
   changing to cross hair cursor, 27
palettes, 19
   keyboard shortcuts, endpaper, 332
Panel Display menu (Paint Style palette),
   157
Pantone matching system, **166**

Pantone Process Color System, 166
Paragraph (Type menu), 320
Paragraph palette, 294, *319*, 319, 320
   alignment options, 152
   extended, 150
   Hyphenation area, *135*, 135
   letter spacing field, 150, 319
   margin and paragraph indents, 152
   Word spacing, 319
Paste (Edit menu), 49, 51, 296, 305
   for data entry to graph worksheet,
      257
Paste In Back (Edit menu), 305
Paste In Front (Edit menu), 186, 305
Paste Remembers Layers (General
      Preferences dialog box), 28
path, as insertion area for text, 120–121
Path Editing tools, 22
Path Type tool, 23, **120–121**
Pathfinder filters, **229–237**
paths, 31, **72**
   adding anchor points, 77–78
   converting text to art, **121–122**
   creating guide from, 104
   dividing for woven look, **180–182**
   entering text within, *120*
   moving line segments of, **82–83**
   types of, **73–74**
Pattern (Object menu), 310
Pattern button, and Paint Style palette
      slider bars, 159, *160*, 160
Pattern dialog box, 173, *174*, *312*
patterns, *See* fill patterns
PC file formats, translating to PICT, 101
PDF (Portable Document Format), 11
   opening files in Illustrator, **270–271**
   saving file as, 270
Pen tool, 22, 44, 285, 287, 290
   changing to cross hair cursor, 27
   creating polygon with, 33
   for curved lines, **34–36**
   for straight lines, **32–34**
pencil icon, in Layers palette, 110
personalizing, copy of Illustrator, 15
perspective, in three-dimensional effect,
   188–190
PICT images
   importing, 9, 106
   mosaic effect for, 210–212
   saving, 109
   as template, 101
   translating PC file formats to, 101
Pie graph, 247, *248*
   options for, **250–251**, *251*
Place Art (File menu), 106, 130, 303

Placed Art (Document Information
      dialog box), 115, 225
plug-in filters, **4–5**, **204–244**
   Document Information, 114
Plug-Ins folder, 122
   adding Make Riders filter to, 227
Point Editing tools, 22
point size of type, 145, *146*
points, **72**
   types of, **74–77**
points/picas, as ruler measurement
      unit, 28
polygon, creating with Pen tool, 33
Polygon filter, **212**, *212*
pop cap, 127, 299
Portable Document Format (PDF), 11
portrait orientation, 272
positive image, from Adobe Separator, 273
poster advertisement, **282–290**
PostScript fonts, 143
   Adobe Type Manager for, 8, **268–269**
PostScript printers, 7
PPD (PostScript Printer Definition)
      file, 271
   default settings for, 272–273
preferences
   setting, **25–28**
   setting for pathfinder filters, 237
Preferences (File menu), 25, 135,
      303–304
Preview (View menu), 308
Preview mode, 31, 68, 196
   color changes, 60
Preview option, for rows and columns
      filter, 126
Preview Selection (View menu), 308
Preview Selection mode, 31
Print (File menu), 303
print shops, font selector for, 143
printable section, tiling pages for,
      111–113
PrintCapture, importing text file from, 123
Printer Effects (Page Setup dialog box), 10
printer marks, adding with Adobe
      Separator, **274**
printers, 7
printing
   color separations, **275–276**
   gradient fills, **171–172**
   rider for information for, 227
   troubleshooting problems, 10
   two-color, 165
Process button, in Paint Style palette, 159
process colors, 59, 163
   changing by percentage, 204–205
   converting from color matching
      system, 167

decreasing intensity of, 209
for gradient fills, 172
increasing intensity, 210
Professional Write, importing text· file
    from, 123
Publishing (Edit menu), 305
punctuation
    smart, **137–138**
    smart vs. regular, 138
Punk filter, *242*, *243*

Q

QuarkXPress, 9, 11, 270
    Illustrator file compatibility, 11
Quit (File menu), 304
quotation marks
    opening and closing, 137
    smart punctuation vs. regular, 138

R

radial gradient, *170*, 170
RAM (random access memory), 6
random sizes, scaling objects to, 224
Reader program (Adobe Acrobat), 270
Rectangle tool, 23, 39–40, 45, 65, 279
    and center points, 77
rectangles. *See also* text box
    rotating, **89–90**
    scaling, 90–91
    Shear tool for, 96–97, *97*
    transforming with Reflect tool, **95–96**
Redo (Edit menu), 305
Reflect dialog box, 91, *92*, 92–93
Reflect tool, 24, **91–93**, 299
    to transform rectangles, **95–96**
register marks, 274
Release Wrap (Type menu), 129, 320
Repeat Transformation (Arrange menu),
    306
Repeating Column design type, 263
replacing type, 57
resolution, for Adobe Separator, 273
Reverse trap option (Trap dialog box),
    175, 176
Revert Text Path filter, 122
Revert to Saved (File menu), 302
riders, 227
right alignment, 152, *153*
right tab stops, 153
Rotate dialog box, 85, *86*
Rotate Each filter, *223*, *223*
Rotate tool, 24, **84–86**
    and three-dimensional effect,
        184, 185
rotating
    blended shapes, 199

rectangles, **89–90**
    Twirl filter for, **218–219**, *219*
Roughen filter, 216, *216*
Round Corners filter, **243**
rounded corners
    radius for rectangle corners, 26
    for stroked path, 163
Rounded-Rectangle tool, 23, 39
Rows & Columns dialog box, *126*
Rows & Columns filter, 4, 125
rows of text, 125–126, *127*
RTF (Rich Text Format), importing text
    file from, 123
ruler, 279, 291
    aligning tab ruler with text margin,
        153
    moving zero point on, 66, 279
Ruler Units, setting preferences, 28
rulers guides, **105**, *106*
Rulers (View menu), 18
runaround, *See* text wrap

S

Same Fill Color filter, **238**
Same Paint Style filter, **238**
Same Stroke Color filter, **238**
Same Stroke Weight filter, **238**
Sample Files folder
    Column & Marker file, 261
    Graph Styles file, 261
sans serif font, *142*, 142
Saturate filter, **209–210**
Saturate More filter, **210**
Save (File menu), 46, 302
Save (Find Font dialog box), *144*, 145
Save As (File menu), 108, 302
Save As dialog box, 46
saving
    color-separated document, **275**
    drawing, 46, 53
    files in PDF (Portable Document
        Format), 270
    imported image with file, 107
Scale dialog box, 88
Scale Each filter, **223–224**, *223*
Scale Line Weight (General Preferences
    dialog box), 27
Scale tool, 24, **86–89**
    for grouped circle, 186
    Option key with, 184, 186, 295, 298
scaling rectangles, 90–91
scaling type, horizontal, **151–152**
scanned image
    importing, 106
    as template, 101
scatter graphs, 247, *248*

options for, *251*, 251
    transposing axes, **258**
Scissors tool, 22, 78, 195, 197, 287
screen angle, in rider, 227
screen frequency, in rider, 227
screen size, restoring 100 percent, 57
Scribble filter, **217**, *218*
script, 9
script font, *142*, 142
Select All (Edit menu), 50, 305
Select All Unused button (Custom Color
    dialog box), 165
Select Inverse filter, **238–239**
Select Masks filter, **239**
Select None (Edit menu), 305
Select Stray Points filter, **239**
selecting
    filters for, **237–239**
    type, **55–56**
Selection tool, 47, 285, 290
    ⌘ Command key for, 48
    and compound paths, 181
    for font changes, 143, 145
    for transforming objects, 184
    for type, 57
Selection tools, 21
Send to Back (Arrange menu), 44,
    192, 307
Separator Setup window, *272*, 272
serial number, 15
serif font, *142*, 142
service bureau, and font selection, 8
shape blends, 197–199
shapes, **39–42**
    constrained, **41–42**
    dialog box to create, 40–41
    moving, 47
Shear dialog box, for setting precise
    angles, 94, *95*
Shear tool, 24, **93–94**
    for rectangles, 96–97, *97*
    and three-dimensional effect, 184,
        185
Shift key, 20
    to constrain rectangle position, 124
    to constrain shape to circle or
        square, 41
    to select multiple objects, 49
Show (Arrange menu), 307
Show Clipboard (Edit menu), 305
Show Placed Images (Document Setup
    dialog box), 107
Show Rulers (View menu), 105, 309
Show Template (View menu), 308
Show/Hide Character
    (Window menu), 328

Show/Hide Gradient (Window menu), 328
Show/Hide Info (Window menu), 328
Show/Hide Layers (Window menu), 327
Show/Hide Paint Style (Window menu), 328
Show/Hide Paragraph (Window menu), 328
Show/Hide Tab Ruler (Window menu), 328
Show/Hide Toolbox (Window menu), 327
Single Full Page option (Document Setup dialog box), 111, *112*
size
    constraining design to specific, 105
    of graph worksheet cells, 259
    of graphic, and text wrap, 129
    of Illustrator pages, 111
    Scale tool to adjust object's, 86
    of type, 64, 145, *146*
Size/Leading (General Preferences dialog box), 27
skewed objects, Shear tool to create, 93
Skip (Find Font dialog box), *144*, 144
slider bars
    in document window, 18
    for mixing colors, 59, *60*
    in Paint Style palette, 159
Sliding Column design type, 263
smart punctuation, **137–138**
Smart Punctuation dialog box, *138*
Smart Punctuation filter, 4
smooth points, 76, *76*
Snap box (Tab Ruler palette), *153*, 153
Snap to Point (General Preferences dialog box), 27
Soft filter, **235–236**, *236*
software requirements, 8
spaces, smart punctuation vs. regular, 138
Spacing (Type menu), 319
special effects, **180–201**. *See also* type special effects
    Blend tool, **197–201**
    dividing paths for woven look, **180–182**
    three-dimensions, **183–190**
speed, and Preview mode, 31
spelling checker, **133**, *134*, **135**
Spiral filter, **213**
spot color printing, 165
spot function, in rider, 227
spread, 175
spreadsheet, for graph data, *254*, 254
squares, 23, 41
Stacked column graph, 247, *248*
    options for, 249, *250*

stacking order, vs. Layers feature, 109
standard legends, for pie graphs, 251
Star filter, **213**, *213*
starting Adobe Illustrator, **15**
status bar, 18
Steps field (Blend dialog box), *199*
stroked lines, 61, 69
    corner style, 163
    vs. filling, 73
strokes, custom colors for, 160
styles, **58–64**
    filters for, **239–243**
    for imported images, 107
    of type, **62–65**, **140–141**. *See also* fonts
stylus, 7
subscripting, 151
superscripting, 151
Switch XY button (Graph Data dialog box), 258
System 7 software, 8

T
Tab Ruler palette, 4, 153
tabs, in text, **152–154**
technical support line, 10
Tekton font, *141*
templates, **100–104**
    creating, **101–102**
    preferences for tracing, 27
    removing from view, 104
    tracing, 102
    tracing portion of, 103
    for two page spread, *293*
text, *See* type
text blocks
    adding to magazine spread, **294–295**
    linking, **124–125**, 320
    selecting type by, 55
text box
    adding for additional text, 124
    in columns and rows, *127*
    for imported text, 123
    overflow text indicator, *123*, 123
    Type tool to draw, 119, 123, 130
Text Flow, *128*
    in Rows & Columns filter, 126
text objects, deleting, 125
text paths, converting to art paths, **121–122**
text wrap, around graphics, **127–129**, *128*, 131,**295–296**
text-handling, 4
Thickness option (Trap dialog box), 176
three-dimensional effect, **183–190**
    for box, **183–185**

cylinders, **185–187**, *187*
gradient fills for, 168
perspective in, **188–190**
spheres, **187–188**, *188*
in woven look, *182*
Tile Full Pages option (Document Setup dialog box), *112*, 112–113
Tile Imageable Areas (Document Setup dialog box), *113*, 113, 291
Tile Spacing, for mosaic filter, 211
tiling, pages, **111–113**
Tint Reduction option (Trap dialog box), 176
Tool Behavior controls (General Preferences dialog box), **26–27**
Toolbox palette
    20-25, *21*, *See also specific tools*
    Color tools, 24
    Drawing tools, 22–23
    Graph tool, 25
    Measure tool, 23
    Page tool, 25
    Point and Path Editing tools, 22
    Selection tools, 21
    Transformation tools, 24
    Type tools, 23
    Viewing tools, 22
Toyo Ink Electronic Color Finder 1050, 166
tracing
    preferences for, 27, 103
    templates, 102
trackball, 7
tracking, **148–149**, *149*
Tracking (General Preferences dialog box), 27
Tracking/Kerning (Type menu), 318
Transfer (PPD file setting), 273
Transform Pattern Tiles (General Preferences dialog box), *27*
transformation dialog box, 84
Transformation tools, 24
    for imported images, 107
transforming objects, **83–97**
    with Reflect tool, **91–93**
    with Rotate tool, **84–86**
    with Scale tool, **86–89**
    with Shear tool, **93–94**
    for three-dimensional effect, **183–185**
translation software utility, 101
transposing
    graph worksheet rows and columns, **258**
    scatter graph axes, **258**
Trap filter, 5, **236**, *237*

dialog box, *175*, 175
trapping
  color, **174–177**
  text, **176–177**
Trim filter, **233**, *233*
Trim Marks filter, **214**, *214*
troubleshooting
  compatibility problems, 9
  lost artwork in gutters, 113
  printing problems, 10
TrueType fonts, 143
Trumatch Color Swatching System, **167**
tutorial files for, 130
Tweak filter, **218**, *218*
Twirl filter, **218–219**, *219*
two-color printing, 165
Type 1 fonts, 8, 143
type, 118–154
  adding, **53–65**, 56, 67–68
  adding other elements to, **196–197**
  adding to poster, **288–289**
  alignment of, 105, **152**
  changing case, 4, **139**
  editing, 56
  entering, 54
  fonts for, 63, *64*
  importing, **122–124**
  inserting, **118–122**
  keyboard shortcuts for editing,
    endpaper, 331–332
  moving, **57–58**
  as outlines before transforming,
    183–184
  outlines for, 176–177, **190–191**
  selecting, **55–56**
  selecting and editing, 57
  sizing, 64, 145, *146*
  styles of, **62–65**
  tabs in, **152–154**
  trapping, **176–177**
Type menu, **316–320**, *316*
  Alignment, Center, 281
  Create Outlines, 177
  Link Blocks, 124
  Make Wrap, 129, 131, 296
  Outlines, 184
  Release Wrap, 129
  Unlink Blocks, 125
type special effects, **190–197**
  drop shadows, **192–193**, *193*
  embossed or chiseled, **193–194**, *194*

masking, **191–192**, *191*
metallic type, **194–196**, *194*
Type tool, 54, 56, **119**, 288
  for business card, **280–281**
  to change font, 143
Type tools, 23
Type units, setting preferences, 28
typefaces, *See* fonts
typesetter's punctuation, 4, 137

U

Undo (Edit menu), 33, 96, 304
  for scale command, 89
Undo Levels (General Preferences
    dialog box), 28
undos, displaying number available, 18
Ungroup (Arrange menu), 307
ungrouped graphs, 257
Uniformly Scaled Column Design Type,
    262
Unite filter, **229**, *229*
United Kingdom, Focoltone Colour
    System, **167**
Unlink Blocks (Type menu), 125, 320
Unlock All (Arrange menu), 307
Use Precise Cursors (General Preferences
    dialog box), 27
Use Ratio button, for Mosaic filter, 211

V

variable line width, with Brush tool, 38
vertical axis
  aligning objects along, 220
  for Reflect tool, 96
vertical distribution of objects, 221
vertical guides, 105, *106*
  for column and row edges, 126
vertical mirror image, 93
vertical percentages, for scaling object, 88
vertical space, between lines of type, 146
Vertically Scaled Column Design Type,
    262
video cards, 6–7
View menu, **307–309**, *308*
  Rulers, 18
Viewing tools, 22
views
  keyboard shortcuts, endpaper,
    330–331
  modes, **30–31**

percentage for, 42
removing templates from, 104

W

wavy lines, creating, 35–36
weight, of stroked line, 61, *62*
white space
  leading for lines of type, **146**, *147*
  between letters, 147
  rivers of, 129
  tracking and, **148–149**, *149*
  between words and letters, **149–151**
widows, 148, *149*
width of graph columns, 249
Window menu, **326–329**, *327*
  Layers palette, 110
  Show Info, 42, 328
  Show Paint Style, 59
  Tab Ruler palette, 153
Windows Adobe Illustrator, saving file
    for, 11
word processing, **133–140**
word processing application, importing
    text file from, **122–124**
WordPerfect, importing text from, 123
words
  keyboard shortcut to center, 67
  spacing for, **149–151**
WordStar, importing text from, 123
woven look, from divided paths, **180–182**
Write Now, importing text from, 123

X

Xywrite, importing text from, 123

Y

Y axis, placement on graph, 248

Z

Zapf Chancery font, *141*
zero point, moving on ruler, 66
Zoom In (View menu), 309
Zoom In tool, 22
Zoom Out (View menu), 309
Zoom Out tool, 22
Zoom tool, 42, 56, 65, 278

[1304] Adobe Illustrator for the Mac Designer's Guide

GET A FREE CATALOG JUST FOR EXPRESSING YOUR OPINION.

Help us improve our books and get a **FREE** full-color catalog in the bargain. Please complete this form, pull out this page and send it in today. The address is on the reverse side.

Name _____   Company _____

Address _____   City _____ State ____ Zip _____

Phone (____) _____

1. How would you rate the overall quality of this book?

❑ Excellent
❑ Very Good
❑ Good
❑ Fair
❑ Below Average
❑ Poor

2. What were the things you liked most about the book? (Check all that apply)

❑ Pace
❑ Format
❑ Writing Style
❑ Examples
❑ Table of Contents
❑ Index
❑ Price
❑ Illustrations
❑ Type Style
❑ Cover
❑ Depth of Coverage
❑ Fast Track Notes

3. What were the things you liked *least* about the book? (Check all that apply)

❑ Pace
❑ Format
❑ Writing Style
❑ Examples
❑ Table of Contents
❑ Index
❑ Price
❑ Illustrations
❑ Type Style
❑ Cover
❑ Depth of Coverage
❑ Fast Track Notes

4. Where did you buy this book?

❑ Bookstore chain
❑ Small independent bookstore
❑ Computer store
❑ Wholesale club
❑ College bookstore
❑ Technical bookstore
❑ Other _____

5. How did you decide to buy this particular book?

❑ Recommended by friend
❑ Recommended by store personnel
❑ Author's reputation
❑ Sybex's reputation
❑ Read book review in _____
❑ Other _____

6. How did you pay for this book?

❑ Used own funds
❑ Reimbursed by company
❑ Received book as a gift

7. What is your level of experience with the subject covered in this book?

❑ Beginner
❑ Intermediate
❑ Advanced

8. How long have you been using a computer?

years _____
months _____

9. Where do you most often use your computer?

❑ Home
❑ Work

❑ Both
❑ Other _____

10. What kind of computer equipment do you have? (Check all that apply)

❑ PC Compatible Desktop Computer
❑ PC Compatible Laptop Computer
❑ Apple/Mac Computer
❑ Apple/Mac Laptop Computer
❑ CD ROM
❑ Fax Modem
❑ Data Modem
❑ Scanner
❑ Sound Card
❑ Other _____

11. What other kinds of software packages do you ordinarily use?

❑ Accounting
❑ Databases
❑ Networks
❑ Apple/Mac
❑ Desktop Publishing
❑ Spreadsheets
❑ CAD
❑ Games
❑ Word Processing
❑ Communications
❑ Money Management
❑ Other _____

12. What operating systems do you ordinarily use?

❑ DOS
❑ OS/2
❑ Windows
❑ Apple/Mac
❑ Windows NT
❑ Other _____

13. On what computer-related subject(s) would you like to see more books?

_____

_____

_____

_____

14. Do you have any other comments about this book? (Please feel free to use a separate piece of paper if you need more room)

_____

_____

_____

_____

- - - - - - - - - - PLEASE FOLD, SEAL, AND MAIL TO SYBEX - - - - - - - - - -

SYBEX INC.
Department M
2021 Challenger Drive
Alameda, CA
94501

Keyboard Shortcuts

Viewing Shortcuts

Hide	⌘-3
Hide All But Selected Objects	⌘-Option-3-any tool
Show All	⌘-4
Preview Mode	⌘-Y
Artwork Mode	⌘-E
Preview Selection Mode	⌘-Option-Y
Show/Hide Template	⌘-Shift-W
Show/Hide Rulers	⌘-R
Hide Edges	⌘-Shift-H
Zoom In	⌘-]
Zoom In (alternate)	⌘-spacebar-any tool
Zoom Out	⌘-[
Zoom Out (alternate)	Option-Zoom tool
Actual Size	⌘-H
Actual Size (alternate)	Double click on Zoom tool
Fit in Window	⌘-M
Fit in Window (alternate)	Double click on Hand tool
New View	⌘-Control-V